TALKING BODIES III

TALKING BODIES III

Transformations, Movements
and Expression

edited by

Michelle D. Ravenscroft,
Bee Hughes, Charlotte Dann
and Paul G. Nixon

University of Chester Press

First published 2021
by University of Chester Press
University of Chester
Parkgate Road
Chester CH1 4BJ

Printed and bound in the UK by the
LIS Print Unit
University of Chester
Cover designed by the
LIS Graphics Team
University of Chester

© University of Chester, 2021
Cover images © Bee Hughes, 2021
Figures 1–5 and 7 © Janine Antoni, 2021
Courtesy of the artist and Luhring Augustine, New York
Figure 6 © Janine Antoni, 2021
Courtesy of the artist, Luhring Augustine, New York
and Anthony Meier Fine Arts, San Francisco

The moral right of the editors
of this work has been asserted

All Rights Reserved
No part of this publication may be reproduced, stored in a retrieval system or transmitted in any form or by any means without the prior permission of the copyright owner, other than as permitted by current UK copyright legislation or under the terms and conditions of a recognised copyright licensing scheme

A catalogue record for this book is available
from the British Library

ISBN 978-1-910481-14-1

CONTENTS

List of Illustrations	vii
Acknowledgements	viii
Foreword Emma L. E. Rees	ix
About the Editors	xi
List of Contributors	xiii
Chapter 1: Introduction Michelle D. Ravenscroft, Bee Hughes, Charlotte Dann and Paul G. Nixon	1
Chapter 2: Body Awareness and Orientation in Midwifery: Moving Towards LGBTQ+ Inclusive Practice Jess McArdle, Teresa Arias and Hannah Rayment-Jones	8
Chapter 3: Bodies in Migration Marked for Exclusion Nancy Hansen	33
Chapter 4: The Bulletproof Black Body: Luke Cage and the Politics of Race and Respectability Esther De Dauw	51
Chapter 5: It's Not Over Until the Fat Professor Sings: Teaching Fat Studies in the 'Fattest Province in Canada' Sonja Boon	75

Talking Bodies III

Chapter 6: Techniques of the Body as Techniques of the 96
Self: Taking Sex Seriously
Chloe Dominique

Chapter 7: "Older Women Masturbate Too": Feminism, 119
Sexuality and the Older Woman in *Grace and Frankie*
Alice Churm

Chapter 8: From Little Women to the 'New Woman': 141
Representations of Female Adolescent Identity
Formation in the Late Nineteenth Century
Michelle D. Ravenscroft

Chapter 9: Between Gender and Tradition: How 166
Normative Crafts-man-ship Causes Role Conflicts
for Travelling Craftswomen
Hannah Rose Bayer

Chapter 10: "My body is your vehicle": Mothering, 189
Relationality and the Transgenerational Bond in Janine
Antoni's Embodied Art
Justyna Wierzchowska

Chapter 11: "Speak of me as I am": Regendering Othello 215
Beth Flanagan

Chapter 12: Conclusion: Bringing it all Together 243
*Michelle D. Ravenscroft, Bee Hughes,
Charlotte Dann and Paul G. Nixon*

Index 246

LIST OF ILLUSTRATIONS

Figure 1: Janine Antoni, *Wean*, 1989/90. Plaster, sheet rock, 12 x 38 x 2 inches (30.48 x 96.52 x 5.08 cm) © Janine Antoni. Courtesy of the artist and Luhring Augustine, New York.   194

Figure 2: Janine Antoni, *Momme*, 1995. C-print, artist's frame, 36 x 29 inches (91.4 x 73.7 cm) © Janine Antoni. Courtesy of the artist and Luhring Augustine, New York.   197

Figure 3: Janine Antoni, *Coddle*, 1999. C-print, hand-carved frame, 21 1/2 x 16 inches (54.61 x 40.64 cm) © Janine Antoni. Courtesy of the artist and Luhring Augustine, New York.   198

Figure 4: Janine Antoni, *Cradle,* 1999 (detail). Two tons of steel, 59 x 58 x 60.5 inches (149.9 x 147.3 x 153.7 cm). Photographed by Larry Lamay. © Janine Antoni. Courtesy of the artist and Luhring Augustine, New York.   200

Figure 5: Janine Antoni, *Umbilical*, 2000. Cast sterling silver of family silverware and negative impressions of artist's mouth and mother's hand, 8 x 3 x 3 inches (20.32 x 7.62 x 7.62 cm). Photographed by John Bessler. © Janine Antoni. Courtesy of the artist and Luhring Augustine, New York.   202

Figure 6: Janine Antoni, *Crowned*, 2013. Plaster molding with plaster pelvic bones. Dimensions variable, site-transferrable installation. Installation view at Anthony Meier Fine Arts, San Francisco, 2015. © Janine Antoni. Courtesy of the artist, Luhring Augustine, New York and Anthony Meier Fine Arts, San Francisco.   206

Figure 7: Janine Antoni, *Rosa,* 2014. Pit fired ceramic 18.5 x 13.5 x inches (46.99 x 34.29 cm) © Janine Antoni. Courtesy of the artist and Luhring Augustine, New York.   206

ACKNOWLEDGEMENTS

Michelle would like to thank
Andy for his patience and support

Paul would like to thank
Professor Jos Beelen, Rebecca Kleiweg de Zwaan
and Michel Hogenes for their continued support
and encouragement

The editors would like to thank
the Talking Bodies research community,
Professor Emma Rees and the team
at the University of Chester,
for the Talking Bodies conference,
and the University of Chester Press
for making this publication possible

FOREWORD

Emma L. E. Rees

In the summer of 2020, the American network CNN ran an advert encouraging people to wear face coverings to slow the spread of COVID-19. "A mask can say a lot about the person who wears it", the voiceover declares, "But even more about the person who doesn't." The ad went further than being merely a public health announcement; it came at a time when the President of the United States was actively disseminating dangerous misinformation about the virus, and was at best ambivalent about the wearing of face masks. The CNN ad, then, was a political statement which made no explicit political statements.

This playful absence/presence captured the ironies inherent in covering part of the body with a mask which, while obscuring half of a wearer's face, ironically revealed much about who they were politically, socially, and culturally. Masks make talking difficult, but they also allow the body to talk without words. The poster for the 2021 Talking Bodies conference showed a masked individual whose steady gaze holds the viewer's attention. Because of the pandemic the conference was postponed not least because of the paradox of the disembodiment so many of us had grown used to – and grown tired of – as our virtual, online lives became daily less distinguishable from 'the real world' than ever.

COVID reconfigured how we read bodies, then, even as it underscored their vulnerabilities. In the months before the creation of the vaccine, the body was a site of susceptibility, and others' bodies, by extension, were viewed as potentially lethal. Only a very few specific bodies could be proximate; others were to be actively avoided. The body, and who and how it could talk to, became legislatively constituted in extraordinary ways. For many, the pandemic meant loss, or anxiety, or a decline in day-to-day productivity. 'Resilience' was exposed as the neoliberal lie it is, and endurance in the face of profound uncertainty was the best that many could manage.

Talking Bodies III

The essays in *Talking Bodies III: Transformations, Movements and Expression* epitomise the interdisciplinarity, inclusiveness, and eclecticism of the Talking Bodies project which I started back in 2013. The contributions, in inventive and distinct ways, in this most anomalous of eras, interrogate 'the norm', from (dis)ability to heteronormativity, and from sex to sexuality. They range across the globe, and through time, as they complicate productively, and challenge constructively.

In their conclusion, the editors state that the Talking Bodies project is "inclusive, diverse, and thought-expanding". The book they've edited also has all of those elements, and I'm delighted that it's being published at a time when we have so much to learn from the body's scripts and inscriptions, its maskings and unmaskings, and its persistence even in the face of existential threat.

Professor Emma Rees
North Wales
July 2021

ABOUT THE EDITORS

Michelle D. Ravenscroft is a graduate of the University of Chester, where she studied English literature, education and nineteenth-century literature and culture. Michelle is an educational consultant working on projects relating to personal and social education and development in the primary and secondary education sectors. She also delivers enrichment sessions in a North Wales primary school. Michelle is currently undertaking doctoral study at Manchester Metropolitan University, researching nineteenth-century and early twentieth-century literature in relation to the Portico Library's collection and archives.

Bee Hughes is an academic, curator and artist. Their recent interdisciplinary work explores non-binary and trans approaches to contemporary art and visual cultures, menstrual art history, materiality, and performativity. Their doctorate 'Performing Periods: Challenging Menstrual Normativity through Art Practice' (2020) explored the ways art can disrupt normative understandings of menstruation and gender. In 2020 Bee began a collaborative project as Artist in Residence at the Centre for Contemporary Art, Institute for Gender Studies, and School of Art History at the University of St Andrews. Bee is a Lecturer in Media, Culture and Communication at Liverpool John Moores University.

Charlotte Dann is a Lecturer in Social and Developmental Psychology at the University of Northampton. Her teaching centres around qualitative, critical, and feminist work – exploring bodies, discourses, and intersectional issues across the lifespan. She received her PhD from the University of Northampton in 2018, exploring the regulation, conformity, and resistance of tattooed women in the UK. She is currently working on two main projects – first, a multi-university project exploring aspects of parenting practices online and second, a funded project focusing on issues of diversity in higher education. She has published work on meaning-making in tattooed bodies, as well as tattooed mothers, with a monograph due to be published in October 2021. She is an editorial assistant for *Psychology of Women & Equalities Review* and a committee member for the Psychology of Women & Equalities Section.

Paul G. Nixon is a Principal Lecturer in Political Science at The Hague University of Applied Sciences, The Netherlands. He has contributed chapters to many edited collections and has co-edited ten previous collections including *Reshaping International Teaching and Learning in Higher Education* (with V. P. Dennen & R. Rawal, 2021) *Sex in the Digital Age* (with I. K. Dusterhoft, 2018), *Digital Media Use Across the Lifecourse* (with Rajash Rawal & Andreas Funk, 2016) and *Gender and Sexuality in the Contemporary Media Landscape*, a special edition of the *Information Communication and Society* journal (edited with Cosimo Marco Scarcelli & Tonny Krijnen), which was published online in 2021.

LIST OF CONTRIBUTORS

Teresa Arias, King's College London, UK

Hannah Rose Bayer, University of Innsbruck, Austria

Sonja Boon, Memorial University of Newfoundland, Canada

Alice Churm, University of Warwick, UK

Esther De Dauw, Independent Scholar, UK

Chloe Dominique, University College London, UK

Beth Flanagan, The Shakespeare Institute, University of Birmingham, UK

Nancy Hansen, University of Manitoba, Canada

Jess McArdle, Lewisham and Greenwich NHS Trust, London, UK

Michelle D. Ravenscroft, Manchester Metropolitan University, UK

Hannah Rayment-Jones, King's College London, UK

Justyna Wierzchowska, University of Warsaw, Poland

CHAPTER 1:
INTRODUCTION

*Michelle D. Ravenscroft, Bee Hughes,
Charlotte Dann and Paul G. Nixon*

Following the first two volumes, *Talking Bodies: Interdisciplinary Perspectives on Embodiment, Gender and Identity* (2017) and *Talking Bodies Vol. II: Bodily Language, Selfhood and Transgression* (2020), this third collection of essays comprises ten chapters by emerging voices, established academics, and early career researchers. *Talking Bodies III: Transformations, Movements and Expression* continues the ongoing discussion around our bodies, and is a timely addition to the vital discussion of what bodies are, how we perceive them, and what they mean. While the subject matter diverges at first glance, all ten essays concern themselves with elements of three central themes – *body images, sex, gender and sexuality*, and *artists and expression* – which link and transcend boundaries to offer challenging, diverse and inclusive narratives of bodies and selfhood. We hope that the interweaving themes will encourage cross-fertilised consideration of the overarching broader ideas and questions of the collection. The work in this volume contributes new perspectives to some of the critical issues that feature in the discourses of contemporary society, aiming to add to a debate that informs and educates, and sparks further discourse with a view to broadening understanding.

Bringing together scholars from across disciplines and continents, this collection further explores questions such as: How do we view our own bodies?; How are they seen by others?; How do we use those bodies to create, demonstrate and constitute our own identities?; And how do we further use them to project thoughts and intentions to others? The notion of our bodies, how we treat them, use them, maintain them, develop them, even recreate and re-engineer them, are topics that have become areas of mainstream debate in modern, post-industrial societies. Those debates also cross and interweave traditional academic disciplines, discourses and boundaries. As the first two volumes posited, the concept of what constitutes the thing we call a 'body' is fundamentally difficult to define, describe, and address. Building on this, body augmentation and technological advances are blurring our conception of whether the body can or should be defined solely by its organic elements. Are we defined by others according to some unfathomable perceived allure or imperfections of our bodies? Or do we define ourselves by the way we use our bodies as a display of persona?

A central theme which spans many of the contributions is challenging heteronormativity, as the expected path of cultural socialisation into naturalised heterosexual relationships and behavioural conventions (Warner, 1993), and the centreing of heterosexuality as a distinct and privileged sexual identity (Mulholland, 2011, p. 123). Importantly, heteronormativity contributes to persistent inequalities which privilege some individuals over others. Rubin developed a typology of sexual practices with marital sex for example being seen as 'permissible' sex, whereas alternate sexual behaviours were viewed as impermissible sex (1984). Responding to cultural shifts Mulholland has built upon Rubin's idea of sex hierarchy aligning this to more modern sexual norms with objects, such as a strap-on, deemed more acceptable; evidently, heterosexuality privileges both certain sexual acts and ways of constructing the self. Mulholland notes how non-normative bodies are often ignored when attempting to present idealised sexual content such as porn. Although a wider variety of sexual acts are now deemed more acceptable, heteronormativity often deprives individuals of sexual subjecthood and instead limits acceptance of sexual subjects to those who conform to a "conventional gender aesthetic" (2011, p. 127). More than challenging heteronormativity, the contributors to the collection interrogate cultural norms and assumptions with an unflinching yet sensitive analytic gaze. There is acknowledgement of the need to wilfully (Ahmed, 2017, p. 71) unpick

Introduction

these difficult subjects and reorientate (Ahmed, 2006) our analysis and practices in our rapidly changing world.

The motif of body images, or bodily images, is explored through a number of the collection's chapters. From the critique of the dehumanised image of the disabled refugee's body in Nancy Hansen's chapter through to the poetic-ethnographic imagery of the European travelling craftswoman in Hannah Rose Bayer's work, these chapters address an area of persistent importance in contemporary life. Body and self-image are seen as key issues in terms of identity and perceptions both by others and of one's self. These chapters tease out the narratives that define body image and the ways in which such narratives can be used to subtly – or sometimes more directly – seek to suppress individuals or to more radically empower them to reject standardised norms and to be comfortable in their own skin.

A number of the chapters examine sex, gender and/or sexuality as sites where individuals challenge the stereotypes that are imposed upon them. The contributions challenge both the hegemony of heteronormativity, stable binary gender, and the bastions of ageist culture that often prevail in much of Western society. Two chapters present a queered reading (see e.g. Barker & Scheele, 2016) of canonical literary genres. Beth Flanagan's innovative work contributes to the theorisation of Shakespearean gender relations through the framework of 'regendering' Othello. Moving to the late nineteenth century, Michelle D. Ravenscroft's chapter presents an excavation of the formation of female adolescent identity at a time of rapid social and cultural upheaval.

Turning to the examination of sexual pleasure and sexual agency, which are not solely the prerogative of the young, we find Alice Churm's sensitive and celebratory chapter exploring sexual (self) pleasure in the series *Grace and Frankie*. This theme is approached through a sociological lens in Chloe Dominique's confident and sensitive ethnographic study of queer sexuality and sexual practices. Sonja Boon brings us from ethnography to autoethnography in her self-reflexive chapter on her embodied experience as a fat professor teaching fat studies in Canada.

Talking Bodies III

Though these chapters differ in their disciplinary field, methodology and subject matter, they are linked by an unshaking insistence that the bodies, sexualities, and subjects they discuss are valid and intelligible despite the insistence of contemporary society that they are not. Many of the contributions to this collection advocate strongly for those who do not physically conform to displaying the 'ideal' body form, size and shape. Instead of inhabiting a position of resignation, they present subjects – fictional and actual – who ultimately revel in the sheer pleasure of their experiences, the contributions allowing the reader a glimpse into the kaleidoscopic possibilities of human sexual desire and affirm the equality of their validity.

Many of our contributors explore representations of the body and the expectations inherently underpinning assumptions that certain bodies suit certain roles. These normative assumptions around bodies, bodily acts and performances are challenged by the contribution of Jess McArdle, Teresa Arias, and Hannah Rayment-Jones. Their chapter opens up discussion about the physicality of midwives in the medicalised yet highly gendered and often (though implicitly) sexualised act of giving birth. Bringing our discussion of transgenerational bodies to bear on contemporary art practices, Justyna Wierzchowska analyses the practice of American visual artist Janine Antoni. In this chapter Wierzchowska interrogates the way the artist disrupts the individualist narrative of the self that has become dominant in neoliberal societies. The work of Esther De Dauw links graphic arts and media representations of the Black body through a comparative analysis of the Marvel character Luke Cage. This chapter offers a critique of the re-presentation of the 'bulletproof' Black body in the context of the #BlackLivesMatter movement and the American prison-industrial complex.

The impact of cross-disciplinary research relies partly on its ability to reach out to other disciplines by offering new and different perspectives. Its "multiplicity of methods ... gives researchers more options from which to choose" (O'Rourke, 2017, p. 276). This broad-ranging appeal offers a flexibility that encourages innovation.

Introduction

However, O'Rourke (2017), argues that cross-disciplinary research is "highly contextual" and that the "responses combine many disciplines and professions, and so have no natural home; as a result contributions to the published and gray literatures are widely dispersed" (p. 276). Bringing together a variety of cross-disciplinary papers can begin to address the problematic dispersal of research, methods and practice. As a response, edited collections are becoming a 'natural home' for cross-disciplinary research, providing easy access to wide-ranging research methods and practices under a common theme. Collating this research in an eclectic, yet relevant, way is important in encouraging exploration of alternative, interdisciplinary researcher-led approaches. This collection not only showcases global considerations of gender and identity, but the increasing practice of cross-disciplinary informed research across multiple disciplines, such as social, art, media and literature studies, and healthcare. This allows for many of these areas to expand beyond their traditional methodologies and encourages exploration of more globally informed practices to add to and enrich our understanding of the complexity of the ways in which we interpret the body. Accessing a variety of research, from multiple disciplines, can also encourage an interdisciplinary approach; increasingly an area of particular focus in higher education institutions.

Cross-institutional knowledge exchange and dissemination can enable the exploration of a diverse range of research practices. Being open to other research perspectives encourages exploration of research practices and methods, and increases understanding of how different approaches can interact. Institutions and organisations are becoming acutely aware of the opportunities and flexibility created by cross-disciplinary and interdisciplinary research, in an ever-changing educational and social climate. A 2016 Higher Education Funding Council for England funded case study review suggests that factors for supporting interdisciplinary research include the "need to address complex social changes" (HEFCE, 2016, p. 5). The review also found that ways of growing interdisciplinary research, such as networking events, can not only "encourage communication and collaboration between researchers from different disciplines", but also "stimulate new interdisciplinary activity" (HEFCE, 2016, pp. 5–6). This collection provides a cross section of often interdisciplinary work that addresses complex social changes, from a cross-disciplinary network of researchers at the 2019 Talking Bodies conference. It also highlights how the successful combination of organisation-led and researcher-led events can create interesting and innovative content for publication which encourages debate and a potential reinterpretation of bodies of knowledge.

It is collections like this that encourage researchers to explore and develop their skills and ideas; especially important for continued engagement, particularly for early career researchers. Collections of cross-disciplinary research can support this developmental process by providing multiple examples of original and innovative research that appeal to all levels. The increasing self-efficacy of students undertaking innovative research is echoed in the HEFCE review, which suggests that "researchers can create their own culture" with an approach that can be "rewarding and exciting because of its potential to drive forward solutions to prevent problems, resulting in continued motivation" (HEFCE, 2016, p. 21). Although the exploration of new and innovative research practice and methodology is vital to testing boundaries, with the review suggesting that "many major discoveries and breakthroughs have occurred at the boundaries between disciplines" (HEFCE, 2016, p. 8), the dissemination of this research is also important. This allows researchers to "create their own culture" to have their work debated and perhaps challenged, and develop their research communities.

Our contributors utilise and draw from a range of divergent methodologies and take different theoretical perspectives, but all interrogate the notion of how we identify and are identified, categorised and defined by our bodies and the usages to which we put them. Many of the contributions show, and indeed outwardly challenge, the notion of norms in relation to the ways in which our bodies are often seemingly gendered, their perceived capabilities, or are in some ways seen as falling short of an abstract and unattainable notion of perfection. This

Introduction

collection considers the many ways people disrupt expectations and delight in transposing the way we almost imperceptibly unconsciously assign roles and actions to certain bodies or personas. These chapters occasionally confound our expectations, cause us to rethink our learned perceptions of how the world 'should' be in terms of bodies, genders and the interactions between the two. Spanning subjects from art, gender, disability and race, to history, sociology, medicine, politics and law, amongst others, *Talking Bodies III* contributes to the ongoing deliberations of the contribution of the body as a focus of investigation to address the ethical, cultural, political and social issues that continue to preoccupy many sections of society.

References
Ahmed, S. (2006). *Queer phenomenology: Orientations, objects, others*. Duke University Press.
Ahmed, S. (2017). *Living a feminist life*. Duke University Press.
Barker, M.-J., & Scheele, J. (2016). *Queer: A graphic history*. Icon.
Higher Education Funding Council for England (HEFCE). (2016). Case Study review of Interdisciplinary Research in Higher Education Institutions in England: A report for HEFCE by Technopolis. https://emps.exeter.ac.uk/media/universityofexeter/emps/research/cee/news/Technopolis-Case_study_of_interdisciplinary_research_in_HEIs_in_England.pdf
Mulholland, M. (2011). When porno meets hetero – sexpo, heteronormativity and the pornification of the mainstream. *Australian Feminist Studies*, 26(67), 119–135.
O'Rourke, M. (2017). Comparing methods for cross-disciplinary research. In R. Friedman, J. Thompson Klein, & R. C. S. Pacheco (Eds.). *The Oxford handbook of interdisciplinarity* (2nd ed., pp. 276–290). Oxford University Press.
Rubin, G. (1984). Thinking sex: Notes for a radical theory of the politics of sexuality. *Social Perspectives in Lesbian and Gay Studies; A reader*, 1, 100–133.
Warner, M. (Ed.). (1993). *Fear of a queer planet: Queer politics and social theory*. University of Minnesota Press.

CHAPTER 2:
BODY AWARENESS AND ORIENTATION IN MIDWIFERY: MOVING TOWARDS LGBTQ+ INCLUSIVE PRACTICE

Jess McArdle, Teresa Arias and Hannah Rayment-Jones

Abstract

This research considers the introduction of an awareness of sexuality and gender diversity in the midwifery curriculum. Based on a social model, the research relates the experiences and expectations of both the service users and the student midwives and how these interact within a medical setting. This chapter explores how the physical experience of midwifery could be a resource for and pathway towards changes to midwifery practice, in particular, making it a practice that is inclusive of all genders and sexualities. Pregnancy and birth hold so much cultural, imaginative and experiential weight in shaping understandings of gender and sexuality, that it seems relevant to consider how people's various expressions and experiences of gender and sexuality might alter the course of their journeys through maternity services. There is a growing body of literature that considers how to make healthcare curricula more inclusive of LGBTQ+ people's needs and desires (Bosse et al., 2015; Carabez et al., 2015; Lim et al., 2015; McCann & Brown 2018; Taylor et al., 2018; Walker et al., 2016; Yingling et al., 2017), and only one of these papers offers suggestions specifically for midwives (Walker et al., 2016). This chapter adds to the body of literature from the specific perspective of midwifery care. Furthermore, and as this chapter attempts to show, it is difficult, and at times unhelpful to separate from one another the intimate, physical, highly gendered and sexualised, as well as obfuscating and medicalised, processes and aspects of pregnancy and birth. With this in mind, this chapter does not offer specific examples of better care for LGBTQ+ people ready to be copied and pasted into midwifery practice. It does, however, offer ways of thinking about the intimate care that midwives provide, which

Body Awareness and Orientation in Midwifery

is already charged with notions of sex, sexuality and gender, as a way of proposing that what may seem uncomfortable or challenging is an essential part of midwifery care.

Key words: midwives, midwives' bodies, inclusion, LGBTQ+, healthcare, birth

Introduction

This chapter explores how bodies of midwives could be resources for and pathways towards changes to midwifery practice, in particular, making it a practice that is inclusive of all genders and sexualities. Pregnancy and birth hold so much cultural, imaginative and experiential weight in shaping understandings of gender and sexuality, that it seems relevant to consider how people's various expressions and experiences of gender and sexuality might alter the course of their experiences of midwifery care. There is a growing body of literature that considers how to make healthcare curricula more inclusive of LGBTQ+ people's needs and desires (Bosse et al., 2015; Carabez et al., 2015; Lim et al., 2015; McCann & Brown, 2018; Taylor et al., 2018; Walker et al., 2016; Yingling et al., 2017), yet only one of these papers offers suggestions specifically for midwives (Walker et al., 2016). The work described in this chapter adds to this body of literature from the specific perspective of midwifery care. Furthermore, and as this chapter attempts to show, it is difficult, and at times unhelpful to separate aspects of pregnancy and birth that are simultaneously intimate, physical, gendered and sexualised, as well as medicalised. With this in mind, this chapter does not offer specific examples of better care for LGBTQ+ people, ready to be transferred into midwifery education and practice. It does however offer ways of thinking about the intimate care that midwives provide already charged with notions of sex, and understandings of sexuality and gender, and proposes that what may seem uncomfortable or challenging is an essential part of midwifery education and care.

We are grateful for and indebted to the work that has already begun to assess the maternity care needs and desires of LGBTQ+ people and the barriers they face in multiple and specific forms (Dutton et al.,

2008; Hoffkling et al., 2017; Light et al., 2014; MacDonald et al., 2016; Obedin-Maliver & Makadon, 2016).

Midwifery researchers working with lesbian women have, for many years, made appeals for curricula to reflect, more widely, the sexual diversity of service users who report a lack of specific antenatal education for their parenting needs, embarrassment on the part of midwives providing their care (Röndahl et al., 2009), heteronormative environments that contribute to lingering feelings that any negative care encounters are related to homosexuality (Goldberg et al., 2011; Lee et al., 2011) and that as lesbian women they feel unable to provide loving and intimate support to their partners (Wilton & Kaufmann, 2001). More recently, researchers have begun to explore the diverse range of experiences and values of trans men in relation to maternity care. There are few legal barriers to trans pregnancy in the UK, however there is little acknowledgment of trans fertility (Pearce, 2018). Low levels of knowledge and awareness among healthcare providers (Light et al., 2014) being cited, among other things, are part of the institutional and structural barriers to safe care, and the potential for trans men to play active roles in creating safe and affirming environments (Hoffkling et al., 2017). In medical and social environments, trans men report feeling both hypervisible, when perceived as 'pregnant Dad', and invisible when assumed to be a woman or a fat man (Pearce, 2018).

Methodology

As researchers, we came together under the research project title, 'Cultivating Awareness of Sexual and Gender Diversity for a Midwifery Curriculum'. We hoped to gain understanding of student midwives', faculty members' and practising midwives' awareness of gender and sexual diversity and how this could relate to a midwifery curriculum. A number of events, coincidences and conversations sparked this coming together: a speech given by a trans man and his midwife at a midwifery conference in Canada, a request for physiological breech birth videos to use gender-neutral terminology, discussions between colleagues, an opportunity for student midwives to be involved in research, and many meetings since. One of the results has been a realisation that focusing on variations of sexuality and gender requires constant shifting and refocusing, and it is with frustration as well as pleasure that we acknowledge how this work has not been straightforward.

The project outlined above employed a qualitative research method. First, we conducted a fact-finding survey of student midwives' knowledge and understanding of LGBTQ+ people's experiences of maternity care, and then focus groups with midwifery students and educators, each building on one another. We were unsuccessful in recruiting practising midwives for a focus group which may reflect the sensitive nature of the content, as well as the burden of workload for midwives. This chapter diverges from the initial project to explore the physical and intimate experience of midwifery care as articulated by a group of student midwives in the first focus group. We shared with the focus group participants concerns and perhaps a preoccupation with our own levels of comfort, knowledge and skill in relation to research questions about sexuality and gender. This process moved us to consider the bodies of knowledge that midwives bring with them, at times literally how they carry themselves in their bodies, when caring for people and their families. These observations broadened our horizons while working with the data, and, gradually phenomenology came into view. Influenced by the work of Goldberg et al. (2011), the focus of study turned to the movement and actions of midwives in shared spaces with recipients of midwifery care. In their paper, "Queering the birthing space: Phenomenological interpretations of the relationships between lesbian couples and perinatal nurses in the context of birthing care", Goldberg, et al. (2011) explain that phenomenology guides an understanding of how "gendered bodies of lesbian birthing couples and perinatal nurses navigate their locatedness within the institutional and hierarchical environments in which they reside" (2011, p. 176). We are similarly interested in the verbal and physical enactment of midwifery practice through the institutionally situated bodies of midwives and the pregnant and birthing people they work with. In this piece phenomenology guides our attention to moments when student midwives' articulations of midwifery practice are interwoven with ideas of gender and sexuality, opening up ways of thinking about physical experiences of midwifery.

In her book *Queer Phenomenology: Orientations, Objects, Others*, (2006) Sara Ahmed thinks about how the invisible, everydayness of heteronormativity reinforces behaviours and ways of being that privilege Whiteness and straightness, and obscure queerness. Phenomenology offers a way of thinking not only about how bodies move and act in certain spaces and time, but how those spaces are, (literally) in turn, (or) simultaneously shaped and shifted by the bodies that move within, above, beside and around them. With phenomenology in mind, we consider how the first focus group participants (student midwives) situated themselves physically and linguistically within discourses of pregnancy, birth and queerness. Ahmed draws the readers' attention to the way in which physical and social bodies relate to one another and permit certain types of (often White, heteronormative) behaviours to take place, while making other types of behaviour seem deviant, queer or "slantwise", and she draws attention too to how that feels (2006, p. 107). In other words, what it feels like when White, heteronormative space is disrupted, the "everyday negotiation" required to deal with the invisible lines that have been drawn and that have ordered things in a straight way, and how those lines are revealed through the actions, behaviours, ways of being that bend them (2006, p. 107). Guided by Heyes et al., and their handling of it (2016), we also consider queer phenomenology – its way of attending to the invisible lines of power that shape bodies and spaces – a method that asks what the dizzying work of midwifery feels like and, when working with people, including LGBTQ+ people, what we can do with those feelings.

Bodywork
It is perhaps taken for granted that midwives work with other people's bodies, in their many unstable and contingent forms. Pregnant and birthing bodies have been figured as bloody, mushy, leaky, unstable,

Body Awareness and Orientation in Midwifery

vulnerable, monstrous, mutilated (de Beauvoir, 1953/1997; Ferrante, 2008; Hanson, 2015; Kirkham, 2007; Ussher, 2006). In a medicalised model of pregnancy and birth, caregivers (midwives, maternity support workers and to some extent obstetricians) work to contain much of this leakage, or protect bodies from the effects of vulnerability – cleaning up, sanitising, drawing curtains, seeking consent (Davis-Floyd, 1990); albeit in a healthcare system where often the distance to or from bodies is determined by, and reinforces, hierarchies of knowledge and power (Lawler, 1991). But birth workers also create this vulnerability; they invite, or demand that someone open up, acknowledge but encourage spillage, even pain, and the loosening of control (Kirkham, 2007; Stewart, 2005). The concept of 'bodywork' in nursing, "work focused on the bodies of others, manipulating, touching, cleaning, adjusting otherwise managing bodies" (Wolkowitz, 2002, p. 497), connects, through movement, the bodies of caregivers with the bodies of the persons in their care. Billie Hunter (2001, p. 441) suggests that this work differs for midwives as they work, not with "the bodies of ill individuals" but "with healthy women experiencing a normal life event, who may only very temporarily lose control of some of their bodily functions" (Hunter, 2001, p. 441).

Some of the attention paid to the way in which bodies of midwives go about performing this care comes from an anthropological perspective. Sheila Kitzinger gives examples of some of the different types of presence, absence and attention a midwife can give. A time-pressed hospital midwife coming and going is, "unable to give focused care if she has to rush from one patient to another" (2012, p. 130) in contrast to a "warm and understanding midwife … [who] holds back and leaves space for the mother to respond to the rush of hormones in her bloodstream" (2012, p. 130). Robbie Davis-Floyd, writing from a North American perspective, cites midwives knowing they must tend to or noticing their own physical needs – lying down and having a rest during a homebirth as a way of opening up to a birthing experience, and a midwife getting diarrhoea as a sign that something in the birth may require more attention (1996, p. 247). The physicality of this knowing is part of what she calls an intuition that involves "the body, psyche, and spirit" in a way that is "essential to receiving intuitive messages" about the birthing experience (1996, p. 247). In these examples, physical experiences of midwifery relate to how one approaches the birthing person or experience. In the English language, the word for midwife comes from Anglo-Saxon meaning *with woman* (Donnison, 1977, p. 11). There is no one definition or understanding of being *with woman*. Instead, the etymological mantra is repeated as a philosophy of midwifery practice (Bradfield et al., 2019; Thorstensson et al., 2012), and a "dynamic and developing construct" (Bradfield et al., 2018, p. 150), that has at times proved difficult to achieve (Kirkham & Stapleton, 2000; McCourt & Stevens, 2009). As being *with woman* is reinterpreted and reappears in multiple iterations – "evolved trust-two-way relationship" (Lewis et al., 2017, p. 49), "relational care" (Sandall et al., 2016, p. 11), "work in partnership with" (Nursing and Midwifery Council, 2009, p. 28) to name some – in this chapter we will attend to moments of midwives *being with* all genders of pregnant and birthing people.

Being with pregnant and birthing people is emotional as well as physical work (Hunter & Deery, 2008). Midwives may find it distressing to be with people who are in pathological, not physiological pain (Niven, 1994); there may be both joy and frustration in the relationships formed with clients (Hunter, 2006); low staffing and high workloads can contribute to low emotional wellbeing (Cramer & Hunter, 2019); and competing ideologies within midwifery pit rewarding moments for some midwives against moments of emotional regulation and control for others (Hunter, 2004). Much of this work has been undertaken by Billie Hunter, who, when she began to consider the emotional terrain of midwives, considered how midwifery "involves intimate knowledge of another's body which normally includes physical contact" (2001, p. 441). She touched on the "under-investigated" (2001, p. 441) issue of sexuality in pregnancy and how there are few references in midwifery literature to "midwives' personal reactions to pain, bodywork and sexuality" (Hunter, 2010, p. 256).

Body Awareness and Orientation in Midwifery

Guided by Ahmed's queer phenomenology, this chapter aims to push the door propped open by Hunter's initial thoughts a little wider, opening onto moments of intimacy by drawing the reader's attention to some of the more subtle ways that focus group participants – student midwives – talked about their bodies. This requires a shifting of attention not *away* from pregnant and birthing people, including LGBTQ+ people – bodies of those seeking and receiving care – but to the relationship between bodywork as attending to others and the bodies of those doing the attending. Our initial readings of the focus group transcript found that through conversations about gender and sexual diversity in midwifery, assumptions about midwifery and its various types of bodywork were thrown into question, including the way that midwives think of their own bodies while caring for the bodies of others.

Conversations in the focus group, framed by questions that tried to find links between midwifery, sexuality and gender, also necessarily brought in race, age and ability. Though outside the scope of this chapter, the multiple and overlapping gendered, sexualised, racialised, marginalised ways of being in the world and in one's body, the intersecting politics and identities of and within midwifery, the people who work as midwives, and those who access midwifery care, need to be explored in more detail. In the UK, Black people are five times more likely, and Asian people are twice as likely to die of pregnancy-related causes than White people (Knight et al., 2018). While much grassroots work has already been done to raise awareness of and to change this disparity, more work urgently needs to be done to integrate this into research and into healthcare institutions. It is a limitation of this chapter, and also the research process, that we did not consider more deeply the interconnectedness of race, and ability, and sexual orientation and gender identity. We did not, for instance, ask for demographic information from the student midwives participating who so generously gave their time and thoughts to this work and whose words make a significant contribution to the chapter. To situate our work, the authors of this chapter identify as White, gay, queer and heterosexual cis women, and two of us have given birth in the UK, all of which shape our analysis of the focus group transcript and understandings of embodied midwifery.

Analysis

The following quotations and analysis are from a focus group with six student midwives from two central London universities, and across the three years of midwifery training. This focus group was the first of three put together as part of a research project entitled 'Cultivating an awareness of gender and sexual diversity in a midwifery curriculum' in which the authors of this chapter were involved. Questions and discussion within the first focus group built on findings from a survey sent out to all midwifery students at the same London university. The facilitators asked about the participants' experiences of working with LGBTQ+ people as well as what preparation they thought they had been given for this from the midwifery curriculum. Midwifery training differs from many other non-healthcare-related undergraduate courses in that the time is divided between attending university and participating in clinical practice. Participants brought in examples from their practice in hospital and in the community as well as their university courses. With a combination of free-flowing conversation, guidance from the facilitators and some visual-textual prompts, the student midwives showed a great deal of sensitivity, knowledge and curiosity about midwifery care for LGBTQ+ people, discussing for example gendered pronouns, making assumptions about people's sexuality, and using the term chestfeeding as well as breastfeeding.

The focus group discussion was recorded and then transcribed by members of the research team. The transcription was checked by multiple members of the team for accuracy, and for greater immersion in the data. Using NVivo (qualitative data analysis software), researchers looked for patterns, repetition and emphasis to group the data into various themes which were checked and agreed upon at regular team meetings. Data from the first focus group informed the questions and discussion of the second focus group (a meeting of midwifery educators) of the project 'Cultivating awareness of gender and sexual diversity within a midwifery curriculum'. That participants had already begun to think about LGBTQ+ inclusivity in maternity, both within the university course and in their practice, are important findings in and of themselves. The themes presented below – 'Being intimate and being professional', 'It's about my body as a midwife too' and 'Reflecting on bodies of midwives' – emerged as secondary or incidental findings to the original research project, and though they did not fit with the main themes that emerged, we felt they warranted further exploration. We have focused on metaphorical articulations of the physicality of midwifery, thinking about what is implied by the language used, attempting to get a sense of not only what participants think but how they feel caring for LGBTQ+ people.

In a paper entitled "Discomfort, Judgement and Healthcare for Queers", authors Harbin, Beagan and Goldberg (2012) explain how a preoccupation with care provider comfort when working with LGBTQ+ people creates a burden that is shared between healthcare providers and LGBTQ+ people; to work out a safe and comfortable environment for them both. However, they noticed that many of the strategies placed much more of that burden on LGBTQ+ people than on the care providers to, for example, be more comfortable with themselves or to seek out LGBTQ+ friendly healthcare providers (Harbin et al., 2012). We hope that our analysis demonstrates, not a preoccupation with midwives' bodies over and above the comfort of LGBTQ+ clients, but the beginning of a way for midwives to think of midwifery as a physical, embodied, relational practice and, seeing it as such, how they might be responsible for and bear more of the burden of creating a safe and comfortable environment when caring for LGBTQ+ people.

Midwifery emotion work as bodywork
When discussing the use of appropriately gendered pronouns, one participant in particular brought her own body into discussion:

> It's just really disorientating to have to kind of question your own assumptions all the time. Like ... isn't it? Like it's just a bit tiring sometimes.
> Participant B

The participant suggests, with the words like 'disorientating' and 'tiring', that a physical effort is required to challenge her assumptions about the gender of pregnant and birthing people. Later on she says:

> It's a bit overwhelming to think about diversity, let alone sexual diversity ...
> Participant B

The participant goes some way to identify the pervasive gender and heteronormativity of healthcare spaces, where people are assumed to have one of two available genders. For those genders to be easily identifiable and obvious, where someone is assumed to be heterosexual unless otherwise signalled or declared. Heyes et al. write about how "people's desires, beliefs, and attitudes congeal into habits that define an orientation" (2016, p. 142). Healthcare spaces, too, created by, inhabited, and brought to life by healthcare workers, may be orientated towards straight people in a way that makes them 'unwelcoming' or 'threatening' to someone who is queer (Heyes et al., 2016). Under-recognition of this heterosexism and homophobia can make even the most well-intentioned healthcare practices "fraught" and further contributes to homophobia in those spaces (Goldberg, et al., 2011, p. 174).

The physical metaphors also tell us something about what happens when gender and heteronormative assumptions are named or questioned. Ahmed writes that "it is in this mode of disorientation that one might begin to wonder: What does it mean to be orientated?" (Ahmed, 2006, p. 6). Moments of disorientation become moments in which those things that we assume (perhaps gender or sexuality), that we are familiar with, that appear "within reach" (Ahmed, 2006, p. 6) are only so because we have already orientated ourselves towards them. In finding that those assumptions cannot always be made, the familiarity with social form, with the way we think the world looks and feels, because we have only orientated ourselves towards it in a particular way, is lost, as other possible vistas open up (Ahmed, 2006, p. 7). Disorientated, the student midwife begins to situate themselves within discourses of gender and sexuality – albeit finding themselves a bit lost – bringing their own body into the discussion, perhaps without even realising it.

Being intimate and being professional
Not wanting to feel overwhelmed, tired or disorientated, a preoccupation with the body in these terms of (dis)comfort is related to a desire for midwives to move with ease through people's pregnancies and birthing experiences – to carry oneself in a confident and professional manner. This is highlighted by awkwardness and embarrassment when things are misunderstood, or are being worked out, or even when they have been understood too well. The same student midwife talking about sexually transmitted infection (STI) screenings begins her contribution with nervous laughter then realises that she's blushing as though in revealing an interest in the sexual practices of others she has revealed too much of herself:

> No, I'm laughing because I'm not the person to ask because I used to work in a sexual health clinic and I just keep talking about it all the time and I'm always asking people, "Do you want to get STI screenings?" And I'm always asking people about sexual activity. Well, not always, obviously, but like I really relish that conversation during booking. I'm blushing.
> Participant B

Laughing and blushing, the participant demonstrates how one's attitudes, understandings and approaches to midwifery care are often carried in the body. She voices her approach to midwifery; to communicate a professional level of understanding and interest in sexual healthcare. But her tentativeness also conveys a sense that even as a midwife you can be too open-minded, too open to the physical intimacies of pregnancy and birth – in this example, acknowledging that pregnant people are also sexually active and may benefit from STI screening – in a way that seems to overstep a boundary. One reason this boundary might exist, at least in popular culture, is that scenes of birth, "especially the moment of crowning (when the foetus reaches the vaginal opening), and maternal experiences of pain and pleasure" (Tyler & Baraitser, 2013, p. 1) have still not been widely portrayed or discussed. Jacqueline Rose writes that "Mothering [is] one of the ways a culture purifies itself of the sexuality that mostly still brings motherhood about today" (2018, p. 64). What begins as a hint that mothering bodies could be reimagined as sexually active bodies, continues in a vein that suggests we may have to completely shed our assumptions about who becomes a mother, and who becomes pregnant, and how they got there. As Rose writes telescopically in the words of Elena Ferrante citing Elsa Morante, "no one, starting with the mother's dressmaker, must think that a mother has a woman's body" (2018, p. 64). Midwives may still blush or laugh in discomfort on their way to shedding these assumptions as, just as there is little guidance for teaching about midwifery care for LGBTQ+ people, there is also little available research into the physical intimacies of birth to support midwives in their training. Elisabeth Bolaza highlights how few studies exist of some of the particular intimacies of birth that fall under what she terms "birth pleasure" (2020, p. 130). In her conclusion she calls for pleasure to be included in fuller understandings of birth as a light shining on pathways towards reproductive justice (2020, p. 133). A fuller spectrum of pregnancy, birth and postnatal experiences exists outside the imagination and expectation of many birth workers, and if these remain partly occluded by cultural depictions, lack of research and training, then birth workers' care practices and understandings of who they care for will limit both themselves and the pregnant and birthing people they work with. We suggest that being open to the physical intimacies of birth extends the scope of professional midwifery care to people of all genders and sexualities.

Body Awareness and Orientation in Midwifery

It's about my body as a midwife too

We have begun to think about how midwives carry knowledge and practices within their body, and some things that allow them to do this and what hinders them. In midwifery practice there are moments of overlap between providing professional care and being sensitive and open to the various intimacies of birth. The focus group provided a space for the participants to think about some of these moments of overlapping professionalism and intimacy as moments where midwives are physically present and implicated too:

> I looked after a same sex female couple having a baby, and I think my experience was quite positive, and the midwife I was with was really great. But one thing was that she, the midwife, like went in to see the couple and then came back to the other midwives, and she was like, "Oh, they always think I'm a lesbian …" Because this midwife thought that's how she came across. I dunno. [Laughter from group] But that was just interesting.
> Participant A

Though midwives are almost always working in one realm of sex or another, this example stands out for the participant as a moment when working with a lesbian couple has brought the midwife's own sexuality into the care episode (and perhaps how that might even be relevant to, or beneficial to the care they are giving). As with previous quotations, the speaker implicitly reveals the heteronormativity of maternity care. There is a sense that homosexuality in birthing spaces is different, noticeable, *felt*, and that this draws attention to the intimacy of birth (in a way that heterosexual intimacy in the birth space may not). The midwife attempts to locate herself in the care episode through ambiguously referring to her own sexuality, reminding us that within the framework of sexual orientation, heterosexuality is thought of as neutral and homosexuality as the deviation from this (Ahmed, 2006, p. 69). However, we could interpret the ambiguity of the midwife's statement as carrying within it the possibility of her own deviation, leading us to wonder how encounters – and which encounters – with birthing and pregnant people cause midwives to question their sexual orientations, gender identities, experiences and surroundings to orientate themselves within their practice.

When prompted, for example in a lecture about chestfeeding, participants gave examples of how student midwives assert their gender identities as cis women in ways that presume gender identity is determined by biological and physical characteristics such as having breasts and being able to breastfeed.

> ... when it came to the subject of chestfeeding, I think that people were expressing that they didn't also want to lose their identity as a woman. So we kind of looked at ways as to how that can coexist.
> Participant E

For the moment, the encounters remain ambiguous; it is not clear how awareness of one's sexuality or of one's gender identity as a midwife is relevant, *beneficial* even, to care episodes, or, if professionalism, sexuality and bodies of midwives make for uncomfortable bedfellows. To explore this, it may be helpful for student midwives to come across these moments – when their gender identities are brought into question – within the context of midwifery care. This is reminiscent of Brueggemann and Moddelmog's pedagogical strategy of coming out as queer and as disabled to their students which opens the students up to the "temporality and slipperiness of identity" (2003, p. 229) and maybe even have them question: "Is it possible for me to be that way too?" (Brueggemann & Moddelmog, 2003, p. 212).

Thinking about a pedagogic setting we might ask how to teach and how someone learns to bridge thinking about their own body, intimacy, and professionalism in midwifery. One participant gave an example from a lecture attended by student nurses and student midwives, where participants were invited to fill the space with the sounds of words for parts of (their) bodies:

> That lecture was very good and it really ... we were talking about the way we view our bodies as well. The lecturer was, he had a very ... he was very engaging and very dynamic and he had us shouting out quite vernacular words for different parts of the body,

which was really good fun ... although I couldn't shout some of them, I was too embarrassed, I just had to mime them. I still felt my mum's eyes on me: "Don't say that word in public!"... It helped me personally as well; it made my mind more open.
Participant C

Midwifery education will not be able to prepare midwives for all encounters, but perhaps it could include space for student midwives to explore their relationships to their own bodies – which may lead onto reflections of their sexual orientations and gender identities – in ways that invite and encourage them to question assumptions about the bodies of those they work towards *being with*.

Reflecting on bodies of midwives
Goldberg et al., writing about the experiences of lesbian mothers and perinatal nurses, offer the idea that "creating birthing spaces that better reflect the needs of lesbian mothers in particular might require that people within those spaces face fruitful discomfort" (2011, p. 187). Below, Participant E articulates the cold hostility of clinical spaces, and wonders, when they bring their own bodies and sexuality into their practice, what is the potential for midwives to recognise how their practices might need to change?

> Providing an environment where you are inviting people to share their intimacy with you. Sometimes it doesn't feel that what I've seen with bookings that the environment is sometimes really kind of cold. I mean, I wouldn't want to talk about my sexuality in that kind of atmosphere.
> Participant E

The student midwife is able to recognise discomfort, through bringing her own sexuality and experience into the space, and in some ways in contact with the sexuality of the pregnant and birthing people that she works with. Bringing sexuality (back) into maternity spaces may be uncomfortable for midwives as it invites them to consider their own bodies as feeling, sensitive, desiring in a way that is perhaps considered taboo. After all, midwives are in close contact with the bodies of pregnant and birthing people in ways that bring to mind Sara Ahmed's thoughts that lesbian desire is "contingent as a way of reflecting on the relation between sexual and social contact" (2006, p. 103). As Ahmed further develops her thought, lingering on the etymology of the word contingent, we think of how this echoes the *being with (woman)* namesake and ideology of midwives. She writes, "'Contingent' has the same root in Latin as the word 'contact' (*contingere: com,* with, *tangere,* to touch). Contingency is linked in this way to the sociality of being 'with' others, to getting close enough to touch" (Ahmed, 2006, p. 103). In linking Ahmed's thoughts on the contingency of lesbian desire to the *being with (woman)* of midwifery practice we suggest that for midwifery students and educators part of locating themselves in the discussion, of building a relationship with LGBTQ+ people, as with all people, involves thinking and working and practising and orientating through physically *being with* pregnant and birthing people.

With this in mind we wonder if midwifery, intimacy and body awareness, while brushing social and sexual practices uncomfortably close to one another, might all coexist with a discomfort full of potential, one that could allow midwives to *improve* their care for LGBTQ+ people. For when the bodies of midwives too are brought into midwifery care, then perhaps midwives are more open and attuned to "hav[ing] their expectations disrupted and practices reworked" (Goldberg et al., 2011, p. 188). Before we leap to conclusions, we remember that not all disorientation is radical; "bodies that experience disorientation can be defensive, as they reach out for support or as they search for a place to reground and orientate their relation to the world" (Ahmed, 2006, p. 158). For some people an experience of midwifery mediated through what we call 'the body' requires more support than is often available. Discomfort as a pedagogical strategy may be more fruitful or even more possible for White, able-bodied, cisgendered or straight midwives and it is necessary to think and act with this in mind.

Conclusion

In this chapter we have given examples of how thinking about LGBTQ+ inclusive care in midwifery involves understanding midwifery as a contingent, relational and embodied practice. This chapter outlines an unpredicted pathway of thought that formed when reading through a focus group transcript where student midwives articulated their bodies in(to) relation to the midwifery care that they give to LGBTQ+ people. The participants expressed how at times, when caring for or when thinking about caring for LGBTQ+ people they feel, or expect to feel out of place, giving shape to and sometimes reinforcing the hetero- and gender-normative healthcare space of maternity at present. Student midwives desire to work as professionals who are comfortable in their work environments, yet they know they will be working with people whose ways of becoming or being pregnant do not follow the heteronormative or gender-normative paths often taken for granted, thus leaving midwives feeling disorientated. Pedagogical strategies that acknowledge and incorporate this disorientation into midwifery curricula may help midwives to take steps towards improving their care and their ability to be *with* LGBTQ+ people.

This chapter also demonstrates how bodies of midwives carry their own kinds of knowledge. This has been acknowledged elsewhere in healthcare literature. Jan Savage's ethnographic work on nurse-patient interaction encourages a reading of the nurse's body through metaphor, suggesting that the social and physical meanings behind words that the nurses use to describe their practice, such as "'closeness'", bear witness to an unutterable embodied knowledge (1995, p. 85). Conversely, the action of nurses sitting and squatting with patients, who "by virtue of being unwell and vulnerable, are in a different place from nurses but, nevertheless, one that nurses can attempt to gain access to" (1995, p. 85), reveals a familiar metaphorical and utterable concept of feeling 'down'. By linking the physical movement of nurses and metaphor, Savage opens a way for nurses' use of their bodies to inform us of their lived experience. There is an opening here for pedagogical strategies that involve working with bodies as somatic research in its own right. These strategies may include verbal articulations of the body, such as the example of shouting out names of body parts in a lecture as shared by one focus group participant. It may also include physical articulations of the body, for example, through opportunities for midwives to move, gesture, perhaps even dance or be still while reflecting on discomfort and disorientation experienced in practice.

Changes to practice must be supported by more research, deeper explorations, and louder exclamations about the disparities in healthcare experienced by marginalised people. Without losing the urgency and specificity needed to care for LGBTQ+ people, we hope this chapter can engender a shift away from models of teaching difference as otherness as well as a shift away from focusing so much on healthcare practitioner comfort as a marker of successful LGBTQ+ curriculum content, and a move towards being more embracing of, and more importantly, responsible for, discomfort in midwifery care.

Author biographies
Teresa Arias BSc, MSc, PGCEA, Senior Fellow of the Higher Education Academy, has been a midwife for over twenty years and has worked in many different roles in the community as a caseload and independent midwife and as a consultant midwife at King's College Hospital. For the last seven years, Teresa has been involved in delivering preregistration and postgraduate education and is currently the lead for Postgraduate Diploma Midwifery and MSc programmes in Midwifery and Maternal and Newborn Health at the Faculty of Nursing, Midwifery and Palliative Care at King's College London. Teresa is committed to preparing future midwives to deliver personalised, compassionate and effective midwifery care.

Jess McArdle is a midwife currently working in the community at Lewisham and Greenwich NHS Trust. She is interested in embodied experiences of midwifery, and relationships between caregiving and receiving. In her spare time she attends as many contemporary dance classes as she can.

Body Awareness and Orientation in Midwifery

Hannah Rayment-Jones is a midwife in the final year of a full-time, NIHR-funded PhD, researching how maternity care can improve clinical outcomes and experiences for women with social risk factors. She has also worked in a range of clinical midwifery settings, including the award-winning caseload team at Imperial College NHS Trust, providing continuity of care for socially vulnerable families and a successful homebirth service. Her research interests focus on improving perinatal morbidity, mortality and clinical care experiences for women with low socioeconomic status and those living socially complex lives. She is committed to ensuring the patient voice is heard in the research, design and delivery of clinical care.

References
Ahmed, S. (2006). *Queer phenomenology: Orientations, objects, others.* Duke University Press.
de Beauvoir, S. (1997). *Le deuxième sexe*, [The second sex]. (H. M. Parshley, Ed. & Trans.). Vintage. (Original work published 1953)
Bolaza, E. B. (2020). Birth pleasure: Meanings, politics, and praxis. *Journal of the Motherhood Initiative for Research and Community Involvement, 11*(1), 123-135.
Bosse, J. D., Nesteby, J. A., & Randall, C. E. (2015). Integrating sexual minority health issues into a health assessment class. *Journal of Professional Nursing, 31*(6), 498-507. https://doi.org/10.1016/j.profnurs.2015.04.007
Bradfield, Z., Duggan, R., Hauck, Y., & Kelly, M. (2018). Midwives being "with woman": An integrative review. *Women and Birth, 31*(2), 143-152. https://doi.org/10.1016/j.wombi.2017.07.011
Bradfield, Z., Hauck, Y., Kelly, M., & Duggan, R. (2019). "It's what midwifery is all about": Western Australian midwives' experiences of being 'with woman' during labour and birth in the known midwife model. *BMC Pregnancy and Childbirth.* https://doi.org/10.1186/s12884-018-2144-z
Brathwaite, C. (2020). *I am not your baby mother.* Quercus.
Brueggemann, B. J., & Moddelmog, D. A. (2003). Coming-out pedagogy: Risking identity in language and literature classrooms. In D. P. Freedman & M. Stoddard Holmes (Eds.), *The embodiment, authority, and identity in the academy* (pp. 208-233). State University of New York Press.

Carabez, R., Pellegrini, M., Mankovitz, A., Eliason, M. J., & Dariotis, W. M. (2015). Nursing students' perceptions of their knowledge of lesbian, gay, bisexual, and transgender issues: Effectiveness of a multi-purpose assignment in a public health nursing class. *Journal of Nursing Education, 54*(1), 50–53. https://doi.org/10.3928/01484834-20141228-03

Cramer, E., & Hunter, B. (2019). Relationships between working conditions and emotional wellbeing in midwives. *Women and Birth, 32*(6), 521–532. https://doi.org/10.1016/j.wombi.2018.11.010

Davis-Floyd, R. E. (1990). The role of obstetrical rituals in the resolution of cultural anomaly. *Social Science & Medicine, 31*(2), 175–189. https://doi.org/10.1016/0277-9536(90)90060-6

Davis-Floyd, R., & Davis, E. (1996). Intuition as authoritative knowledge in midwifery and homebirth. *Medical Anthropology Quarterly, 10*(2), new series, 237–269.

Donnison, J. (1977). *Midwives and medical men: A history of the struggle for the control of childbirth*. Heinemann Education.

Dutton, L., Koenig, K., & Fennie, K. (2008). Gynecologic care of the female-to-male transgender man. *Journal of Midwifery and Women's Health, 53*(4), 331–337. https://doi.org/10.1016/j.jmwh.2008.02.003

Ferrante, E. (2008). *The lost daughter* (Ann Goldstein, Trans.). Europa.

Goldberg, L., Harbin, A., & Campbell, S. (2011). Queering the birthing space: Phenomenological interpretations of the relationships between lesbian couples and perinatal nurses in the context of birthing care. *Sexualities, 14*(2), 173–192. https://doi.org/10.1177/1363460711399028

Hanson, C. (2015). The maternal body. In D. Hilman & U. Maude (Eds.), *The Cambridge companion to the body in literature* (pp. 87–100). Cambridge University Press.

Harbin, A., Beagan, B., & Goldberg, L. (2012). Discomfort, judgment, and health care for queers. *Journal of Bioethical Inquiry, 9*(2), 149–160. https://doi.org/10.1007/s11673-012-9367-x

Heyes, C., Dean, M., & Goldberg, L. (2016). Queer phenomenology, sexual orientation, and health care spaces: Learning from the narratives of queer women and nurses in primary health care. *Journal of Homosexuality, 63*(2), 141–155. https://doi.org/10.1080/00918369.2015.1083775

Hines, S., Pearce, R., Pfeffer, C., Riggs, D., Ruspini, E., & Ray White, F. (2018). Trans pregnancy: Implications for policy and practice. Poster presented at *World Professional Association of Transgender Health Symposium*, Buenos Aires, Argentina.

Hoffkling, A., Obedin-Maliver, J., & Sevelius, J. (2017). From erasure to opportunity: A qualitative study of the experiences of transgender men around pregnancy and recommendations for providers. *BMC Pregnancy and Childbirth, 17*(S2), 332. https://doi.org/10.1186/s12884-017-1491-5

Hunter, B. (2001). Emotion work in midwifery: A review of current knowledge. *Journal of Advanced Nursing, 34*(4), 436–444. https://doi.org/10.1046/j.1365-2648.2001.01772.x

Hunter, B. (2004). Conflicting ideologies as a source of emotion work in midwifery. *Midwifery, 20*(3), 261–272. https://doi.org/10.1016/j.midw.2003.12.004

Hunter, B. (2006). The importance of reciprocity in relationships between community-based midwives and mothers. *Midwifery, 22*(4), 308–322. https://doi.org/10.1016/j.midw.2005.11.002

Hunter, B. (2010). Mapping the emotional terrain of midwifery: What can we see and what lies ahead? *International Journal of Work Organisation and Emotion, 3*(3), 253–269. https://doi.org/10.1504/IJWOE.2010.032925

Hunter, B., & Deery, R. (2008). *Emotions in midwifery and reproduction*. Palgrave Macmillan.

Kirkham, M. (2007). *Exploring the dirty side of women's health*. Routledge.

Kirkham, M., & Stapleton, H. (2000). Midwives' support needs as childbirth changes. *Journal of Advanced Nursing*. https://doi.org/10.1046/j.1365-2648.2000.01497.x

Kitzinger, S. (2012). *Birth & sex: The power and the passion*. Pinter & Martin.

Knight, M., Bunch, K., Tuffnell, D., Jayakody, H., Shakespeare, J., Kotnis, R., Kenyon, S., & Kurinczuk, J. J. (Eds.) on behalf of MBRRACE-UK. (2018). *Saving lives, improving mothers' care – lessons learned to inform maternity care from the UK and Ireland Confidential Enquiries into Maternal Deaths and Morbidity 2014–16*. National Perinatal Epidemiology Unit, University of Oxford.

Lawler, J. (1991). *Behind the screens: Nursing, somology, and the problem of the body*. Churchill Livingstone.

Lee, E., Taylor, J., & Raitt, F. (2011). "It's not me, it's them": How lesbian women make sense of negative experiences of maternity care: A hermeneutic study. *Journal of Advanced Nursing, 67*(5), 982–990. https://doi.org/10.1111/j.1365-2648.2010.05548.x

Lewis, M., Jones, A., & Hunter, B. (2017). Women's experience of trust within the midwife–mother relationship. *International Journal of Childbirth, 7*(1), 40–52. https://doi.org/10.1891/2156-5287.7.1.40

Light, A. D., Obedin-Maliver, J., Sevelius, J. M., & Kerns, J. L. (2014). Transgender men who experienced pregnancy after female-to-male gender transitioning. *Obstetrics & Gynecology, 124*(6), 1120–1127. https://doi.org/10.1097/AOG.0000000000000540

Lim, F., Johnson, M., & Eliason, M. (2015). A national survey of faculty knowledge, experience, and readiness for teaching lesbian, gay, bisexual, and transgender health in baccalaureate nursing programs. *Nursing Education Perspectives, 36*(3), 144–152. https://doi.org/10.5480/14-1355

MacDonald, T., Noel-Weiss, J., West, D., Walks, M., Biener, M. L., Kibbe, A., & Myler, E. (2016). Transmasculine individuals' experiences with lactation, chestfeeding, and gender identity: A qualitative study. *BMC Pregnancy and Childbirth, 16*(1), 106. https://doi.org/10.1186/s12884-016-0907-y

McCann, E., & Brown, M. (2018). The inclusion of LGBT+ health issues within undergraduate healthcare education and professional training programmes: A systematic review. *Nurse Education Today, 64,* 204–214. https://doi.org/10.1016/j.nedt.2018.02.028

McCourt, C., & Stevens, T. (2009). Relationship and reciprocity in caseload midwifery. In B. Hunter & R. Deery (Eds.). *Emotions in midwifery and reproduction* (1st ed., pp. 17–35). Palgrave Macmillan.

Niven, C. (1994). Coping with labour pain: The midwife's role. In S. Robinson & A. M. Thomson (Eds.), *Midwives, research and childbirth Volume 3* (pp. 91–119). Chapman and Hall.

Nursing and Midwifery Council (Great Britain). (2009). Standards for pre-registration midwifery education. Nursing & Midwifery Council. https://www.nmc.org.uk/globalassets/sitedocuments/standards/nmc-standards-for-preregistration-midwifery-education.pdf

Obedin-Maliver, J., & Makadon, H. J. (2016). Transgender men and pregnancy. *Obstetric Medicine, 9*(1), 4–8. https://doi.org/10.1177/1753495X15612658

Pearce, R. (2018). *Understanding trans health: Discourse, power and possibility.* Policy Press.

Body Awareness and Orientation in Midwifery

Rose, J. (2018). *Mothers: An essay on love and cruelty*. Faber & Faber.

Röndahl, G., Bruhner, E., & Lindhe, J. (2009). Heteronormative communication with lesbian families in antenatal care, childbirth and postnatal care. *Journal of Advanced Nursing, 65*(11), 2337–2344. https://doi.org/10.1111/j.1365-2648.2009.05092.x

Sandall, J., Coxon, K., Mackintosh, N., Rayment-Jones, H., Locock, L., & Page, L. (writing on behalf of the Sheila Kitzinger symposium) (2016). Relationships: The pathway to safe, high-quality maternity care. Report from the Sheila Kitzinger Symposium at Green Templeton College, October 2015. Green Templeton College, Oxford.

Savage, J. (1995). *Nursing intimacy: An ethnographic approach to nurse-patient interaction*. Scutari.

Stewart, M. (2005). "I'm just going to wash you down": Sanitizing the vaginal examination. *Journal of Advanced Nursing, 51*(6), 587–594. https://doi.org/10.1111/j.1365-2648.2005.03543.x

Taylor, O., Rapsey, C. M., & Treharne, G. J. (2018). Sexuality and gender identity teaching within preclinical medical training in New Zealand: Content, attitudes and barriers. *The New Zealand Medical Journal, 131*(1477), 35–44.

Thorstensson, S., Ekström, A., Lundgren, I., & Hertfelt Wahn, E. (2012). Exploring professional support offered by midwives during labour: An observation and interview study. *Nursing Research and Practice*. https://doi.org/10.1155/2012/648405

Tyler, I., & Baraitser, L. (2013). Private view, public birth: Making feminist sense of the new visual culture of childbirth. *Studies in the Maternal, 5*(2), 1–27. https://doi.org/10.16995/sim.18

Ussher, J. M. (2006). *Managing the monstrous feminine: Regulating the reproductive body*. Routledge.

Walker, K., Arbour, M., & Waryold, J. (2016). Educational strategies to help students provide respectful sexual and reproductive health care for lesbian, gay, bisexual, and transgender persons. *Journal of Midwifery & Women's Health, 61*(6), 737–743. https://doi.org/10.1111/jmwh.12506

Wilton, T., & Kaufmann, T. (2001). Lesbian mothers' experiences of maternity care in the UK. *Midwifery, 17*(3), 203–211.

Wolkowitz, C. (2002). The social relations of body work. *Work, Employment and Society, 16*(3), 497–510. https://doi.org/10.1177/095001702762217452

Yingling, C. T., Cotler, K., & Hughes, T. L. (2017). Building nurses' capacity to address health inequities: Incorporating lesbian, gay, bisexual and transgender health content in a family nurse practitioner programme. *Journal of Clinical Nursing, 26*(17–18), 2807–2817. https://doi.org/10.1111/jocn.13707

CHAPTER 3:
BODIES IN MIGRATION
MARKED FOR EXCLUSION

Nancy Hansen

Abstract

The United Nations Refugee Agency has stated that there are more people on the move than ever before (UNHCR, 2017) and the current political understanding is of refugees and migrants as dangerous, fearful and unwelcome (Dolmage, 2018). It is estimated that as many as 22% of the world's refugees have some form of disability and disabled people comprise one of the world's largest minority groups: over one billion in number. Yet, for the most part, disabled people remain largely marked for exclusion as the vast majority of migration legislation reflecting disabilist/ableist understandings of disability and disabled people excludes disabled people from the outset. Almost four million of the world's displaced peoples are disabled and the Women's Refugee Commission estimates this proportion to be one fifth of the total number (Women's Refugee Commission, n.d.). However, despite these compelling numbers little is known of their (disabled people's) daily lived experience in post-conflict situations. Several funding agencies and non-governmental organisations geared to rebuilding in post-conflict/disaster situations have disability access as part of the organisation's philosophy or mission statement. Yet, in practice during the reconstruction phase disability access considerations rarely feature. Similarly, a significant number of countries are signatories to the UN Convention on Rights of Persons with Disabilities. However, progress on the ground remains markedly slow.

Key words: disability, displacement, exclusion, migration, armed conflicts, refugees

Talking Bodies III

Introduction: Fleeing Syria in a wheelchair

> My name is Nujeen Mustafa and I am 18 years old. I am from Syria and I grew up in Aleppo. When the war started, we could not evacuate easily because of my disability, particularly as we were living on the 5th floor of a building with no elevator. I felt like I was a barrier for the safety of my family. Everybody was trying to be strong for me. It was very stressful and depressing. Our worst fear was that the army would break into the city and that we wouldn't be able to leave after that, so we fled. It turned out to be a wise decision. We first fled to Turkey and in August 2015, crossed the Mediterranean Sea, got to Greece and from there to Germany.
> (Mustafa, 2017)

Across the globe there are more people on the move than ever before. In 2019 the United Nations Refugee Agency estimated the number of migrants to be 272 million (UNHCR, 2019). The reasons for this mass migration are many and varied: armed conflict, political unrest, famine, discrimination or economic necessity (Hughes, 2017). Migrant populations are not homogeneous and they reflect the natural diversity that is humanity. Disabled people have always been part of that diversity and disabled persons themselves are diverse. They comprise the world's largest minority group – over one billion people worldwide (World Health Organization, 2011). The Women's Refugee Commission estimates that of the world's seventy million displaced people, over fourteen million are disabled (Women's Refugee Commission, n.d.).

Estimates indicate that as many as 80% of disabled refugees are without access to food, water, sanitation and medical services (Humanity & Inclusion, 2013). Few, if any, facilities are built with disability access in mind. Disabled refugees remain largely marked for exclusion. Often, the action of migration itself is so arduous and difficult that disability is acquired in the process (Humanity & Inclusion, n.d.). However, despite these compelling numbers little is known of their (disabled people's) daily lived experience in post-conflict situations (Humanity & Inclusion, 2013).

Bodies in Migration Marked for Exclusion

Context

There is a disturbing silence, a lack of engagement and general absence of consideration of the situation regarding disabled migrants (Soldatic, 2013). In general, disabled people remain unexpected in these on-the-ground situations. Their appearance seems to take us by surprise and thus the services that they might require, which one might ordinarily expect (or hope) to find in other societies, are not available to them.

Disabled people are present in conflict zones throughout the world. If there is a conflict, it is safe to assume that there are disabled people affected by it as well as those who will become disabled as a direct consequence of that conflict (Byrne et al., 2017). Hospital activities, so vital to many disabled people, can be severely curtailed as well as other damage and/or disruption to major infrastructure, such as public transport, roads and footpaths, which can have a detrimental effect on the physically disabled. The noise, danger and displacement inherent in conflict situations can also add to the stresses of all disabled people but particularly those whose disability relates to mental health or cognitive ability. Inclusion and Humanity (previously known as Handicap International), estimates that as many as 22% of refugees in Syria, Lebanon and Jordan are disabled (Calvot, 2014). Disability is still largely perceived as an individual medicalised problem as opposed to a social justice issue (Jaffee, 2016). Fear, ignorance, ableism, myth and misconceptions regarding disability mean that disabled refugees are between four to ten times more likely to experience violence than non-disabled refugees (Pearce, 2015).

At present, we find ourselves in an era where difference is often frowned upon, greeted with fear and suspicion (Dolmage, 2018; Baynton, 2016). Those individuals who have historical privilege feel threatened and fear displacement and a shift in the 'natural' order of things (Nario-Redmond, 2020). As a result, we can view current political understandings of refugees and migrants as being seen as dangerous, fearful and unwelcome (Dolmage, 2018). Populist governments have introduced highly restrictive immigration legislation and disabled people have been disproportionately affected by its application (Kim,

2019). In France, Spain and Italy, citizenship can be restricted or denied on the basis of disability (Fries, 2019). Recent changes to US immigration legislation would disqualify individuals receiving public assistance from obtaining a 'green card' (documentation enabling people to live and work in the United States) (Kim, 2019).

The onset of the COVID-19 pandemic has only served to worsen the situation for disabled refugees (Mustafa, 2020). Services and facilities in refugee camps are rarely accessible to physically disabled people at the best of times and the required sanitation, hygiene and social distancing are next to impossible in such a situation (Mustafa, 2020). Emergency confinement and disaster preparedness protocols that place restrictions on access to food, transportation, support services and other resources often fail to account for the needs of disabled people (Qi & Hu, 2020). Consequently, disabled people are disproportionately impacted by lack of access and the virus itself (Mustafa, 2020). The vast majority of deaths attributed to COVID-19 are among people with disabilities and underlying health conditions (UNHCR, 2020). According to recent statistics two-thirds of the deaths attributed to COVID-19 in the UK are people with disabilities (Webster, 2020). Similarly, in Canada "Today, four out of five Canadians who have died from COVID-19 in Canada are linked to long-term care homes"(Black, 2020).

Most disabled people are located in areas of limited resources and fragile economies, and 80% of disabled people are located in countries with extremely limited resources (WHO, 2011). Most disability that is acquired can be seen as being the result of ageing, poverty, malnutrition and conflict. Often the very same causes can compel individuals to migrate in the hope of better living conditions elsewhere, or in the most severe of cases to hope to ensure survival in the face of impending death. Many acquire disability, or have their pre-existing conditions worsened, as a consequence of the living conditions they have to endure as a consequence of that migration (Mirza, 2011a).

Historical roots, myths and misconceptions
These situations are often made worse by discriminatory cultural

understandings of disability in their homeland (WHO, 2011). In various regions worldwide, disabled people are perceived as sub-human (Rau-Barriga, 2016). Disabled people's bodies are thought to have magical powers and they are killed for their body parts as they purportedly bring good luck (Reimer-Kirkham et al., 2019). In times of conflict, families are often forced to make difficult decisions, on the spot, and disabled family members may be left behind as a result (Human Rights Watch, 2019). Consequently, disabled people often face a perilous existence in the countries where they live or the ones they are migrating to (Hansen et al., 2017). Discrimination from outwith and within their cultural groups is often presented as natural, accepted practice and is not seen as oppression or discrimination (Harris, 2003).

It would seem that human disability – the mere presence of it as well as its representation – somehow disturbs the accepted 'natural' cultural aesthetic of public space (Siebers, 2010). Indeed, the so called 'ugly laws' passed in late nineteenth and early twentieth century North American cities were geared to keeping the 'unsightly' (read disability) out of public space so as not to offend public sensibilities (Schweik, 2010). These retrograde statutes remained in place in various jurisdictions throughout North America until the mid 1970s (Schweik, 2010). This lack of understanding works to justify ongoing inequities and lack of acceptance and accommodation (Yeo, 2017). Disabled people have not experienced the same degree of legislative advancement that has been generally accorded to other marginalised populations (racialised, gender or LGBTQ+) groups (Anani, 2001). Many policies, particularly those related to immigration, remain instilled with ableism (El-Lahib, 2016).

The discriminatory language found in Australian immigration legislation is one example, where:

> The Department of Immigration and Border Protection (DIBP) currently implements a policy that deems "significant cost" to be $40 000 throughout the visa applicant's stay in Australia. A visa applicant whose projected care costs exceed this amount can be refused a visa on the grounds of failing to meet the Public Interest

> Criteria, unless they are able to obtain a waiver (in PIC 4005). Moreover, this cost ceiling applies regardless of whether the health care or community services will actually be used by the applicant.
> (Cookman, 2018)

Despite the significant advances in the legal recognition of the rights of persons with disabilities at international and national levels, the deeply rooted negative perceptions about the value of their lives continue to be a prevalent obstacle in all societies. Those perceptions are ingrained in ableism (Devandas-Aguilar, 2019, p. 3). Determinations of capacity are often highly subjective, based on so-called abhorrent physicality and outdated understandings of disability and misconceptions of the body as machine with disability being characterised as burdensome and useless (El-Lahib, 2016; Hughes, 2017).

The United Nations Convention on the Rights of Persons with Disabilities (CRPD) marks one of the few instances where people with disabilities have been substantively involved from the development and implementation of disability specific legislation.

> The Convention follows decades of work by the United Nations to change attitudes and approaches to persons with disabilities. It takes to a new height the movement from viewing persons with disabilities as 'objects' of charity, medical treatment and social protection towards viewing persons with disabilities as "subjects" with rights, who are capable of claiming those rights and making decisions for their lives based on their free and informed consent as well as being active members of society.
> (United Nations, n.d.)

Structural invisibility
Traditionally, disability is seen in one of two ways: exceptional or unexpected. Either way it is regularly framed as unnatural and disruptive to established practices (Hansen & Philo, 2007). This perspective has in effect enabled a form of social absolution presenting disability as dismissable, difficult, individualised and avoidable. Complicating or problematising disability has direct negative consequences for disabled people (Berghs, 2015; Cherney, 2019)

Bodies in Migration Marked for Exclusion

Statistical categorisations rarely include data on disabled refugees (Naseef, 2018). Therefore, disabled refugees are not viewed as real or important and do not count literally or figuratively, demeaning their status as human beings and further adding to their exclusion. Disabled people are not regularly identified in statistical and other data collection and assessment exercises. Those disabled individuals who are displaced many times, who live in dispersed or urban settings, who remain isolated in their homes, or with invisible disabilities (such as those with hearing, visual, intellectual and psychosocial impairments) are very often omitted. Disabled children often remain unregistered at birth, owing to negative social cultural beliefs thereby exposing them to even further risks (UNHCR, 2019).

Consequently, they remain present but invisible. That is, because disabled people are rarely enumerated, they do not *count* officially and remain unexpected. Furthermore, people with disability are frequently reduced to some sort of block identity or singular identifying factor, such as the elderly or vulnerable people. Identifying a group in this manner can signify a lack of importance or value (CBM, 2018). Again, the value of disabled people as individuals is negated. Characterisations of this type may also work to conceal ongoing abuse, neglect or marginalisation (Yeo, 2017). Knowledge of disability and capacity remain for the most part superficial and narrow. The standard approach to disabled access, where it exists, maintains isolation through segregation in that universal access is not usually part of infrastructure design. As a result, access may be incremental and disabled people are placed together in specific areas or locations. Most countries have restrictive, discriminatory immigration policies related to disabled people. Some refugee resettlement agencies provide specialised care but it is limited with little consistency, add on or afterthought.

Several refugee support and funding agencies and non-governmental organisations geared to rebuilding in post-conflict/ disaster situations have disability access as part of the organisation's philosophy or mission statement (CBM, 2017). However, in practice during the reconstruction phase these tenets are rarely followed

(CBM, 2013). Often, personnel in the field are placed in difficult emergency, post-conflict or disaster situations. Established protocols rarely include disability accommodation as part of their framework. Minimal attention is paid to the creation of accessible programmes, services and facilities (CBM, 2018). It is as if disabled people are not expected as part of the migrant population (CBM, 2017). Furthermore, there remains a perception that some type of expertise is required to 'deal with' disability and/or impairment (Mirza, 2011b). As a result, a type of social amnesty has developed where officials believe that some unknown specialised organisation will 'take care' of 'those people' (Women's Refugee Commission, 2008). In doing so, individuals absolve themselves of social responsibility. Therefore, little, if anything, is done to facilitate access or inclusion of disabled migrants. Similarly, a significant number of countries are signatories to the UN Convention on Rights of Persons with Disabilities. However, the signing of the documentation has not translated to implementation in many countries and progress on the ground remains markedly slow (Waldschmidt & Sépulchre, 2019). Subsequent monitoring by the United Nations Rapporteur documented serious gaps and weaknesses in execution in some of the world's most resource rich countries (Canada and the United Kingdom are only two examples (Roberts, 2000; Hansen et. al., 2017)). Much of the daily life experience of disabled migrants seems to remain in a mysterious vacuum.

With poor accessibility, and limited access to services and facilities, the disabled remain among the most at risk of displaced persons. Accounts of physically disabled people having to crawl to the toilet and other public facilities are not uncommon (Mustafa, 2020). Food and water distribution and healthcare access often remain inaccessible (Karanja, 2009). This is a manifestation of structural ableism. That is, the arbitrary privileging of certain forms of physicality and blithely assuming that everyone has the capacity to be able to climb stairs or to read printed notices, for example. Excessive cost is regularly attributed as a reason for denying people with disabilities access to services and facilities. It is interesting to note that disability accommodation cost is often targeted in this manner. Whereas costs associated with other types of accommodation are seen as natural, those associated with disability are often labelled extravagant; as is the rationale used by the British Government for the cessation of the programme allowing disabled children to enter the country citing a lack of resources (Agerholm, 2017).

At times, individual determinations are resolved by ministerial intervention (intersession by a public official on behalf of an individual). However, this action is a highly individualised and unregulated process (CBC, 2016). This crisis response approach minimises the extent of this issue and reinforces the naturalness of invisibility. There are numerous documented cases where immigration status has been denied based on the perceived disability or impairment of immediate family members (spouse or child). Furthermore, non-disabled family members may be denied entry based on the perceived health status (or lack thereof) of family members (Fries, 2019). Although some jurisdictions, such as Canada, for example (Government of Canada, 2018), have relaxed somewhat, many of the underlying tenets remain the same (Wright, 2018). Although these changes will improve immigration opportunities, for some, medicalised understandings of disability present a significant obstacle.

Throughout most immigration history, impairment and disability have been used as a screening mechanism to deny entry (Soldatic & Fiske, 2009; Baynton, 2016; Dolmage, 2018; Capurri, 2020). For example, the vast majority of disability-related legislation reflects systemic ableism (disabilist/ableist understandings of disability): "Despite the significant advances in the recognition of the rights of persons with disabilities at international and national levels, the deeply rooted negative perceptions about the value of their lives continue to be a prevalent obstacle in all societies." Those perceptions are ingrained in what is known as 'ableism' (Devandas-Aguilar, 2019, p. 3), thereby excluding disabled people from the outset (Fries, 2019).

As this recent article underscores:

> Immigration to many countries is already difficult for those with disabilities. In 2007, when I applied for permanent residency in Canada, I learned that medical requirements were waived only if I were married to a Canadian citizen. Fortunately, Canada had recently recognised gay marriage, so I was able to live as a permanent resident with the Canadian citizen who, for the past 12 years, has been my husband …
> (Fries, 2019)

Regarding health status, the Canadian Immigration and Refugee Act states that people with disabilities can be denied a visa because they "might reasonably be expected to cause excessive demand on health or social services" (Fries, 2019). Disabled immigrants are largely perceived as passive recipients of care and are not seen as having capacity value in their own right, but rather only in their association with non-disabled people. The United States and Canada are not unique in their restrictive interpretations, with the United Kingdom, France and Australia and many other European countries adopting similarly prohibitive legal interpretations (Fries, 2019). When disabilities have been caused by the experience of forced relocation, migration or dislocation, the process of relocation is slower and more complicated as a result, because services, facilities and housing are not accessible (Mirza, 2011a). These factors often result in social, cultural and/or environmental restrictions (Pearce, 2015). Consequently, family and friends are the means of access to goods and services for the majority of disabled people in the midst of fractured infrastructure (Dockery, 2018).

Marginalised groups such as disabled or LGBTQ+ peoples are often overlooked and are not part of the process or programming in post-conflict situations (Byrne et al., 2017). Health professionals have little exposure, training or real understanding of disability or disability issues in this context (Rohwerder, 2013). According to statistics, less than 16% of refugee support agencies have disability-related programming (Pearce, 2015). There is limited or difficult accessibility to sexual healthcare support (Tanabe et al., 2015). Disabled people are often seen as 'less worthy' or cursed. Living in cultural social isolation is accepted practice. Able-bodied privilege is largely unrecognised. Social citizenship of disabled people may be formally recognised but rarely substantively implemented (dos Santos-Zingale & McColl, 2006).

The way forward
To date, the existing system shows few signs of substantive inclusion of disabled people (CBM, 2013). Until very recently disabled people have had little if any input into policies and programmes that directly impact them (UNHCR, 2018). As a result, we (disabled people) find ourselves caught up in and grappling with a legislative system that is not of our making (UNHCR, 2017). Yet, all too often we are expected to fix it, and in doing so a great deal of physical and emotional energy is expended. The concept of programme development or adaptation for disabled people is rare and where they exist at all, segregation is the order of the day (CBM, 2017). Information is seldom shared between and among government or non-governmental agencies (UNHCR, 2017). Universal design and budget elements are not usually included in development schemes (CBM, 2017). Disability-led organisations remain aliens on the scene. Though rarely included, these organisations can provide valuable insights concerning inclusive protocol development, expertise and disability awareness training (CBM, 2018). A disability-inclusion lens is essential going forward and disability must be included from the outset (CBM, 2018).

Conflict is a significant source of disability responsible for both physical and psychological impairment (Byrne et al., 2017). We also need to recognise that people with newly acquired disabilities may be very different from those individuals with lifelong disability experience. Thus, programmes must be developed and personnel trained accordingly in order to acknowledge this consideration (CBM, 2017). An intersectional approach is the key to moving forward.

Although progress is being made thanks to the CRPD, problems remain with interpretation and implementation on the ground on the part of the signatories (Duell-Piening, 2018). It should be noted that there are no penalties for non-compliance with the agreement.

Conclusion

The naturalness of exclusion for disabled refugees and their disadvantaged status is alarming. There are important questions that must be asked going forward and uncomfortable conversations that must be had in order to substantively improve and rectify the current situation. Whose bodies count? Why are certain bodies (read disabled) so readily made invisible, discounted and disappeared? The respect that should be accorded to disability issues and to disabled people is largely missing. At best, we are slowly moving toward tolerance, which is simply not good enough. Mere tolerance is not acceptance and certainly does not constitute inclusion. The social discomfort that permeates and often accompanies disability is based on embedded understandings. Fear and ignorance have not led to a solid framework of policy development. With few exceptions, development in this arena has been haphazard and disorganised with little substantive impact. Despite our numbers, disabled people are dealt with as a fringe element on an ad hoc basis. Quite simply, going forward we must expect disability. We have a very long way to go and, until that time, we remain marked for exclusion.

Author biography

Nancy Hansen, PhD is an Associate Professor and Director of the Interdisciplinary Master's Programme in Disability Studies at the University of Manitoba. Nancy obtained a PhD (Human Geography) from the University of Glasgow. Her research interests in disability studies are varied including: disability in spaces of culture education, literacy social policy, employment healthcare access and experiences of disabled and LGBTQ+ communities in post-conflict areas. Nancy is a former President of the Canadian Disability Studies Association. She is co-editor of the *Routledge History of Disability* and *Untold Stories: A Canadian Disability History Reader*. Nancy has written numerous book chapters and contributed to various international academic journals.

References

Agerholm, H. (2017, 9 February). Disabled child refugees entry to UK through resettlement scheme suspended by Home Office. *The Independent.* https://www.independent.co.uk/news/uk/home-news/disabled-child-refugees-uk-suspend-entry-home-office-resettlement-unhcr-united-nations-lord-dubs-a7571451.html

Anani, L. (2001). Refugees with disabilities: A human rights perspective. *Refuge, 19*(2), 23–30.

Baynton, D. (2016). *Defectives in the land: Disability and immigration in the Age of Eugenics.* University of Chicago Press

Berghs, M. (2015). Radicalising "disability" in conflict and post-conflict situations. *Disability and Society, 30*(5), 743–758. https://doi.org/10.1080/09687599.2015.1052044

Black, D. (2020). BC's swift response to long-term care crisis sets the bar for other provinces. *Broadbent Institute.* https://www.broadbentinstitute.ca/bc_s_swift_response_to_long_term_care_crisis_sets_the_bar_for_other_provinces

Byrne, S., Mizzi, R., & Hansen, N. (2017). Living in a liminal peace. Where is the social justice for LGBTQ and disability communities residing in post peace accord Northern Ireland? *Journal of Peace and Justice Studies, 27*(1), 24–51. https://doi.org/10.5840/peacejustice20172712

Calvot, T. (2014). Hidden victims of the Syrian crisis: Disabled, injured and older refugees. HelpAge International and Handicap International. https://data.unhcr.org/en/documents/details/41843

Capurri, V. (2020). *Not good enough for Canada: Canadian public discourse around issues of inadmissibility for potential immigrants with diseases and/or disabilities, 1902–2002.* University of Toronto Press.

CBC (2016, 10 August). York University prof denied residency over son with Down syndrome returning to Canada, *CBC News.* https://www.cbc.ca/news/canada/toronto/professor-granted-permanent-residency-1.3715416

CBM (2013, 31 October). CBM is supporting refugees with disabilities. https://reliefweb.int/report/jordan/cbm-supporting-refugees-disabilities

CBM (2017). Disability-Inclusive Development Toolkit. https://www.cbm.org/fileadmin/user_upload/Publications/CBM-DID-TOOLKIT-accessible.pdf

CBM (2018, 11 November). Oasis of accessibility. https://www.cbm.org/news/blog/blogs/blogs-2018/oasis-of-accessibility/

Cherney, J. (2019). *Ableist rhetoric: How we know, value, and see disability*. Penn State University Press.
Cookman, D. (2018). How does Australia's migration system deal with disability? https://www.shglawyers.com.au/how-does-australias-migration-system-deal-with-disability/
Devandas-Aguilar, C. (2019, 17 December). Rights of persons with disabilities: Report of the Special Rapporteur on the rights of persons with disabilities. United Nations. https://digitallibrary.un.org/record/3872393
Dockery, W. (2018, 25 May). Support for disabled refugees in Germany. https://perma.cc/WE8X-5Q8F
Dolmage, J. (2018). *Disabled upon arrival: Eugenics, immigration and the construction of race and disability*. Ohio State University Press.
Duda-Mikulin, E., Scullion, L., & Currie, R. (2019). Wasted lives in scapegoat Britain: Overlaps and departures between migration studies and disability studies, *Disability and Society*, 9(35), 1373–1397. https://doi.org/10.1080/09687599.2019.1690428
Duell-Piening, P. (2018). Refugee resettlement and the Convention on the Rights of Persons with Disabilities. *Disability and Society*, 23(5), 661–684. https://doi.org/10.1080/09687599.2018.1444582
El-Lahib, Y. (2016). Troubling constructions of Canada as a "land of opportunity"for immigrants: A critical disability lens. *Disability and Society*, 33(5), 758–776. https://doi.org/10.1080/09687599.2016.1200460
European Disability Forum. (n.d.). Migration & refugees with disabilities. https://www.edf-feph.org/migration-and-refugees-with-disabilities
Fries, K. (2019, 5 February). Crossing the border while disabled. https://howwegettonext.com/crossing-the-border-while-disabled-e19fa81cd91d
Government of Canada. (2018, 16 April). Government of Canada brings medical inadmissibility policy in line with inclusivity for persons with disabilities. https://www.canada.ca/en/immigration-refugees-citizenship/news/2018/04/government-of-canada-brings-medical-inadmissibility-policyin-line-with-inclusivity-for-persons-with-disabilities.html
Hansen, N., & Philo, C. (2007). The normality of doing things differently: Bodies, spaces and disability geography. *Tijdschrift voor Economische en Sociale Geografie*, 98(4), 493–506. https://doi.org/10.1111/j.1467-9663.2007.00417.x

Bodies in Migration Marked for Exclusion

Hansen, S., Wilton, R., & Newbold, K. (2017). "There is always this feeling of otherness": Exploring the lived experiences of visually impaired immigrant women in Canada. *Disability and Society, 32*(8), 1121–1141. https://doi.org/10.1080/09687599.2017.1343128

Harris, J. (2003). "All Doors are Closed to Us": A social model analysis of the experiences of disabled refugees and asylum seekers in Britain. *Disability and Society, 18*(4), 395–410. https://doi.org/10.1080/0968759032000080968

Hughes, B. (2017). Impairment on the move: The disabled incomer and other invalidating intersections. *Disability and Society, 32*(4), 467–482. https://doi.org/10.1080/09687599.2017.1298991

Human Rights Watch. (2019). UN: Focus on civilians with disabilities in wartime. https://www.hrw.org/news/2019/05/28/un-focus-civilians-disabilities-wartime

Humanity & Inclusion. (n.d.). 1/5 Syrian Refugees has disability. https://hi-canada.org/en/news/1-5-syrian-refugees-has-disability-

Humanity & Inclusion. (2013). Hidden victims of the Syrian crisis: Disabled, injured and older refugees. https://blog.hi.org/hidden-victims-of-the-syrian-crisis-disabled-injured-and-older-refugees/

Jaffee, L. J. (2016). Disrupting global disability frameworks: Settler-colonialism and the geopolitics of disability in Palestine/Israel. *Disability and Society, 31*(1), 116–130. https://doi.org/10.1080/09687599.2015.1119038

Karanja, M. (2009). Disability in contexts of displacement. *Disability Studies Quarterly, 29*(4). http://dsq-sds.org/article/view/969/1177

Kim, S. (2019, 13 August). Trump's New Green Card Policy disproportionally affects immigrants with disabilities. *Forbes.* https://www.forbes.com/sites/sarahkim/2019/08/13/trumps-new-green-card-policy-disproportionally-affects-immigrants-with-disabilities/#c0a52f34a115

Mirza, M. (2011a). Disability and cross-border mobility: Comparing resettlement experiences of Cambodian and Somali refugees with disabilities. *Disability and Society, 26*(5), 521–535. https://doi.org/10.1080/09687599.2011.589188

Mirza, M. (2011b). New Issues in Refugee Research. Research Paper No. 212. Unmet needs and diminished opportunities: Disability, displacement and humanitarian healthcare. https://www.unhcr.org/4e0dbdb29.html

Mustafa, N. (2017, April). Fleeing Syria in a wheelchair, *Disability Voice,* 3. https://us9.campaign-archive.com/?u=865a5bbea1086c57a41cc876d&id=17efe4335c&e=[UNIQID]

Mustafa, N. (2020, 10 April). COVID-19 doesn't discriminate against refugees with disabilities. Neither should our response. *Euronews*. https://www.euronews.com/2020/04/10/covid-19-doesn-t-discriminate-refugees-with-disabilities-neither-should-our-response-view

Nario-Redmond, M. (2020). *Ableism: The causes and consequences of disability prejudice*. Wiley.

Naseef, K. (2018, 18 August). Support for refugees with disabilities and other specific health care needs. http://www.reflaw.org/support-for-refugees-with-disabilities-and-other-specific-health-care-needs/

Pearce, E. (2015). "Ask us what we need": Operationalizing guidance on disability inclusion in refugee and displaced persons programs. *Disability and the Global South*, 2(1), 460–478.

Pisania, M., & Grechb, S. (2015). Disability and forced migration: Critical intersectionalities. *Disability and the Global South*, 2(1), 421–441.

Qi, F., & Hu, L. (2020). Including people with disability in the COVID-19 outbreak emergency preparedness and response in China. *Disability and Society*, 35(5), 848–853. https://doi.org/10.1080/09687599.2020.1752622

Rau-Barriga, S. (2016, 20 June). We need to stop treating people with disabilities as less than human. *The Guardian*. https://www.theguardian.com/global-development-professionals-network/2016/jun/20/we-need-to-stop-treating-people-with-disabilities-as-less-than-human

Reimer-Kirkham, S., Astle, B., Ikponwosa, E., Panchuk, K., & Dixon, D. (2019). Albinism, spiritual and cultural practices, and implications for health, healthcare, and human rights: A scoping review. *Disability and Society*, 34(5), 747–774. https://doi.org/10.1080/09687599.2019.1566051

Roberts, K. (2000). Lost in the system? Disabled refugees and asylum seekers in Britain. *Disability and Society*, 15(6), 943–948. https://doi.org/10.1080/713662008

Rohwerder, B. (2013). Intellectual disabilities, violent conflict and humanitarian assistance: Advocacy of the forgotten. *Disability and Society*, 28(6), 770–783. https://doi.org/10.1080/09687599.2013.808574

dos Santos-Zingale, M., & McColl, M. (2006). Disability and participation in post-conflict situations: The case of Sierra Leone. *Disability and Society*, 21(3), 243–257. https://doi.org/10.1080/09687590600617428

Schweik, S. (2010). *The ugly laws: Disability in public*. New York University Press.

Siebers, T. (2010). *Disability aesthetics*. University of Michigan Press.

Soldatic, K. (2013). The transnational sphere of justice: Disability praxis and the politics of impairment. *Disability and Society, 28*(6), 744–755. https://doi.org/10.1080/09687599.2013.802218

Soldatic, K., & Fiske, L. (2009). Bodies "locked up": Intersections of disability and race in Australian immigration. *Disability and Society, 24*(3), 289–301. https://doi.org/10.1080/09687590902789453

Straimer, C. (2011). Between protection and assistance: Is there refuge for asylum seekers with disabilities in Europe? *Disability and Society, 26*(5), 537–551. https://doi.org/10.1080/09687599.2011.589189

Tanabe, M., Nagujjah, Y., & Rimal, N. (2015). Intersecting sexual and reproductive health and disability in humanitarian settings: Risks, needs, and capacities of refugees with disabilities in Kenya, Nepal, and Uganda. *Sexuality and Disability, 33*, 411–427. https://doi.org/10.1007/s11195-015-9419-3

United Nations. (n.d.). Convention on the Rights of Persons with Disabilities (CRPD). https://www.un.org/development/desa/disabilities/convention-on-the-rights-of-persons-with-disabilities.htm

UNHCR (2017). Migrants and refugees with disabilities must be priority in new Global Compact on Migration. https://www.ohchr.org/EN/NewsEvents/Pages/DisplayNews.aspx?NewsID=21495&LangID=E

UNHCR (2018, 8 March). *UNHCR Policy on age, gender and diversity.* https://www.refworld.org/docid/5bb628ea4.html

UNHCR (2019). *Working with persons with disabilities in forced displacement.* https://www.unhcr.org/publications/manuals/4ec3c81c9/working-persons-disabilities-forced-displacement.html

UNHCR (2020, 29 April). COVID-19 and the rights of persons with disabilities: Guidance. https://www.ohchr.org/Documents/Issues/Disability/COVID-19_and_The_Rights_of_Persons_with_Disabilities.pdf

Waldschmidt, A., & Sépulchre, M. (2019). Citizenship: Reflections on a relevant but ambivalent concept for persons with disabilities. *Disability and Society, 34*(3), 421–448. https://doi.org/10.1080/09687599.2018.1543580

Webster, L. (2020). Coronavirus: Why disabled people are calling for a Covid-19 inquiry. *BBC News.* https://www.bbc.com/news/uk-53221435

Women's Refugee Commission. (n.d.) Disability Inclusion. https://www.womensrefugeecommission.org/focus-areas/gender-social-inclusion/disability-inclusion/

Women's Refugee Commission. (2008). Disabilities among refugees and conflict-affected populations. https://www.womensrefugeecommission.org/wp-content/uploads/2020/04/disabilities_report_02-10_web.pdf

World Health Organization. (2011). *World report on disability.* https://www.who.int/disabilities/world_report/2011/report.pdf

Wright, T. (2018, 16 April). After 40 years, federal government ending barriers to disabled immigrants. *CVT News.* https://www.ctvnews.ca/canada/after-40-years-federal-government-ending-barriers-to-disabled-immigrants-1.3887123

Yeo, R. (2017). The deprivation experienced by disabled asylum seekers in the United Kingdom: Symptoms, causes, and possible solutions. *Disability and Society, 32*(5), 657–677. https://doi.org/10.1080/09687599.2017.1320268

CHAPTER 4:
THE BULLETPROOF BLACK BODY: LUKE CAGE AND THE POLITICS OF RACE AND RESPECTABILITY

Esther De Dauw

This chapter focuses on the character Luke Cage, and the way his body is framed as the nexus of the politics of both race and respectability in the *Luke Cage* Netflix series (Murray et al., 2016–2018). As a bulletproof Black character in the age of #BlackLivesMatter, the mass incarceration of African–American men through the school-prison pipeline (Wald & Losen, 2003) and the over-policing of Black urban communities, Luke Cage attempts to challenge the stereotype surrounding Black male characters while asking if it is even possible for a Black superhero to exist outside of those stereotypes. Focusing on the preconception of Black male characters as inexhaustible rage and work machines, and how respectability politics are infused with Whiteness, this chapter examines how the representation of an indestructible Black body functions as a power fantasy within the context of White Supremacy and the White gaze, and their invisibility. Luke Cage's origin story as an incarcerated, but innocent, man, who consents to undergo (illegal) medical experiments frames prison or abuse as an empowering experience. After all, the only reason Luke has become a superhero is because of his time in prison, thus framing prison as a necessary tool to 'improve' or 'correct' Black men. This chapter questions whether it is possible for such a narrative to challenge the current bio-political ideology that justifies the mass incarceration of Black people.

Considering Kenneth Ghee's concept of the real Black superhero, who works to empower their own community and thus, inevitably challenges the status quo of White-as-norm culture, this chapter works to analyse the series' racial politics (Ghee, 2014, pp. 230–231). The series' storyline simultaneously focuses on the need for Black communities to be empowered in order to resist systemic racism and on the politics of respectability and 'acting White' as the route towards empowerment. Using Critical Race Theory, this chapter will explore how 'acting White' is clearly aligned with the moral high ground and the greater good, even as it is placed in direct opposition to the Black community. This reveals how respectability politics, as a strategy of resistance, can serve the individual on a temporary basis, but cannot empower the community at large in the long term. The Black superhero who functions within that context is trapped by the demands of Whiteness and the White gaze.

Key words: race, respectability, politics, Blackness, bodies

Introducing: Luke Cage in Print

The first African-American superhero without the 'Black' tag in his superhero name *and* to have his own titular comic was Luke Cage in the eponymous *Luke Cage, Hero for Hire* (1972-1974) and *Luke Cage, Power Man* (1974-1978). Brought into existence during the popularity of Blaxploitation films, the emergence of benign neglect and the rise of the prison-industrial complex alongside the school-prison pipeline, the Luke Cage comics featured White, rich villains as well as Black gangsters; with Luke as the sole hero standing between them and the impoverished community of Harlem (Kruse, 2013, pp. 263-265). Comics scholar, Adilifu Nama, describes Luke Cage as "the superhero that has epitomized Blaxploitation" and also the "most inherently political and socially profound Black superhero to ever emerge" (Nama, 2011, pp. 53-55). Blaxploitation, initially a term used to describe a variety of films, includes Black protagonists who are "socially and politically conscious" while "the conflict operates as a metaphor in which Whites represent the oppressive establishment" (Lawrence, 2008, p. 20). Initially, Blaxploitation films were created by Black film makers and often portrayed the experiences of Black audiences and their struggle with a White establishment. However, soon this became co-opted by mainstream film studios and, with the increase in violence and sexual imagery, Black audiences began to reject the Blaxploitation genre (Lawrence, 2008). The character of Luke Cage was designed to embody

The Bulletproof Black Body

the Blaxploitation genre in order to draw in a (new) Black audience as well as appeal to the 1960s fan-base, which demanded more socially progressive storylines (Regalado, 2015, p. 171). Despite Luke's political and social significance, his comics have struggled to remain in print. In 1978 the series was rebranded as *Power Man and Iron Fist* and Luke Cage became partners with the White Iron Fist. At this time, the storylines increasingly move further away from the Blaxploitation elements present in the previous *Luke Cage, Power Man* comics and doing so, "the comics lose the Black community and Luke's social and political consciousness" (De Dauw, 2020, p. 130). This series was cancelled in 1986 and Luke Cage only reappeared in print in limited series or various ensemble titles. As a result, the 2016 Netflix *Luke Cage* series is the first time in fifteen years that Cage has been the titular character of the media he is appearing in.

Luke Cage's return as a titular character in the Netflix series is both a return to the character's origins and a rejection of Luke's initial and radical status as a superhero. While the series is invested in a Black community and incorporates various elements of the Blaxploitation genre (the politically conscious superhero, the Black community under threat, a violent urban setting, etc.) just like the original comics, the series continues to de-emphasise Luke's identity as a superhero by removing Luke's costume. Blair Davis, in his analysis of the first issue of *Luke Cage, Hero for Hire* (1972), discusses how Luke's original costume, and the scene that introduces this costume, invites the reader to look at the Blackness of Luke's body. The costume, although theatrical enough with its silky yellow shirt, pirate boots and silver headband and chains, is not the standard superhero costume. The mask, tights and chevron or chest insignia are missing, but it is "hokey" as Luke says and it is this hokeyness that Luke consciously constructs in order to pass as a superhero (Davis, 2015, pp. 196–198). Davis (2015) points out that:

> Cage therefore intends his costume to serve as a sort of uniform, one that identifies him as a protector, rather than an offender, and as a member of a higher rank that typically carries with it a certain

amount of social status, respect and/or fear – much as the uniform of a police officer does. (p. 198)

The comics use the costume, not only to highlight how Luke stands out from other superheroes, but also to differentiate him from the "civilian" population (Davis, 2015, pp. 196–198). This is further underlined when the narrative turns away from action-filled panels to show Luke changing into costume. Luke needs the costume to pass as a legitimate superhero and without it, he cannot become Power Man.

However, throughout the years, creators increasingly portray Luke without his costume; the yellow shirt is replaced by a red T-shirt and black jacket in the 1990s, followed by the removal of the headband and chains. Eventually, Luke only wears a yellow T-shirt and a pair of jeans in the 2000s. As a member of the Avengers, he is increasingly noticeable for his lack of costume. This rejection of the "hokey" costume is interpreted by some as a rejection of Luke Cage's Blaxploitation origins. Removing the costume's political implications works to de-politicise Luke's status as a Black hero. But, considering the power of the White hegemony which frames the White body as 'normal' and the Black body as 'abnormal' or 'other' (Martin, 2013), is it even possible for a Black character to be a superhero while simultaneously existing as an apolitical body? (Davis, 2015, pp. 196–198). If we consider the original costume as a signification of Luke's superhero status, which grants him access to privileged (White) spaces, what does the lack of a superhero costume achieve? Within a White hegemony which continuously politics and politicises the existence of Black people, it is not possible for a Black superhero to exist apolitically. After all, the inclusion of a Black character incites the rage of those who cry out that 'forced diversity' and 'pandering to the liberal agenda' is ruining a franchise previously dominated by White characters. In other words, a Black superhero is always politicised due to the context of White Supremacy in which they are published and the audience's response to that context. This does not change depending on the character's commercial achievements. For instance, the *Black Panther* (2018) film was, both commercially and culturally, an immense success and many considered it a new milestone for what Black superheroes are capable of. This success was, in part, due to the politics of the Black Panther character and the status of Wakanda as a non-colonised African nation. Many Black people went online and spoke of the importance of the character, both from a personal and political point of view. On the other hand, the film also gave rise to online debates about Western media packaging and commodifying African cultures in order to sell them to Western audiences, and led to coinage of the term 'Wakandification' by Jade Bentil on Twitter (Joseph, 2020). The film launched Black Panther from a firmly B-list character to cultural prominence due to its cultural and political messages. Both to those who read it as a pro-Black celebration or a reconceptualisation of Afrofuturism, and those who consider it as part of a racist and rising trend of bundling African cultures together to project a biologically essential 'Black' identity, consider *Black Panther* to have important political messages concerning Black identities within a global landscape that is dominated by Whiteness. Audiences very rarely read Black superheroes as being devoid of political messages in the way that White, straight and male characters are considered apolitical characters. Therefore, it is not possible for Luke to be a Black man who is also a superhero and remain devoid of a political message.

Luke Cage on screen
Live action formats usually change the superhero's costume in favour of more 'realistic' battle wear or no costumes at all, with the *Jessica Jones* Netflix series (2015–2019) even poking fun at Jess' original costume. However, costumes and superhero names do persist, and in the case of the Netflix series, that privilege is reserved for the White, male and straight Daredevil. Davis (2015) writes that, due to the loss of Luke's costume in the comics, "[to] unfamiliar readers, Cage appears to be just an average man; perhaps this is exactly the point: that the average person can indeed be a hero" (p. 201). However, Davis suggests that, "given the minuscule number of black superheroes in existence, perhaps the fact that Cage is a black man is meant to be a 'costume' in and of itself – his skin color alone is enough to distinguish him visually from

the overwhelming number of White heroes that surround him" (Davis, 2015, p. 201). In the comics, where Luke is part of the predominantly White Avengers team, Luke's lack of costume does make him stand out from his peers. But, Luke is not surrounded by a White cast in the Netflix series. While 1970s-era Luke had a "hokey" costume in an effort to both highlight Luke's Blackness and show off his chest, it also clearly identified Luke as a superhero. Because of the lack of a costume, the Netflix series is intensely obsessed with Luke's body as the signifier of his super-heroic identity and superhero masculinity.

The opening sequence demonstrates an obsession with Luke's body by overlapping it with images of Harlem, not only equating the community with Luke's body and framing Luke's body as the shield for the neighbourhood, but also foreshadowing the multiple tightly framed and close-up images of Luke's body throughout the episodes, while other characters are compelled to touch him or comment on his size. In the very first episode, Luke meets the series' villains, Cottonmouth and Mariah, and they immediately comment on his body:

> Cottonmouth: You're a big one, he?
> Mariah: He's got a little jacket.
> *they both laugh*
> Cottonmouth: You want a job? I can find something more suitable for a man your size. Better paying too. You ever carried a gun?
> (Coker, 2016a)

Because he is a big Black man, people immediately assume he is more suited to violence than bartending. This scene is not an isolated incident. Throughout the series, men and women frequently comment on Luke's body. Men see it as a tool for violence and women as a tool for sex. In the *Jessica Jones* Netflix series, where Luke is a recurring character, the sex scenes between Luke and Jessica focus on the vigorous and furniture-destroying nature of Luke's sexual prowess and appetite. The sex scene between Claire and Luke in Season Two of the *Luke Cage* series is very similar. The only sex scene that differs slightly is the one between Luke and Misty Knight in the first episode

The Bulletproof Black Body

of the first season, where the camera focuses on the female body for the visual pleasure of the audience. But, it does so by highlighting Luke's ability to touch her, lift her and hold her up.

The focus on Luke's body and its capacity for sex and violence fits into damaging stereotypes of Black men as both violent and hypersexual. These stereotypes were used liberally in Blaxploitation movies produced by mainstream (and White controlled) studios and more recently in shows such as NBC's *Parenthood* (Howard et al., 2010–2015), as discussed by Gina Castle Bell and Tina M. Harris, and Fox's *Empire* (Strong et al., 2015–2020). Meya Joyell Hemphill (2017) also notes how Luke's body is part of the "recurring trend of the hypersexualisation of Black superheroes" with serial close-ups of Luke's body while the series works to de-emphasise Luke's intellectualism (p. 6). Combined with a focus on emotional stoicism, Luke's capacity for violence and his body's indestructability, the series presents an image of Luke as the Black Brute stereotype: unnaturally strong, silent and violent. Ronald L. Jackson II describes the Black Brute as "a tall, darkskinned, muscular, athletically built character and often either bald or with a short haircut" whose beast-like nature, in contrast, emphasises the civilised, cerebral and human nature of the White body (Jackson, 2006, p. 41). Hemphill identifies how most Black Brute characters are "nameless stock characters" in "television series such as *Law and Order, ER* and *NYPD Blue*", with few named exceptions such as B. A. Baracus from *The A-Team* (Hemphill, 2017, p. 24). Hemphill identifies Luke as part of this Black Brute tradition, as the show highlights his strong, silent and violent nature, which obfuscates Luke's intellectual capacity. While Luke clearly engages with Black history, articulates the complex nature of crime in his Black neighbourhood, and juggles the various expectations other characters put on him, the show consistently focuses and highlights Luke's physical strength and macho cool as his defining characteristic. This contrasts with the series' focus on the Harlem Renaissance, which is a period characterised by the poetry and writings of Black Harlemites and is considered a golden age of Black intellectual output. The use of the Harlem Renaissance as a symbol

Talking Bodies III

is wielded predominantly by Mariah Stokes, who is clearly identified as a member of the Black middle class in Harlem in the series' first episode. This immediately frames her as a villain through her contrast with the heroes, who are mostly working class. Luke, the titular hero, is a member of the working poor who needs to work two jobs to pay rent and both of those jobs are at the bottom of their respective industries' hierarchy, the lowest valued and lowest paid: a sweeper at the barbershop and a dishwasher at a nightclub. Luke's status as a working-class man is in line with the series' overall fixation on the need for Black men to be seen doing physical work. The show's focus on Luke's body not only works to establish Luke as the Black Brute, but also works to underscore the class politics at play in Luke's Black, working-class superhero status.

Working hard: respectability and performativity
The first episode of Season One emphasises the importance of Black men working through one of the first scenes in the barbershop. Claudia, a single Black mother who is picking up her son, watches Luke sweep the floor and says, "Black man working, ain't nothing wrong with that" (Coker, 2016a). This sets the tone for the series' attitude to physical labour, with an emphasis on the necessity of the visibility of Black men doing an honest day's work. Specifically, the series focuses on the need for young Black boys to see Black men working as an example of good Black masculinity, in contrast to the bad masculinity widely demonstrated by gang members. In a scene between Luke and Pop, the owner of the barbershop, Pop explains the role of the barbershop in the community. It serves as neutral territory, where Black gangs can meet to negotiate terms and decrease the violence taking place within the community, but also as a place where young Black boys can be given work to prevent them from being idle, and therefore, being tempted by the streets. The self-control that hard work generates, as modelled in the barbershop, provides a gateway to true, mature and good masculinity. The series implies that if there are no examples of Black men visibly at work, young Black men fall prey to gangs, violence and crime.

The Bulletproof Black Body

The series' implication that Black men are working machines who give in to crime and lawlessness when left idle is one of the many historical stereotypes used to justify slavery, and is still used to justify enforced labour in the prison-industrial complex (Alexander, 2010, pp. 14–16). In *Luke Cage,* young Black boys need to be protected from their own Blackness by learning how to work; and through work, learn self-control. This theme, present in Season One, crystallises in Season Two, when Luke and Claire fight over Luke's increased use of violence after he puts a man in hospital. During the fight, Luke loses his temper and punches the wall. Claire, who is Luke's girlfriend at the time, explains that she recognises such an act as a precursor to, or an element of, domestic violence because her father exhibited similar behaviour towards her mother. As a result, Claire decides to leave him. Discussing this incident with Bobby, an older Black man who frequents the barbershop, the following conversation occurs:

> Bobby: As long as you're being pulled in so many directs, you're ... You're going to lose your temper. Every man struggles with that
> Luke: But I'm not every man.
> Bobby: Precisely my point. You're a grown-ass man, yes. But you're also a grown-ass man who can throw a Volkswagen. So, you have to be more careful than your average man 'cause if you lose your shit, people's lives could be at stake.
> (Coker, 2018)

In this conversation, and throughout the rest of the season, Black men are presented as inherently violent and it is only through self-control that they become respectable heroes. Luke's strength presents him as being doubly at risk and he must have twice the self-control that other men have.

The ability of Black men to control their inherent violence is thus framed as a sign of maturity and good masculinity. However, it is also reminiscent of macho cool, a phrase coined by bell hooks to discuss the way Black men are taught to suppress positive, tender emotions (especially towards each other), as well as all expressions of anger, to avoid retaliation from a White environment which, historically, has taken any emotion in a Black man as a threat resolved through lynching, prison or other forms of abuse. According to hooks, Black men are required to always act cool, as if nothing ever bothers them, while performing a 'tough' masculinity. The oppression of all emotion required by Whiteness is another way for the hegemony to dehumanise Black men and rob them of their agency (hooks, 2004, pp. 142–143).

Alongside the threat of reprisal, there is also the promise of reward, the illusion that adhering to the demands of Whiteness will provide access to privileged and institutional spaces without White harassment. This is where respectability politics come in. Historically, respectability politics was a self-presentation strategy initially developed by Black American women, which involved the conscious adoption of behavioural patterns that "downplayed sexuality and emphasized morality and dignity to reject White America's stereotypes" (Pitcan et al., 2018, p. 164). Specifically, this catered to 1950s era White, middle-class morality and gender roles. It focused on personal behaviour and self-censorship as a gateway to overcoming racism through appealing to Whites' sympathy by actively demonstrating that Black people are good people and do not deserve discrimination or ill-treatment. However, this "emphasis on individual uplift ignores structural inequalities" and through its adherence to 'respectable' values does not challenge the values that determine Black people to be unequal to Whites (Pitcan et al., 2018, p. 164).

This is similar to Critical Race Theory and its notion of White performance, which describes the White behavioural standards Black people are pressured to adopt in White spaces. Delgado and Stefancic suggest it is essential to recognise that Whiteness is "normative: it sets the standard in dozens of situations", and is invested in privileging White hegemony (Delgado & Stefancic, 2012, p. 84). Karla Martin considers Whiteness as the norm by which all racial minorities are judged, which bars non-White people from White social, cultural and economic spaces (Martin, 2013, p. 53). Whiteness as the behavioural norm creates the illusion that acting White will provide access to institutionalised White privilege and is the good road to equality instead of political organisation or direct action, which is characterised as disruptive, pointless and damaging to both the country and the racial minority community. One of the clearest examples of how Black people are expected to perform Whiteness at all costs is the way that White behavioural norms are projected onto natural Black hair, which is seen as unprofessional and dirty, even when clean and well-cared for. This forces Black women to straighten or relax their hair in ways that are highly damaging and toxic in order to conform (Nasheed, 2019). Therefore, Whiteness requires Black women to damage their bodies and risk their health in order to approach Whiteness. Respectability politics further pushes the idea that approaching Whiteness, or White performance, as well as respectable behaviour – not responding to racist provocation and always remaining polite, deferential and being the bigger person – will allow Black people to defeat racism and discrimination instead of engaging in organised action. The Netflix series is heavily invested in respectability politics as a route to empowerment. However, even while it highlights why respectability politics is a strategy doomed to fail, it plays into and reinforces Whiteness as the norm instead of resisting Whiteness and, thus, liberating Blackness from having to twist itself into something it should not have to be.

Black history and White Supremacy
One of the ways in which respectability politics plays out in the Netflix *Luke Cage* series is through the glorification and de-radicalisation of the Harlem Renaissance. As mentioned previously, the Harlem Renaissance is considered a golden age of Black intellectual output. It was a social, artistic and intellectual movement throughout the 1920s and mid-1930s, powered by the Black Harlem community, which spread to African and Caribbean francophone writers living in Paris. It resulted in an unprecedented number of publications by Black writers, poets and artists (Hutchinson, 1995, pp. 1–28). The *Luke Cage* Netflix series aligns the Harlem Renaissance with Black middle-class respectability, de-radicalising the movement in a way that mirrors the

Talking Bodies III

way Fox News and other White establishments have, for instance, co-opted Martin Luther King as a way to identify a supposedly 'correct' way to do Black activism that is palatable to a White establishment. This obscures the fact that there is no way for an oppressed minority to protest their oppression in a way that is considered appealing by the oppressing majority. Consider Fox News' glorification of Martin Luther King and his strategy of non-violence as the 'right way' to be an activist, in comparison to their vilification of Colin Kaepernick's kneeling during the national anthem as a peaceful protest against police brutality (Beydoun, 2016).

The history of the Harlem Renaissance is also used to highlight Black excellence in order to erase the context of White Supremacy and the institutional oppression of Black peoples. This allows the *Luke Cage* series to put the onus on the Black person to educate themselves and to rise above. This is clear in episode five of the first season, when Luke tracks down a thief who robbed a Black-owned store:

> Luke: Think about where you are. It's hallowed ground this park, named for Jackie Robinson, It's here. It's all around you, if you respect yourself enough to take a look.
> Zip: At what?
> Luke: Our legacy.
> (Coker, 2016b)

The idea of respecting yourself enough to know and understand Black history ties into one of the ideas at the core of respectability politics: if you resist racism and respect yourself by acting respectably (which is code for acting White), you can be successful. This oversimplifies how White Supremacy has hollowed out Black communities, through municipal disinvestment and benign neglect, the Whitewashing of America's history of racial segregation and slavery, and the systematic imprisonment of Black people in the prison-industrial complex. As a consequence, there is a lack of opportunity, well-funded schools, and infrastructure to support young Black men to whom gang life seems like the only way out of abject poverty. But instead of highlighting these

The Bulletproof Black Body

issues, interactions, such as the scene above, frame Black communities and people as infighting and lacking the respect to educate themselves on their history. They are framed as the destructors of their own community. In a telling scene, one of Cottonmouth's henchmen tries to discuss Moynihan and Nixon's policy of 'benign neglect' of urban communities, but before a proper explanation of that historical context is provided, Cottonmouth kills him, silencing the evidence of White institutions' oppression of Black communities. The series discusses Black history, but not White history's destruction of it. Of course, it is the Black villain who recruits from the poor Black community who does the silencing, as he benefits from the dismantling of equal opportunity policies. This drives the community further into poverty, which eventually accords him more power. But, this only emphasises the image of the Black community as self-destructive and the cause of their own disenfranchisement.

The lack of context around White Supremacy extends towards the way that the series engages with police brutality and the historical veneration of the police in TV shows. Misty Knight, the good cop and female lead of the series, expresses the idea that police officers serve a higher purpose and, when using minority characters to express this sentiment, it erases the police's function as a tool to uphold White Supremacy and its history as a slave catching/control mechanism. In *Luke Cage,* most of the police force is Black, which obscures the fact that police brutality against minorities and racial profiling is a common and widespread tactic and serves to uphold White Supremacy and its institutions (Garrido, 2018, p. 2). For instance, in episode nine, a White police officer is murdered by a Black civilian and the police start arresting people at random. One of the Black police officers arrests a young Black child, Lonnie, who was walking home from school. He asks for his mother and, although he is a minor, his request is denied and he is questioned without an adult present. During the interrogation, Lonnie refuses to be cowed, talks back to the police officer and raises the fact that he is there illegally. The Black police officer 'snaps' and beats him. This frames the confrontation between a child and an adult police officer as a Black man unable to control his inherent violence. Thus, Misty's role as the good cop is emphasised through the contrast with such 'bad apples' as the police officer that beats Lonnie, which allows the show to frame the police as a respectable force for good that is impeded by a few bad apples and endless bureaucracy. In this way, the show obfuscates the police's fundamental function as a tool of the White Supremacist state and, through this obfuscation, supports it as White Supremacy derives much of its power from its invisible normalcy.

Near the end of Season One, this erasure of White Supremacy becomes increasingly clear through Luke's origin story. The audience knows at the start of the series that Luke was framed and sent to prison. That in itself is reflective of the disproportionate levels of incarceration in the African-American community. Michelle Alexander documents how the police are encouraged to target African-American communities through the War on Drugs and monetary incentives connected to arrest quotas. The system encourages police officers to detain and arrest African-Americans, while prosecutors' near limitless powers of discretion allow them to overcharge African-Americans, who are disproportionately disenfranchised throughout this entire process (Alexander, 2010). However, near the end of the series, the viewer discovers that Luke was not the victim of a biased system protected from critique through the Supreme Court. Instead, he was framed by his own brother. Once again, the White institution is rendered invisible through the presence of Black-on-Black crime.

The series depicts prison as a harrowing time for Luke, made even more difficult by the prison's predominantly White guards who brutally abuse their mostly Black inmates, which is one of the rare moments the show engages with the realities of White Supremacy's visible power. This eventually results in Luke being put into a tank of experimental medical liquids, that one of the White guards sabotages in an attempt to kill him. Instead, Luke gains superpowers. On the one hand, Luke's heroism allows him to make the best out of a bad situation and become empowered despite the abuse he has suffered.

The Bulletproof Black Body

On the other hand, the experimentation and trauma of his experience empowers him to break out of prison, punish evil doers, and become a hero. In the context of a narrative that consistently frames Black people as destructive, with White behaviour or respectability as the tools to control that destruction, this origin story is troubling. In *Luke Cage*, White Supremacy is erased, Black-on-Black crime is the cause of Black people's disenfranchisement, and the Black individual needs to be controlled by White behavioural standards, science and respectability. In this context, can Luke Cage, a Black man, serve as a powerful superhero? Consider Ghee's concept of the culture bound hero as the only true hero of colour as he "is working to save *his own* people *first*, in the context of saving humanity" (Ghee, 2014, pp. 230–231). Ghee proposes that a Black superhero needs to fight the conditions that have caused Black oppression in order to be a true Black superhero. While showcasing Black talent through a predominantly Black cast, the obfuscation of the White hegemony from the context of the Netflix series and its use of respectability politics, make it impossible for Luke to become a true Black superhero (Ghee, 2014). As the series progresses into Season Two, Luke moves further away from the true Black superhero as he becomes increasingly violent and, in the series' finale, assumes the position within the community formerly occupied by the villains, Cottonmouth and Mariah.

The signification of the suit
Throughout the series, Luke's body has been the main signifier of his superhero identity. Instead of a superhero costume, he wears regular casual clothes: T-shirt and jeans. The suit he wears in the first episode is borrowed and too small for him. He is literally too big for the accoutrements of middle-class masculinity, money and wealth. Comparatively, his villains do not wear costumes either, but they wear middle-class respectability like a disguise. Cottonmouth always wears beautifully tailored suits to signal his middle-class respectability. While he is known within the community as a drug dealer, in public he attempts to cultivate the image of a successful club-owner and

businessman. In a series where working-class work is considered a requirement for Black people to control themselves, the suit not only signals the corrupting influence of wealth and luxury, it becomes the mark of the villain. All the middle-class and wealthy Black characters are villainous and corrupt in some ways, while working-class occupation and attire are marks of the hero. The closing shot of Season Two focuses on Luke wearing a suit and standing in the same spot where Cottonmouth used to observe the Club he owned, which is now Luke's property. We see Luke moving from attempting to restore the barbershop – the site of respectable and hard-working masculinity – to taking over the Club. This image is the opposite of how Luke appears for most of the series: in a T-shirt and a hoodie.

There is a contradiction that needs to be resolved here. On the one hand, the series very clearly presents the Black man as someone who requires hard work to drive off his natural tendency towards crime and excess. This is portrayed through the barbershop, Luke's status as a working-class hero, and the portrayal of middle-class characters as villains. On the other hand, the show's heavy-handed foregrounding of respectability politics reveals a reverence for the middle class. This intersects with the use of the Harlem Renaissance as evidence of the 'Exceptional Black' myth, which promotes a trickle-down approach to enfranchisement from the individual to the community. The Exceptional Black person is "a black person who to white people seems unlike other black people they use as a reference point" (O'Neal, 2018, p. 2). This Black person deviates from the stereotypes of thugs and brutes that proliferate throughout mainstream culture. This person is "often well-educated, always articulate, cultured" and able to move comfortably within White spaces (O'Neal, 2018, p. 2). The idea is that this person is exceptional, unlike other Black people, and through their exceptionality, provides evidence that the Black community is uncultured, uneducated and consists of thugs and brutes. The myth of the Exceptional Black sustains the belief that racism is over because Black success is possible and because US law does not criminate based on race, the disproportionate impact of these laws on communities of

The Bulletproof Black Body

colour must be the fault of the communities themselves. As Alexander writes, "[highly] visible examples of black success are critical to the maintenance of a racial caste system in the era of colorblindness" (Alexander, 2010, p. 235). The glorification of a few select Black individuals who have reached a higher socio-economic status, fame and success helps to conceal the ongoing oppression, marginalisation and disenfranchisement of communities of colour. The Netflix series uses the Harlem Renaissance to consistently highlight exceptional Black individuals and, combined with its use of respectability politics, the show also promotes the idea that socio-economic status *is* enfranchisement and 'having made it'.

The *Luke Cage* series does the same thing through its use of the Harlem Renaissance, the depiction of Black-on-Black crime, and the absence of the White hegemony. So, what does it mean when the hero is working class and the villains are, for all appearances, middle class, while the show's politics venerates the middle class? A significant aspect of White, middle-class masculinity (as the ideal masculinity), incorporates a transformation: from working class to middle class. This demonstrates the ability to master and dominate your surroundings, a prerequisite for masculinity, to access social mobility (Kimmel, 1998, pp. 20-25). This is also a significant aspect of respectability politics; the ability to lift oneself out of poverty through strength of character as a demonstration of your race's potential. This tenet automatically implies a distrust of generational wealth and unearned luxury as a corrosive force that eats away at the hardness generated by working-class labour, which the series taps into through its focus on the Stokes family's standing in Harlem. Cottonmouth and Mariah are the inheritors of wealth and standing, gleaned from criminal activities. While both Mariah and Cottonmouth work to present a respectable front, Cottonmouth is known (within the community) as a drug dealer and gang leader, instead of the legitimate Black businessman persona he adopts. Mariah, as an elected official, has managed to craft a respectable public persona, but she is haunted by her family's legacy, accusations of corruption (which are true), and being inauthentic.

Her efforts to improve the community are portrayed as a way for her to ensure re-election and continued success, and not a legitimate desire to support her community. Cottonmouth and Mariah publicly adhere to respectability politics, but have failed to internalise it. Their respectability is not genuine and instead of lifting up, they oppress other Black people through murder, drug dealing and theft. For Cottonmouth, the suit also symbolises this outward projection of respectability while covering all manner of sins. Mariah's wardrobe signals this respectability as she is almost always seen wearing formal business dresses or suits. Luke's wearing of the suit in Season Two is a sign that he is losing his way. Luke briefly wears a suit in Season One, but this is destroyed while he attempts to protect the neighbourhood and he goes back to wearing a hoodie and T-shirt.

Luke's T-shirt and hoodie directly tie into the class and racial politics of the series. Garrido writes that "[the] black hoodie has become one of the symbols of the Black Lives Matter movement after 17-year-old Trayvon Martin was shot by George Zimmerman in 2012" (Garrido, 2018, p. 15). Throughout the ensuing media attention and the legal trial, the hoodie became equated with Black criminality, and Trayvon Martin's wearing of it became a reasonable justification for his murder according to many conservative media outlets (Wemple, 2013). In *Luke Cage*, there are many moments where the camera zooms in on Luke's hoodie, showcasing how the hoodie becomes riddled with bullets, but Luke's body is unharmed. In response, local shop owners distribute black hoodies with bullet holes to confuse the police and allow Luke to pass unseen. As Garrido writes: "the hoodie is transformed from a sign of alleged criminality into a symbol of Black empowerment that is used subversively by Black subjects in the city space of Harlem" (Garrido, 2018, p. 16). In this instance, the hoodie becomes a powerful symbol. However, reconsider Davis' analysis of the "hokey" superhero costume, which serves "as a sort of uniform, one that identifies him as a protector, rather than an offender, and as a member of a higher rank that typically carries with it a certain amount of social status, respect and/or fear" (Davis, 2015, p. 198). In the original comics, Luke Cage obtained increased social status through his costume, which identified him as someone capable of protecting people in the community. In the Netflix version of *Luke Cage,* his clothing signals the reverse. In order to work as a hero, he has to pass unnoticed and uses the paraphernalia of victimhood to pass invisibly through the streets. While this works as social critique and a demonstration of how the bigotry of the hegemony can be used in direct action against it, the context of the series is what makes this suspect. How can the hoodie function as a sign of Black heroism if the series continually refuses to name and shame the White hegemony against which the hoodie is meant to protest?

Conclusion: The (a)political Black hero and his audience
Perhaps the answer lies in who is actually watching *Luke Cage*. Netflix does not release viewing information, but the website *Screen Rant* reports that independent data, including media attention and online commentary, indicates that Luke Cage was a big success when first released in 2016 (Dodd, 2016). The show generated a considerable amount of attention on social media, with some viewers claiming that the lack of White characters made the show racist and that the show itself was too Black (McKinney, 2016; Lang, 2016). The discussions around *Luke Cage*'s Blackness expressed the sense that the show was written for Black people and, because of this, could not appeal to White audiences. This tied into the commonly accepted (yet un-evidenced) wisdom that White people do not watch TV shows with a predominantly Black cast and that shows such as *Family Matters* (1989-1998) and *The Fresh Prince of Bel Air* (1990-1996) are outliers that should not be counted. However, many also expressed the sentiment that *Luke Cage* failed to truly tap into Blackness. As Angelica Jade Bastién writes, "The problem with *Luke Cage* is that it implicitly endorses the mythical perfection of men like Martin Luther King Jr., then deploys similar mythologising to craft its own hero" (Bastién, 2016, para. 5) and, as such, the series created a hollow symbol that lacks humanity. After *Luke Cage*'s cancellation in 2018, many expressed the sentiment that the show had not been Black enough and that, through its attempts

Talking Bodies III

"to please everyone – black and non-black audiences alike", it said nothing worth saying (Ransome, 2018, para. 4). Produced by Coker, a Black man, it is possible that the show was written for a Black audience who are already aware of the White hegemony and do not require its presence in order to accurately interpret the political messages of the show. In interviews, Coker has repeatedly discussed the importance of Luke Cage's symbolism as a bulletproof Black man for Black audiences and expressed his desire to write a Black story (Bastién, 2018; Moss, 2016; Carter, 2016). Regardless, it seems that, similar to much Black content that has entered into the mainstream, Luke has been stripped of his most radical elements to make him more palatable to a White, mainstream audience and assuage White guilt. The result is a character that is simultaneously too Black for White audiences and not Black enough for Black audiences. Gone is his original costume, meant to signal his clear existence as a superhero, and while he remains deeply embedded in a community, the end of Season Two sees him lifted out of and possibly set against that community. Very few of his storylines dealt with explicit racism performed by White people or White institutions, making this 2016 series less radical than the 1970s comic book series.

The Netflix series is a culmination of the increased de-politicising of Luke's character throughout his publication history even while the writer, Coker, attempts to use him as the main character in a Black story. Davis writes that "many feminist scholars see the cinematic gaze as being 'male' (…). In turn, then, it is worth asking if a 'comic book gaze' exists and, if so, whether this gaze is a 'White' one, particularly regarding depictions of ethnic diversity" (Davis, 2015, p. 199). This White gaze is not limited to comic books, but also extends to other media formats in which the superhero appears. Therefore the superhero is always constructed within a 'White gaze' as the superhero works to protect the status quo and defend the greater good, which is defined by the respectable values and morals set out by White Supremacy. For Luke Cage, it is clear that both print and screen iterations catered to a

The Bulletproof Black Body

White gaze, which is both facilitated and evidenced by the invisibility of the White hegemony and the damage it does to Black individuals and communities.

Author biography
Esther De Dauw is a comic scholar who focuses on the intersection of gender and race, with publications such as *Missing Panels* and 'Seeing White: Normalization and Domesticity in Vision's Cyborg Identity' in *Unstable Masks: Whiteness and American Superhero Comics*. She was awarded her PhD by the University of Leicester in 2018.

References
Alexander, M. (2010). *The new Jim Crow: Mass incarceration in the age of colorblindness*. The New Press.
Bastién, A. J. (2016, 6 November). Luke Cage recap: The Ballad of Luke Cage. *Vulture.com*. https://www.vulture.com/2016/11/marvels-luke-cage-recap-season-1-episode-12.html
Bastién, A. J. (2018, 28 June). *Luke Cage*'s showrunner on criticism, black Hollywood, and that explosive season finale. *Vulture.com*. https://www.vulture.com/2018/06/luke-cage-cheo-hodari-coker-season-2-interview.html
Bell, G. C., & Harris, T. M. (2017). Exploring representations of black masculinity and emasculation on NBC's *Parenthood*. *Journal of International and Intercultural Communication, 10*(2), 135–152. https://doi.org/10.1080/17513057.2016.1142598
Beydoun, K. A. (2016, 2 September). Colin Kaepernick: Mix of racism, anti-Islam rhetoric are increasingly toxic. *The Undefeated*. https://theundefeated.com/features/colin-kaepernick-mix-of-racism-anti-islam-rhetoric-are-increasingly-toxic
Carter, K. L. (2016, 28 July)."Luke Cage" showrunner Cheo Hodari Coker says it's as dangerous as it ever was. *The Undefeated*. https://theundefeated.com/features/luke-cage-showrunner-cheo-hodari-coker-says-its-as-dangerous-as-it-ever-was/
Coker, C. H. (Writer), Jackson, N. L. (Writer), Owens, M. (Writer), & McGuigan, P. (Director). (2016a). Moment of truth [TV series episode]. In A. Cooper (Producer), *Luke Cage*, Netflix.

Coker, C. H. (Writer), Jackson, N. L. (Writer), M. Owens (Writer), Horwitch, J. (Writer), & Jobst, M. (Director). (2016b). Just to get a rep [TV series episode]. In C. Murray et al. (Executive Producers). *Luke Cage* [TV series]. Marvel Television; Netflix.

Coker, C. H. (Writer), Lopes, M. (Writer), & Richardson-Whitfield, S. (Director). (2018). I get physical [TV series episode]. In C. Murray et al. (Executive Producers). *Luke Cage* [TV series]. Marvel Television; Netflix.

Davis, B. (2015). Bare chests, silver tiaras, and removable afros: The Visual design of black comic book superheroes. In F. Gateward & J. Jennings (Eds.), *The blacker the ink: Constructions of Black identity in comics & sequential art* (pp. 193–212). Rutgers University Press.

De Dauw, E. (2020). *Hot pants and spandex suits: Gender representation in American superhero comic books*. Rutgers University Press.

Delgado, R., & Stefancic, J. (2012). *Critical race theory: An Introduction*. New York University Press.

Dodd, G. (2016, 16 November). Luke Cage is Marvel's biggest Netflix hit of 2016. *Screen Rant*. https://screenrant.com/luke-cage-netflix-ratings-viewership/#:~:text=Independant%20viewing%20data%20reveals%20that,biggest%20Netflix%20success%20of%202016

Garrido, L. A. (2018). Luke Cage as postpost-9/11 TV: Spatial negotiations of race in contemporary U.S. television. *Current Objectives of Postgraduate American Studies*, *19*(1), 1–20. https://doi.org/10.5283/copas.292

Ghee, K. (2014). "Will the 'Real' Black superheroes please stand up?!": A critical analysis of the mythological and cultural significance of Black superheroes. In S. Howard & R. L. Jackson II (Eds.), *Black comics: Politics of race and Representation* (pp. 223–238). Bloomsbury Academic.

Hemphill, M. J. (2017). *The anti-black hero: Black masculinity media representations as seen in Netflix Series Luke Cage and Fox Series Empire* [Unpublished Master's thesis], Kennesaw State University.

hooks, b. (2004). *We real cool: Black men and masculinity*. Routledge.

Howard, R., Grazer, B., Katims, J. Trilling, L., Watson, S., & Nevins, D. (Executive Producers). (2010–2015). *Parenthood* [TV series]. True Jack Productions, Imagine Television, Universal Media Studios, Universal Television, Open 4 Business Productions; NBC.

Hutchinson, G. (1995). *The Harlem Renaissance in Black and White*. Harvard University Press.

The Bulletproof Black Body

Jackson, R. L. (2006). *Scripting the Black masculine body: Identity, discourse and racial politics in popular media*. State University of New York Press.

Joseph, C. (2020, 31 July). Black Is King review – Beyoncé's love song to the black diaspora. *The Guardian*. https://www.theguardian.com/film/2020/jul/31/black-is-king-review-beyonce-disney-plus-lion-king

Kimmel, M. (1998). *Manhood in America: A cultural history*. Oxford University Press.

Kruse, K. M. (2013). *White flight: Atlanta and the making of modern conservatism*. Princeton University Press.

Lang, N. (2016, 6 October). "Luke Cage" and the racial empathy gap: "Why do they talk about being black all the time?". *Salon*. https://www.salon.com/2016/10/05/luke-cage-and-the-racial-empathy-gap-why-do-they-talk-about-being-black-all-the-time/

Lawrence, N. (2008). *Blaxploitation films of the 1970s: Blackness and genre*. Routledge.

Martin, K. (2013). Privileging privilege with the hope of accessing privilege. In C. Hayes & N. D. Hartlep (Eds.), *Unhooking from Whiteness: The key to dismantling racism in the United States* (pp. 53–56). Sense.

McKinney, J. (2016, 5 October). People are complaining that "Luke Cage" is "Too Black". *Vice*. https://www.vibe.com/gallery/luke-cage-racist-too-black-netflix-456865/

Moss, C. (2016, 30 September). Luke Cage is truly a hero for his time. *The Atlantic*. https://www.theatlantic.com/entertainment/archive/2016/09/luke-cage-gets-a-new-story/502229/

Murray, C., McGuigan, P., Holland, C., Goss, A., Engel, A., Henigman, K., Fine, A., Lee, S., Quesada, J., Buckley, D., Chory, J., Loeb, J., & Coker, C. H. (Executive Producers). (2016–2018). *Luke Cage* [TV series]. Marvel Television; Netflix.

Nama, A. (2011). *Super Black: American pop culture and Black superheroes*. University of Texas Press.

Nasheed, J. (2019, 9 August). A brief history of black hair, politics, and discrimination. *TeenVogue*. https://www.teenvogue.com/story/a-brief-history-of-black-hair-politics-and-discrimination

O'Neal, T. D. (2018). *The exceptional negro: Racism, White privilege and the lie of respectability politics*. Icart.

Pitcan, M., Marwick, A. E., & Boyd, D. (2018). Performing a vanilla self: respectability politics, social class and the digital world. *Journal of Computer-Mediated Communication, 23*, 163–179. https://doi.org/10.1093/jcmc/zmy008

Ransome, N. (2018, October 24). "Luke Cage" wasn't black enough to be a classic. *Vice*. https://www.vice.com/en_uk/article/evw3x4/luke-cage-wasnt-black-enough-to-be-a-classic

Regalado, A. J. (2015). *Bending steel: Modernity and the American superhero*, University of Mississippi Press.

Strong, D., Grazer, B., Munic, R., Calfo, F., Chaiken, I., Hamri, S., Daniels, L., Hammer, D., & Mahoney, B. (Executive Producers). (2015–2020). *Empire* [TV series]. Imagine Television, Lee Daniels Entertainment, Danny Strong Productions, Little Chicken Inc., 20th Century Fox Television; 20th Television.

Wald, J., & Losen, D. J. (2003). Defining and redirecting a school-to-prison pipeline. *New Directions for Youth Development, 99*, 9–15. https://doi.org/10.1002/yd.51

Wemple, E. (2013, 16 September). Fox News's Bill O'Reilly blames Trayvon Martin's death on hoodie. *The Washington Post*. https://www.washingtonpost.com/blogs/erik-wemple/wp/2013/09/16/fox-newss-bill-oreilly-blames-trayvon-martins-death-on-hoodie/

CHAPTER 5:
IT'S NOT OVER UNTIL THE FAT PROFESSOR SINGS: TEACHING FAT STUDIES IN THE 'FATTEST PROVINCE IN CANADA'

Sonja Boon

Abstract
What does it mean to embody the very subject one is tasked with teaching, particularly when that subject is profoundly stigmatised? In this chapter, I reflect on my embodied experience of designing, developing and teaching the first undergraduate course in Fat Studies in a university located in what has regularly been termed the 'fattest province in Canada' (CBC News, 2015). Taking an autoethnographic approach – through a series of vignettes and reflections – that centres my own embodied subjectivity as a fat professor and drawing on fat pedagogies literature (Cameron & Russell, 2016), I reflect on administrative resistance, physical constraints (such as classroom assignments), embodied identity, and emotional investments (both mine and those of my students). I read all of this through the fat studies and critical obesity literature I assigned for the course; from fat studies theories put forward by scholars such as Cecilia Hartley, Samantha Murray and others, to fat activists such as Charlotte Cooper, Virgie Tovar and Sonya Renee Taylor, and questions of citizenship, representation, and materiality in order to examine what it means to be a fat professor teaching fat studies in the 'fattest province in Canada'.

Key words: fat, teaching, Fat Studies, vulnerability, pedagogy

Introduction
The province of Newfoundland and Labrador, on the easternmost coast of Canada, has been framed, through healthest discourses, as fat. Indeed, Newfoundland and Labrador is regularly positioned as ground zero for the 'obesity epidemic' or 'crisis' (Canning et al., 2004; CBC

News, 2015, 2018; Twells et al., 2014). As a result, Newfoundlanders and Labradorians are surrounded, in all places and at all times, by anti-obesity rhetoric. This emerges in alarmist studies trumpeted in the local media, in public policy, and in educational materials and approaches (McPhail, 2013; Petherick & Beausoleil, 2015; Ward et al., 2017). It also emerges in relation to how the province is seen by outsiders, both in Canada and beyond (McPhail, 2016).

In Newfoundland and Labrador, fat intersects broadly with class. With a historically high rural unemployment rate and comparatively large percentage of the population receiving social assistance in various forms, the province is seen by the rest of Canada as the 'poor cousin' in Confederation. As national newspaper columnist Margaret Wente voiced it in a now infamous 2005 column:

> Because of stupendous political malfeasance, [Newfoundland] is at least $11-billion in debt. And so we send more money so that people can stay in the scenic villages where they were born, [...] there's no more work and never will be [...]. Rural Newfoundland [...] is probably the most vast and scenic welfare ghetto in the world. (Wente, 2005, para. 8)

Fat also intersects with cultural capital, or, rather, a lack thereof. Newfoundlanders and Labradorians are seen as quaint and friendly with cute accents, but also, in this way, as uneducated, backwards, and living in another time, or even, outside of time (Tilley, 2000). In other words, Newfoundlanders and Labradorians are seen as fat and somewhat bumbling extended family members who have yet to be properly assimilated into Canadian bodily citizenship.

In this chapter, I reflect on the experience of teaching Fat Studies in the 'fattest province in Canada'. In addition to drawing on critical literature, I intersperse my own fat histories, in a series of reflections and vignettes (presented in italics) as a way of bringing together the various factors – conceptual, material, embodied and lived – that shaped this journey.

It's Not Over Until the Fat Professor Sings

I'm not a Newfoundlander. Rather, I'm what is known locally as a CFA, or Come From Away. And so, I enter into and move through Newfoundland culture as an outsider. If there is one thing Newfoundlanders and Labradorians and I share, however, it is body size and shape. The experience of fatness.

Language around obesity and fatness operates from the unquestioned 'obesity epidemic' rhetoric, and is fatphobic, patronising, shame and stigma-based. Almost all news articles refer to 'headless fatties', as featured in Cooper's title (Cooper, 2007), or in the accompanying pictures. In one such image, a medical professional (whose professional authority is marked by stethoscope, measuring tape and a white lab coat) is attempting to measure the circumference of a fat stomach (CBC News, 2015). Another, in a slight variation on the headless theme, focuses on the gaping mouth of a child, her fleshy fingers grasping tightly around a hamburger (CBC News, 2018). At play in such imagery is not just the surveilling and disciplining authority of the medical establishment, but also, and more pointedly, the grotesque unruliness of the excessive fat body: a revolting body that resists measurement, and will not be contained or controlled (LeBesco, 2003).

Local news media reported the words of celebrated Norwegian author, Karl Ove Knausgaard. Knausgaard visited St Anthony, a remote community located the northernmost point of the island of Newfoundland, during his 2015 journey that retraced the steps of the first Europeans to set foot in the Americas. In the first of a two-part series titled 'My Saga', published in the *New York Times*, Knausgaard wrote:

> Everyone in the place, except the waiter, was fat, some of them so fat that I kept having to look at them. I had never seen people that fat before. The strange thing was that none of them looked as if they were trying to hide their enormous girth; quite the opposite, several people were wearing tight T-shirts with their big bellies sticking out proudly. (2015, para. 73)

Talking Bodies III

Here, Knausgaard imagines the fat residents of St Anthony as abject, objects of spectacle and display that are alternately fascinating and horrifying. Knausgaard cannot make sense of what he is seeing; for him, these are excessive and ultimately incomprehensible presentations of self and he cannot imagine how Newfoundlanders do not feel shame, or why, indeed, they would feel 'proud'. Showing his utter disgust of and, indeed, dismissive disdain for the people of St Anthony, and, extrapolating from this, the people of Newfoundland and Labrador more broadly.

These comments were received with horror and outrage, on the one hand, but also, simultaneously, with nodding approval. As Robin Whitaker, writing in a St John's-based online newspaper, *The Independent*, wrote, "if one set of reactions was affronted, another can be summarised as, 'the truth hurts'" (Whitaker, 2015, para. 10). Later that same year, the provincial government listed reducing obesity by 5% as a policy plank (Government of Newfoundland and Labrador, 2015). This is the context in which the vast majority of my undergraduate students have been raised. This is the world in which they have come to know and understand their own bodies, and those around them. Most have had almost no exposure to alternative viewpoints and limited access to critical lenses that might allow them to interrogate anti-obesity and fatphobic, shaming messaging. The predominance of biopedagogical discourses of responsibilisation (Petherick & Beausoleil, 2015; Petherick et al., 2015), fed through emotionally manipulative languages of shame and stigma, together with the ubiquity of 'concern trolling', mean that they have only barely – if at all – examined the social, political, cultural and historical context of fatness. Instead, many of my students have internalised a fear of fat, and in some cases, have taken the shame, stigma and hatred inside their bodies.

> Pace *Simone de Beauvoir: One is not born fat. One becomes fat. In my case, it was my parents, and more specifically, my mother, who defined me as fat. These becomings came in myriad forms: Food measuring and monitoring; Weekly weigh-ins, marked on a prominently placed calendar in the kitchen; Locked cupboards and freezer; Cookie jars sealed with duct*

It's Not Over Until the Fat Professor Sings

> *tape; Diet books left, oh so casually, on my bed; Dismissive comments about fat people in the shopping mall, on the television, in politics.*
> *I was a good student. Diligent. Serious. I learned my lessons well. But I was still fat.*

Memorial University is the only university in the province. A comprehensive university, with a Faculty of Medicine and extensive graduate programmes in a range of faculties and disciplines, it has approximately 18,000 students. But until September 2018, it had never had a dedicated course in Fat Studies. While critical approaches to obesity have been introduced, albeit briefly, in medical school modules, in graduate seminars in community health, and in kinesiology courses, and while Fat Studies readings have been included in gender studies courses in feminist theory and activisms, there had never previously been a stand-alone course on the topic. In some respects, this is not surprising. Fat Studies is still a relatively new area of study and such courses are still uncommon at many universities. However, at the same time it seemed to me that examining the social, historical, political and cultural context of obesity and fatness was particularly urgent in a social, political and medical context almost wholly defined by obesity and fatness.

What did it mean to teach the first fat studies course in the fattest province, and further, what did it mean to be the fat professor teaching that course?

> *Looking back through the family photo albums. In one photo, I'm trying to clamber into the bathtub, intent on doing it all by myself. I'm balanced on the toes of my right foot, my left leg extended like a ballerina at the barre, almost up to the bathtub's edge. My naked body towards the tub, my face towards the camera: flirtatious ingénue, loose dark curls around a cherubic face, fleshy toddler legs and bottom exposed to the camera. If I were to title this photo, I'd call it Determination.*

First and foremost, I knew that Fat Studies needed to be taught by a fat professor. As pedagogues, our bodies are, for better or for worse, our storytellers. They mark how we are read in the classroom; they also determine the extent to which we are or are not accepted as authorities (Fisanick, 2007).

> *Another photo. I'm standing in the garden now, patio stones and begonias in earthenware planters. Clothed, this time, my stomach pushing a pinafore dress out from my body, white socks pulled onto sturdy legs, shiny black Mary Janes. Same curls. Same cherubic face. Same fleshy body. Same feet, only this time, they're planted firmly on the ground. Another title: Garden Nymph, or, perhaps more prosaically, Flower Child.*

Our bodies and the way that we inhabit them also shape how our students feel in classroom spaces. Representation, as countless studies have shown, matters. This is equally important in relation to fat pedagogy. While I acknowledge the political relevance of allyship (Bacon et al., 2016; Nash & Warin, 2017), and the impact of sizeism on all bodies, regardless of size or shape (Kannen, 2016), I wanted to centre fatness in the classroom, and part of that centreing involved situating the fat professor as source and site of knowledge; that is, as an expert. This was, for me, particularly important given that fat folks are routinely imagined as lazy, weak-willed and out of control (Murray, 2005); that is, as failed citizens (Biltekoff, 2007; McPhail, 2009; Rinaldi et al., 2017). Given the stigma and shame associated with dominant discourses, I felt that it was very important for students to know that a fat professor would develop and teach a course in fat studies.

> *In early childhood photos, I'm fleshy, round, sturdy. I am, in a word, fat. But I didn't yet have the knowledge of fatness in my body. Fatness – as social concept or stigma – had not yet shaped my movements, my behaviours, my thoughts, my feelings. In these photos, I hadn't yet learned to hate my body. I hadn't learned that my fat nakedness should be shameful, my protruding stomach disgusting.*

What could a single course in Fat Studies accomplish? My opening vision was vast: I was interested in fat theory and methodology (Forth, 2013; Hartley, 2001; McPhail, 2009; Murray, 2005, 2008), fat history (Farrell, 2011; McPhail, 2017; Strings, 2019), fat representation (Asbill, 2009; Beattie, 2014; Elliott, 2016; Kuppers, 2001; Norman et al., 2016), and more. I wanted students to locate fat alongside other axes of identity and oppression, including gender, sexuality, race and class (Bergman, 2009; Biltekoff, 2007; Boero, 2009; Cooper, 2016; Dark, 2014; Ingraham, 2015; McPhail & Lavallee, 2016; Poudrier, 2016; Robinson, 2019; Sarkar, 2019; Strings, 2019; White, 2019). And I wanted to introduce them to fat activisms: both local critical health researchers working to actively change public policy (Beausoleil & Petherick, 2015; Petherick & Beausoleil, 2015; Ward, Beausoleil & Heath, 2016), and also the thriving and vibrant fat community that reached well beyond our shores (Cooper, 2016; Wann, 1998; Taylor, 2018; Tovar, 2018).

My students needed to know that there were alternate discourses available to them, that the anti-obesity rhetoric that had shadowed them since birth was not the only story out there. My students needed to be both thinkers and activists; they needed to develop critical, creative, and activist tools that would allow them not only to respond to, but to actively combat and resist, the fatphobic messaging to which they were overwhelmingly subject.

> *I wasn't a child who talked back to her elders. Among my accomplishments was a carefully-honed ability to hide, to remain silent. I was an observer. I did my work quietly, hoping nobody would notice.*

I recognised from the outset that this was going to be a course that involved not just intellectual growth, but that it would also involve political and emotional commitments. I recognised, too, that students might be vulnerable. However, what I did not realise at the time was exactly *how* much these things would come to matter. Nor did I recognise how teaching this course would affect the fat professor: me.

Fat Studies pushed buttons right from the start, and sometimes in unexpected ways. I experienced resistance throughout the process of proposing, designing and delivering this course. Some of this resistance was expected: for example, I expected this to be a challenge for students; some of it, however, was unexpected. I want to look at three forms of resistance that emerged in the course of developing, planning and teaching this course: structural, everyday and internalised.

Talking Bodies III

As with many universities, my university has a labyrinthine and deeply bureaucratic course approvals process that requires us to seek approval at many levels, from the department to the faculty and from there, right through to the Senate Committee on Undergraduate Studies. Unsurprisingly the proposed course enjoyed full approval at the departmental level. While most colleagues in other departments were also supportive, one departmental head wondered if I was going to deal with thinness, too. On the surface, this sounds like a perfectly logical question. But would I teach about Shakespeare in a course about T. S. Eliot, or the War of 1812 in a course about World War II? This question reminded me of the all too common 'But where are the men?' that still accompanies requests to teach women's literature or history courses.

I experienced the most resistance at middle management levels. The Associate Dean did not like the course title. 'Fat Studies' made him uncomfortable. This was both surprising and, simultaneously, unsurprising. My course proposal was accompanied by a lengthy bibliography which included many titles focused on fat. Nevertheless, the Associate Dean indicated that, before he was willing to send it on for approval, he requested I add a special statement indicating why 'Fat' was appropriate terminology.

And so, while every other course proposal passed through the Dean's office has a standard one-sentence Executive Summary – 'This is a 3000 level course, titled Fat Studies, to be offered by the Department of Gender Studies, Faculty of Humanities and Social Sciences' – I was asked to revise the proposal to justify the title. Implicit in this request was also a challenge to justify both the course and my own expertise in this area of study. In the end, my revised summary read as follows:

> This is a 3000 level course, titled Fat Studies, to be offered in the Department of Gender Studies, Faculty of Humanities and Social Sciences. Fat Studies is a rich and growing field of study that responds to the medicalised language of 'obesity' through a reclamation, reframing, and re-articulation of the word fat (see, for example, the journal *Fat Studies*, as well as such publications as the

It's Not Over Until the Fat Professor Sings

Fat Studies Reader and the *Fat Pedagogy Reader*, among others, see bibliography; Boon 2017).

Resistance did not end there. I knew, too, that my proposal would not be read the same way as other proposals. What Samantha Murray (2005) terms the "negative collective 'knowingness' about fatness" (p. 154) would inherently shape how my colleagues assessed the proposal itself. Would they take this course seriously, or would they read this as flimsy justification for my own body state/condition in a province already beset, if not afflicted with obesity?

Fat Studies also encountered everyday resistance. By this, I mean resistance that is passive, unthinking, but still present. In the context of this course, everyday resistance manifested itself in at least two ways: institutional and social. First of all, it emerged in the form of classroom allocations. I cannot presume malice in this decision; as instructors, we have little to no decision-making power over classroom allocations, rather, they are given to us based on class time and presumed class size and location on campus.

Cat Pausé (2016) has observed that classroom spaces are important to student learning and experience. She writes: "[w]e do a great disservice to our students when we ignore the role that physical comfort plays in their learning" (p. 57). For Fat Studies, I was assigned a room I'd taught in before and hated. 'Designed' – and I put this in quotation marks for good reason – for approximately fifty students, this room has five rows of long fixed tables. Affixed to each of these tables are ten chairs. Apart from inhibiting any possibility of group discussion or work, this classroom design does not acknowledge body diversity of any kind at all; indeed, such spaces serve instead to discipline and shame, something my students noticed immediately after they registered. As Ashley Hetrick and Derek Attig (2009) share:

> Desks hurt us ... [Desks] are highly active material and discursive constructions that seek to both indoctrinate students' bodies and minds into the middle-class values of restraint and discipline, and inscribe these messages onto the bodies that site in them. (p. 197)

Talking Bodies III

Many of my students had previously experienced the disciplining effects of this particular classroom and were baffled upon learning where Fat Studies would be held. The relatively small class size meant that I was able to source another classroom: our seminar room which features fully movable tables and chairs and is not included in central room booking processes. Other everyday resistance emerged in relation to the course poster I put up on my door. Several times, when returning from a meeting or teaching, I would see random students pointing and laughing at it. Some took pictures of it, presumably to share on their social media accounts.

More important though was the resistance that came from the students themselves. This resistance emerged from internalised fatphobia, and, as term progressed, from their need to protect themselves. I would term this internalised resistance. While one student loved the idea of having 'Fat Studies' listed on their transcript, some students were, like our Associate Dean, very uncomfortable with a course titled Fat Studies. They hadn't told family they were taking it. They hadn't told friends. And if they did, they quickly glossed over it, shoving it in the middle of a recitation of all of their courses so that hopefully they would not have to explain. They did not like the word. They did not like what it meant. They did not want to talk about it. They did not want to use it. All of this, even though they made it abundantly clear in class discussions that they were fully committed to the topic.

> *To be honest, I didn't tell my parents what I was teaching either. I didn't want to hear the lack of comprehension, the false joviality, the inevitable sigh. I like to think that I was frustrated. That I didn't have the patience anymore. That I didn't feel the need to have to justify myself. But perhaps, like my students, I was uncomfortable, ashamed, fearful. And perhaps, in this way, I failed them.*

But the resistance also went much deeper. Many students struggled to work through topics about which they were deeply passionate, but which touched very close to the bone. Two students dropped the course because the material was too emotionally charged for them.

It's Not Over Until the Fat Professor Sings

And even those who continued, struggled. At numerous points my class of twelve students dwindled to two or three. This was something I had never previously experienced.

Many of my students, no matter their size, came into class with deeply traumatic body histories. These experiences ranged from microaggressions and more from parents – often mothers – and the school system, to shaming and stigmatising medical encounters that regularly included incorrect diagnoses based entirely on fatphobia, to poor service in shops, and even to experiences of sexual violence. As a result, many students had troubled and troubling relationships with their bodies. Unsurprisingly, these troubles accompanied them into the classroom.

I expect that students in my courses will be intellectually challenged, that they will leave the course in a different place from where they started, and that we will have journeyed far together. I also anticipate that for some students, a course will be as much an emotional journey as it is an intellectual journey; topics hit some students harder than others and resonate in specific ways at specific times in their lives. But what I hadn't expected was the extent of this emotional journey, and along with this, the sheer weight of the emotional and psychological baggage they were already carrying, a weight that some barely knew they were carrying until they started to critically interrogate the notion of fat itself.

Victoria Kannen (2016) observes that "[a]critical pedagogy of the body requires most students to be open to new possibilities for what their bodies may mean and the variety of social spaces they inhabit" (p. 33). But this course hit my students at the point where they were most vulnerable, a place where they had been – often repeatedly – deeply hurt. My students hadn't experienced fat stigma once. They had experienced it repeatedly, from those closest to them – the parents and caregivers entrusted with nurturing and fostering their growth and development – to those who exercised authority over them (doctors, teachers), and those who were part of their everyday encounters in public places. The topic and the readings asked them to excavate, examine and interrogate this painful, bruised, battered and vulnerable core of themselves. Mona Awad's *13 Ways of Looking at a Fat Girl* in particular, because of its intimacy and its refusal of a happy ending, which brought into high relief many of my students' own experiences and insecurities.

For many students, although not all, the tension between the emotional and psychological labour of living a fat life and the intellectual labour of taking a course in fat studies was sometimes too much. While students were usually prepared for class, they did not always have the emotional capacity to engage in the classroom space itself. Reading between the lines of our classroom discussions and their research journals, I could see deep visceral responses to the reading. *Rage. Recognition. Helplessness. Grief. Loss. Determination.* These emotions accompanied their critical journeys through the term. Interrogating fat meant interrogating their very selves, and some of them were frozen into place. Like deer caught in the headlights of an oncoming car, they were completely overwhelmed: they could not unlearn what they had already learned, but were also sometimes incapable of moving forward. Their critical lenses were wide open, but these lenses warred with their vulnerabilities; with the hurts, pains, shame and stigma that they had experienced both throughout their childhoods and in the everyday fatphobia – both conscious and unconscious – that they continued to navigate in their everyday lives. Some of them were struck by the extent to which they had internalised these messages. They had come to see themselves as unworthy, unlovable, and in this way, they felt they had let themselves down. But in these discussions and in their writing, I also sensed determination, a need and desire to move beyond this, to see and think differently, and to work for change.

I had anticipated some of this, of course. This was precisely why I invited local scholars, why I ended the courses with an extended module on fat activisms, and why I felt it was so important that the course be taught by a fat professor. I wanted my students to see the roots of Fat Studies as both a critical and a social justice practice, I wanted them to be able to find and experience fat community, and I wanted them to be able to do this in a space where their professor had likely shared some of their experiences.

What I had not anticipated at all was the way that this course might impact me. I love corporeal feminist theory. I have taught courses on bodies before. Many topics I have taught have touched me deeply, at a personal level, but I have been able to teach them and separate my personal self from my critical self. Fat Studies would not allow me to divide myself in two. I could not hide my fat, embodied self. It accompanied me through my readings and my preparations, and it accompanied me into the classroom. It was part of every discussion I led, every lecture I prepared. Indeed, it had been part of every stage of course development that preceded the class itself.

> *I may not yet know how to love my body, but over the years, I have learned to tolerate it.* In Fat Studies, I wanted to deploy it as a weapon to target fat hatred, but I also wanted to use it as a shield to protect, somehow, against fat shame. I wanted my softness to serve as a cushion against my students' grief, shame, loss, fear, dismay, discomfort, and vulnerability. I wanted to be the 'strong tree' for them. I wanted them to know, explicitly and overtly, that they could count on me to create a generous, open, and nourishing space for discussion and conversation. I wanted to take their vulnerabilities into my own fat body, to carry their weight for them so that they would be able to move forward. Almost subconsciously, I wanted my fat body to stand in for theirs. I wanted so much. And perhaps, then, following Elizabeth, the lead character in Mona Awad's 2016 novel, 13 Ways of Looking at a Fat Girl, *I wanted* too *much*.

Carrying this emotional weight takes its own toll. In December, after the term had finished, I had a conversation with a colleague who teaches a course on the sociology of sexuality. My colleague nodded when I discussed the weight I had carried, the tension between my physical weight and the emotional weight of my students. They nodded, because as a queer sociology professor, they had experienced similar things in their own teaching of the sociology of sexuality. In fact, it was precisely because of these things that they had taken a break from teaching it. They could not keep performing queerness for their students, no matter how much their students needed it. It was too difficult.

> Excel excellence. It's an idea I encountered in Black Canadian playwright Lorena Gale's autobiographical dramatic monologue Je me souviens. Excelling excellence, Gale's mother told her, was one way she could protect herself against the inevitable racism she would encounter. The idea stuck with me because it was so familiar. I know this feeling intimately. As a fat, mixed-race immigrant kid growing up in a small town on the Canadian prairies, excelling excellence offered the possibility of escape. Excelling excellence was an odd sort of invisibility cloak, a way to hide what those around me could never unsee.
>
> Look at me now, the fat professor standing in the front of the class, doctoral degree and all.

I know that my students took much away from this course. All students agreed that the course was important, and, as challenging as some of the readings were, they felt that they were necessary. The students felt that the course gave them new tools and new lenses. It offered ways to push back against anti-obesity rhetoric: they had ammunition to respond to fatphobic 'concern trolling' and dominant anti-obesity commentaries. Students also learned about themselves and about the fatphobia they had internalised. As a result, they began to read their bodies differently. Disruption, unruliness and revolting were not necessarily negative attributes; they could be turned on their heads and directed to activist ends. My students learned that their unruly fat bodies challenged and disrupted dominant gender norms and undermined healthist imperatives of control and containment. They learned that a revolting body is a revolutionary body, whose very presence provokes change.

Students interrogated questions of pleasure and desire, and the ways these have been conventionally denied fat people. They grappled with the complexities of fat representations that move beyond the 'becoming' narratives that require thinness and as part of any 'happy ending'. So too, did they begin to interrogate the tensions between critical engagement and emotional vulnerability, and move beyond the frozen 'deer in the headlights' helplessness that stopped them in their tracks. Some began to have productive – and long overdue – conversations with those closest to them about questions of body size and body image.

When considering how to create transformative learning spaces, Bacon et al. suggest:

> [W]e will have to recognize the vital role of emotion in the classroom so that we can help our students learn in a way where real life including embodiment, is not an afterthought or optional extra, but an integral piece in their conceptual framework. (2016, p. 47)

Many of my students took transformative journeys – but at what cost? In the face of all of this, I still find myself returning to my queer sociologist colleague's comments about the nature of classroom teaching performances. While, like Bacon et al. (2016), I was attentive to my students' embodied and emotional needs, I was not nearly as attentive to my own. What are the implications of taking on our students' vulnerabilities as we strive to make a critical but also nurturing space to discuss deeply intimate and often painful stories? How do we manage the emotional labour of teaching? It may not be over until the fat professor sings, but how long can this fat professor keep singing?

Author biography

Sonja Boon is Professor of Gender Studies at Memorial University. An award-winning researcher, writer and teacher, she is interested in bodies, stories, identities and theories, and has published on a variety of topics, from considerations of gender, class, embodiment, identity and citizenship in eighteenth-century medical letters, to breastfeeding selfies and virtual activism, autobiographies of infanticide, vulnerability as longing in the writing of Hélène Cixous, auto/ethnography and the embodiment of maternal grief, and craftivism in the feminist classroom, among others. She is the author of four books, including

Autoethnography and Feminist Theory at the Water's Edge: Unsettled Islands (with Lesley Butler and Daze Jefferies, Palgrave, 2018) and, more recently, the critical memoir, *What the Oceans Remember: Searching for Belonging and Home* (Wilfrid Laurier University Press, 2019).

References

Asbill, D. L. (2009). "I'm allowed to be a sexual being": The distinctive social conditions of fat burlesque. In E. Rothblum & S. Solovay (Eds.), *The fat studies reader* (pp. 299–304). New York University Press.

Awad, M. (2016). *13 ways of looking at a fat girl*. Penguin.

Bacon, L., O'Reilly, C., & Aphramor, L. (2016). Reflections on thin privilege and responsibility. In E. Cameron & C. Russell (Eds.), *Fat pedagogy reader: Challenging weight-based oppression through critical education* (pp. 41–50). Peter Lang.

Beattie, S. (2014). Bear arts naked: Queer activism and the fat male body. In C. Pausé, J. Wykes, & S. Murray (Eds.), *Queering fat embodiment* (pp. 115–129). Ashgate.

Beausoleil, N., & Petherick, L. (2015). Taking up the vitality message: Health knowledge, feeling good, and pleasure in Newfoundland children's drawings and talk. *Cultural Studies ↔ Critical Methodologies, 15*(5), 407–416. https://doi.org/10.1177/1532708615611722

Bergman, S. B. (2009). Part-time fatso. In E. Rothblum & S. Solovay (Eds.), *The fat studies reader* (pp. 139–142). New York University Press.

Biltekoff, C. (2007). The terror within: Obesity in post 9/11 U.S. life. *American Studies, 48*(3), 29–48.

Boero, N. C. (2009). Fat kids, working moms, and the *"epidemic of obesity"*: Race, class, and mother blame. In E. Rothblum & S. Solovay (Eds.), *The fat studies reader* (pp. 113–119). New York University Press.

Boon, S. (2017). *Revised course proposal for GNDR3026 Fat Studies*. Memorial University.

Cameron, E., & Russell, C. (Eds.). (2016). *The fat pedagogy reader: Challenging weight-based oppression through critical education* (Vol. 467). Peter Lang.

Canning, P., Courage, M. L., & Frizzell, L. M. (2004). Prevalence of overweight and obesity in a provincial population of Canadian preschool children. *Canadian Medical Association Journal, 171*(3), 240–242. https://doi.org/10.1503/cmaj.1040075

CBC News. (2015, 17 June). NL Fattest province in Canada, StatsCan report shows. *CBC News*. https://www.cbc.ca/news/canada/newfoundland-labrador/n-l-fattest-province-in-canada-statscan-report-shows-1.3116832

CBC News. (2018, 9 September). Expert weighs in as NL tops country for most overweight kids. *CBC News*. https://www.cbc.ca/news/canada/newfoundland-labrador/study-finds-nl-kids-most-overweight-1.4813732

Cooper, C. (2007). *Headless fatties*. http://charlottecooper.net/fat/fat-writing/headless-fatties-01-07/

Cooper, C. (2016). *Fat activism: A radical social movement*. HammerOn.

Dark, K. (2014). Becoming Travolta. In C. Pausé, J. Wykes, & S. Murray (Eds.), *Queering fat embodiment* (pp. 27–30). Ashgate.

Elliott, C. (2016). Find your greatness: Responsibility, policy and the problem of childhood obesity. In. J. Ellison, D. McPhail, & W. Mitchinson (Eds.), *Obesity in Canada: Critical perspectives* (pp. 272–91). University of Toronto Press.

Ellison, J., McPhail, D., & Mitchinson, W. (2016). Introduction. In. J. Ellison, D. McPhail, & W. Mitchinson (Eds.), *Obesity in Canada: Critical perspectives* (pp. 3–28). University of Toronto Press.

Farrell, A. E. (2011). *Fat shame: Stigma and the fat body in American culture*. New York University Press.

Fisanick, C. (2007). "They are weighted with authority": Fat female professors in academic and popular cultures. *Feminist Teacher, 17*(3), 237–255.

Forth, C. E. (2013). The qualities of fat: Bodies, history, and materiality. *Journal of Material Culture, 18*(2), 135–154. https://doi.org/10.1177/1359183513489496

Gale, L. (2001). *Je me souviens*. Talon.

Government of Newfoundland and Labrador. (2015). *The way forward: A vision for sustainability and growth in Newfoundland and Labrador*. https://www.gov.nl.ca/pdf/the_way_forward.pdf

Hartley, C. (2001). Letting ourselves go: Making room for the fat body in feminist scholarship. In J. E. Braziel & K. LeBesco (Eds.), *Bodies out of bounds: Fatness and transgression* (pp. 60–73). University of California Press.

Hetrick, A., & Attig, D. (2009). Sitting pretty: Fat bodies, classroom desks, and academic excess. In E. Rothblum & S. Solovay (Eds.), *The Fat Studies Reader* (pp. 197–204). New York University Press.

Ingraham, N. (2015). Queering porn: Gender and size diversity within SF Bay area queer pornography. In H. Hester & C. Walters (Eds.), *Fat sex: New directions in theory and activism* (pp. 115–132). Ashgate.

Kannen, V. (2016). "How can you be teaching this?": Tears, fears, and fat. In E. Cameron & C. Russell (Eds.), *Fat pedagogy reader: Challenging weight-based oppression through critical education* (pp. 31–40). Peter Lang.

Klumbyte, G., & Smiet, K. (2015). Bodies like our own: The dynamics of distance and closeness in online fat. In H. Hester & C. Walters (Eds.), *Fat sex: New directions in theory and activism* (pp. 133–151). Ashgate.

Knausgaard, K. O. (2015, 1 March). My saga, Part 1. *New York Times*. https://www.nytimes.com/2015/03/01/magazine/karl-ove-knausgaard-travels-through-america.html

Kuppers, P. (2001). Fatties on stage: Feminist performances. In J. E. Braziel & K. LeBesco, *Bodies out of bounds: Fatness and transgression* (pp. 277–291). University of California Press.

LeBesco, K. (2001). Queering fat bodies/politics, In J. E. Braziel & K. LeBesco, *Bodies out of bounds: Fatness and transgression* (pp. 74–87). University of California Press.

LeBesco, K. (2003). *Revolting bodies? The struggle to redefine fat identity*. University of Massachusetts Press.

McPhail, D. (2009). What to do with the 'Tubby Hubby': 'Obesity,' the crisis of masculinity, and the nuclear family in early Cold War Canada. *Antipode, 41*(5), 1021–1050. https://doi.org/10.1111/j.1467-8330.2009.00708.x

McPhail, D. (2013). Resisting biopedagogies of obesity in a problem population: Understandings of healthy eating and healthy weight in a Newfoundland and Labrador community. *Critical Public Health, 23*(3), 289–303. https://doi.org/10.1080/09581596.2013.797566

McPhail, D. (2016). Having your jiggs dinner and eating it too: Newfoundland obesity and the affects of tradition. In J. Ellison, D. McPhail, & W. Mitchinson (Eds.), *Obesity in Canada: Critical perspectives* (pp. 320–341). University of Toronto Press.

McPhail, D. (2017). *Contours of the nation: Making the nation and imagining Canada*. University of Toronto Press.

McPhail, D., & Lavallee, B. (2016). Indigenous people's clinical encounters with obesity: A conversation with Barry Lavallee. In J. Ellison, D. McPhail, & W. Mitchinson (Eds.), *Obesity in Canada: Critical perspectives* (pp. 175-184). University of Toronto Press.

Mitchinson, W. (2016). Mother blaming and obesity: An alternative perspective. In J. Ellison, D. McPhail, & W. Mitchinson (Eds.), *Obesity in Canada: Critical perspectives* (pp. 187-217). University of Toronto Press.

Murray, S. (2005). Un/(be)coming out? Rethinking fat politics. *Social Semiotics, 15*(2), 153-163. https://doi.org/10.1080/10350330500154667

Murray, S. (2008). Normative imperatives vs. pathological bodies: Constructing the 'fat' woman. *Australian Feminist Studies, 23*(56), 213-224. https://doi.org/10.1080/08164640802004752

Nash, M., & Warin, M. (2017). Squeezed between identity politics and intersectionality: A critique of 'thin privilege' in fat studies, *Feminist Theory, 18*(1), 69-87. https://doi.org/10.1177/1464700116666253

Norman, M. E., Rail, G., & Jette, S. (2016). 13. Screening the un-scene: Deconstructing the (bio) politics of story telling in a Canadian reality makeover weight loss series. In J. Ellison, D. McPhail, & W. Mitchinson, (Eds.), *Obesity in Canada: Critical Perspectives* (pp. 342-372). University of Toronto Press.

Pausé, C. (2016). Promise to try: Combating fat oppression through pedagogy in tertiary education. In E. Cameron & C. Russell (Eds.), *The fat pedagogy reader: Challenging weight-based oppression through critical education* (53-60). Peter Lang.

Petherick, L., & Beausoleil, N. (2015). Female elementary teachers' biopedagogical practices: How health discourse circulates in Newfoundland elementary schools. *Canadian Journal of Education, 38*(1), 1-29.

Petherick, L., & Beausoleil, N. (2016). Obesity panic, body surveillance, and pedagogy: Elementary teachers' response to obesity messaging. In J. Ellison, D. McPhail, & W. Mitchinson (Eds.), *Obesity in Canada: Critical perspectives* (pp. 245-271). University of Toronto Press.

Petherick, L., Rail, G., & Jette, S. (2015). Shaping the child as a healthy child: Health surveillance, schools, and biopedagogies. *Cultural Studies ↔ Critical Methodologies, 15*(5), 361-370. https://doi.org/10.1177/1532708615611716

Poudrier, J. (2016). The geneticization of Aboriginal diabetes and obesity: Adding another science to the story of the thrifty gene. In J. Ellison, D. McPhail, & W. Mitchinson (Eds.), *Obesity in Canada: Critical perspectives* (pp. 89–121), University of Toronto Press.

Rail, G., & Jette, S. (2015). Reflections on biopedagogies and/of public health. *Cultural Studies ↔ Critical Methodologies, 15*(5), 3273–3336. https://doi.org/10.1177/1532708615611703

Rinaldi, J., Rice, C., Lamarre, A., McPhail, D., & Harrison, E. (2017). Fatness and failing citizenship. *Somatechnics, 7*(2), 218–233. http://dx.doi.org/10.3366/soma.2017.0219

Robinson, M. (2019). The big colonial bones of Indigenous North America's 'obesity epidemic'. In M. Friedman, C. Rice, & J. Rinaldi (Eds.), *Thickening fat: Fat bodies, intersectionality, and social justice* (pp. 15–28). Routledge.

Sarkar, S. (2019). "May my children always have milk and rice": Problematizing the role of mothers in childhood fatness in India. In M. Friedman, C. Rice, & J. Rinaldi (Eds.), *Thickening fat: Fat bodies, intersectionality, and social justice* (pp. 51–63). Routledge.

Strings, S. (2019). *Fearing the Black body: The racial origins of fat phobia.* New York University Press.

Taylor, S. R. (2018). *The body is not an apology: The power of radical self-love.* Berrett-Koehler.

Tilley, S. A. (2000). Provincially speaking: "You don't sound like a Newfoundlander". In C. James (Ed.), *Experiencing difference* (pp. 235–245). Fernwood.

Tovar, V. (2018). *You have the right to remain fat.* Feminist.

Twells, L. K., Gregory, D. M., Reddigan, J., & Midodzi, W. (2014, 3 March). Current and predicted prevalence of obesity in Canada: A trend analysis. *CMAJ Open, 2*(1), E18–E26. https://doi.org/10.9778/cmajo.20130016

Wann, M. (1998). *Fat! So?: Because you don't have to apologize for your size.* Ten Speed.

Ward, P., Beausoleil, N., & Heath, O. (2016). Creating space for a critical examination of weight-centered approaches in health pedagogy and health professions. In E. Cameron & C. Russell (Eds.), *The fat pedagogy reader: Challenging weight-based oppression through critical education* (pp. 81–90). Peter Lang.

Ward, P., Beausoleil, N., & Heath, O. (2017). Confusing constructions: Exploring the meaning of health with children in "obesity" treatment. *Fat Studies, 6*(3), 255–267. https://doi.org/10.1080/21604851.2017.1288494

Ward, P. (2016). Obesity, risk, and responsibility: The discursive production of the "ultimate at-risk child". In J. Ellison, D. McPhail, & W. Mitchinson (Eds.), *Obesity in Canada: Critical perspectives* (pp. 218–244), University of Toronto Press.

Wente, M. (2005, January). Wente says. *The Globe and Mail.* https://www.theglobeandmail.com/news/national/margaret-wente-says/article1112977/

Whitaker, R. (2015, 26 March). Karl's adventures in Newfoundland: Time for a healthy debate? *The Independent Newfoundland and Labrador.* https://theindependent.ca/2015/03/26/karls-adventures-in-newfoundland-time-for-a-healthy-debate/

White, F. R. (2019). Embodying the fat/trans intersection. In M. Friedman, C. Rice, & J. Rinaldi (Eds.), *Thickening fat: Fat bodies, intersectionality, and social justice* (pp. 110–121). Routledge.

CHAPTER 6:
TECHNIQUES OF THE BODY AS TECHNIQUES OF THE SELF: TAKING SEX SERIOUSLY

Chloe Dominique

Abstract

What do techniques of the body do to the self? What are the processes by which sex comes to inform a person's sexual subjectivity, their embodied notions of self, and an identity readable to others? What makes sex, *sex?* This work explores the role that body techniques and material culture play in the emergence of sexual subjectivity. Through an ethnographic account of LGBTQ+ individuals living in London, UK, it is argued that the emergence of the queer subject as ontologically distinct from heteronormativity, is in part constituted by the bodily technique of sex. Queer subjects have historically been *systematically* and *violently reduced* to their genitals, in terms of what they do with them, as well as how they are constituted in relation to normative notions of *personhood, gender identity* and *modernist understandings of sexuality.* Queer subjectivity relies upon – and has historically been forced upon – the *distinction* from their heterosexual counterparts. Expectations of gender identity and presentation, sexuality and desire become *conflated* with the physical composition of their bodies. Despite this history, the literature on sexuality often lacks an analysis of the sexual acts themselves. They are regarded as a backdrop to something more important, more discursive. In short, the social nature of sexual practices is missing. My research proposes a novel way to regard sexual practices, taking the body as a material form through which techniques are enacted. Focusing on the social content of sexual practices, it will be argued that queer sexual practices are a locus for the navigation, contestation and (re)appropriation of social norms. The sexual subject should thus not be treated as a *fait accompli*, but rather one that co-emerges with the material world through the

Techniques of the Body as Techniques of the Self

process of interiorisation, via the body. In short, we must take sexual techniques seriously.

Key words: sex, the body, queer, subjectivity, identity, self, aesthetics

Introduction

> ... we talk about sex – sexual practices and erotic variation – much less than we might imagine, and this is at least partly because we talk a great deal about categories such as "lesbian" and "gay".
> (Halberstam, 1998, p. 113)

> ... we need to know more about sex [...] We need a more precise vocabulary to take us out of Victorian romanticism in sexual matters and toward a new understanding of women's sexual diversity and possibility.
> (Newton & Walton, 1984, p. 174)

> Nothing is more technical than sexual positions. Very few writers have had the courage to discuss this question [...] There are all the techniques of normal and abnormal sexual acts. Contact of the sexual organs, mingling of breath, kisses, etc. Here sexual techniques and sexual morals are closely related.
> (Mauss, 1935/1979, p. 84)

This chapter explores how notions of power, of agency, and structure – in the myriad gendered, classed, raced and other ways these emerge – appear to 'float' above the material experience of being a body (and a subject) in the world. Particularly within queer theoretical frameworks of gender and sexuality, the fear of biological determinism has often meant abandoning the body as a site of enquiry, favouring more meaning-based analyses. The discipline has thus been charged with an "indefensible refusal to name a subject" (Seidman, 1993, p. 132), due to its deconstructionist directive – an imperative to move the analysis of the self and one's subject position, into a "conception of the self radically disarticulated from the social" (Green, 2007, p. 27). Floating like lanterns in the literature, discursive elements of socio-sexual phenomena draw our eyes upwards and outwards. They encourage us to look for and to seize postmodern 'potentialities' of the subject; of imaginings, not affordances, of infinite limits, not finite presents. Within this chapter, the influence of bodily techniques in the emergence of sexual subjectivity will be centred and materialised. I ask the following questions, and by way of employing ethnographic accounts of fieldwork conducted during 2017 and 2018 with LGBTQ+ individuals in London, UK, seek to answer them: What makes the sexual subject? What makes sex, *sex*? What is the embedded nature of sexual practices? How, as social scientists, can we reach and observe them? Sex – even auto-sex – and indeed the absence of sex, is always relational, and therefore always social. I thus employ the term 'sociosexual' to highlight that sex is always concerned with the particular material and social milieu in which it is practised. What are the processes by which (the act of) sex comes to inform a person's sociosexual subjectivity? What are the limits to this question?

In order to produce a holistic image of the material, sociocultural and economic processes that constitute the lives of LGBTQ+ individuals, I argue that we must attend not only to the meanings of social phenomena, but to the techniques and processes of such historically situated phenomena. Indeed, these two elements are indissolubly linked. Through answering the above questions, I aim to marry the distinction between discursive identity and bio-social matter as they substantiate the subject. This chapter explores what can be said about the nature of bodily motricity, techniques, and the absorption of objects as they influence and become entangled in the phenomenological experience of our bodies, ourselves, and of the world around us.

The aesthetics of sexual action
Sexual action is comprised of two initial attributes: the individual decision to act, and the collective influence on such actions. These elements are at many times relational, but can also come into conflict, oppose one another, or create the environment for technical change and adaptation; what Leroi-Gourhan calls technological innovation (1993)

(see Lenay, 2018). We arrive at the concept of action, of techniques, and the concept of the self, and the way these forms recursively govern one another, and so, sexual action can be seen as a microcosmic demonstration of the ongoing formation of one's subjectivity.

Aesthetics of action illustrates the dynamic interplay between structure of social and cultural forms, and how people recognise and evaluate particular phenomena as appropriate (or not). Kris Hardin's work amongst the Kono people in Sierra Leone (1993) illustrates that aesthetics can act as a mediator between structural properties (Giddens, 1979) and action (individual agency). Aesthetics via Hardin's formulation pulls us away from imagining societal structures – and the embedded quality of these within individuals – as concrete, immovable forms. According to Hardin, regarding aesthetic evaluation and change as processual phenomena can produce fundamental insights into the ways in which new forms can be transformed by old ones, and vice versa (1993, p. 3).

From the beginning of the twentieth century, the notion of aesthetics became a major part of the conceptual terrain of the art world (Hardin, 1993), both in the public (and academic) imaginary, in its attempts to reify Western categories of value in art practices. It is possible to redeem the theory of aesthetics away from its employment in problematic 'othering' art practices, however, by ethnographically charting the ways that experiences and practices are understood in their vernacular form, within different contexts. Hardin stresses that "our focus should not be on particular objects and forms and how they are evaluated but rather on *how evaluations take place* and how aesthetic systems articulate with behaviour, especially motives and ideals, in a particular place" (1993, p. 6, emphasis mine). Hardin shifts the focus away from the recursive art/non-art dilemma, into an approach of aesthetics that utilises notions of redundancy, agency and power, in order to examine questions of change and variation of idiomatic forms. In short, signification of particular meanings, in any context, takes place vis-à-vis a framework that individuals interpret, to varying scales of 'success' as being determined by the structure themselves. Bateson

(1972) argues that redundancy acts as a medium through which forms and things are taken to be noteworthy, remarkable and meaningful. Through a repetition of forms of redundancy, aesthetic judgement develops – appreciation and a sense of what is appropriate, what 'fits'. In turn, this produces spheres of value that become attached to social phenomena (Durkheim, 1915/2008; Evans-Pritchard, 1951/2003; Lienhardt, 1961) – which although they may appear to be, and have been theorised as immovable, are in fact being constantly negotiated by individuals.

Hardin's approach to a theory of aesthetics is useful in relation to queer sexual practices; she posits that through aesthetics of action, we can regard how particular structural properties reveal the various ways in which human beings evaluate what is and what is not valued, collectively and individually. What I am particularly interested in here is examining how queer subjects negotiate what can be understood as a 'double bind' of structural properties within their sexual practices. That is, I argue that not only must queer subjects situate themselves in contrast to the total social phenomena of heteronormativity, which marginalises and de-centralises their bodies and ontologies, but they must also navigate the particular idiomatic forms which have come to constitute queer subjectivity (Boyle & Omoto, 2014; Newton & Walton, 1984; Piontek, 2006). This also highlights the ways that sexuality is not simply about sex, but about aesthetical practices, ontological orientations, and relationships to structural and institutional governance. This approach is useful in order to tease out the ways in which a queer aesthetic judgement emerges. As new patterns emerge from *and* away from heteronormativity, and become more frequently practised, they take on a more idiomatic element, and can be found in a variety of domains (of structural properties); in other words, actions that become normalised and thus normalising. As such, their paradigmatic associations become increasingly entrenched, and thus they evolve into a resource for constructing and organising meaning and perception. These meanings in turn permit a composition of specific make-up of other structural properties, and so on. In this

Techniques of the Body as Techniques of the Self

way, structural properties have the capacity to become a blueprint for action, though do not determine it fully. Additionally, and crucially to aesthetics of action as Hardin theorises it, action has also the potential to affect the emergence and solidification of new (and old) structural properties.

Intrinsic to an aesthetics of action approach to the formation of cultural practices (in our case, of sexual practices) is Marcel Mauss' work on techniques of the body. Within Mauss' seminal work on *techniques du corps*, originally published in 1935, he regards how bodily actions and ways of doing things should be considered techniques, ones that require a learnt transmission within a particular society. He forced the attention of anthropologists and sociologists onto the body, demonstrating that body techniques are socially determined, thus providing a framework for understanding how social phenomena are materialised. Although according to Pierre Lemonnier, Mauss' insistence of the centrality of techniques "remained almost without impact or response" until the late 1980s (Lemonnier, 1986, p. 15).

Mauss defines a technique as an action which is both *effective* and *traditional* (Mauss, 1935/1979, p. 75). 'Effective' here concerns the agent's perspective on how efficacious the action is. In other words, does the technique perform the required emic result? 'Traditional' in Maussian terms references the act of transmission: how a technique is learnt and how it becomes embodied into a particular bodily schema and within wider practices. Further, as new techniques and bodily practices are engaged in, they can become the mediators for new subjectivities to emerge, as well as reifying existing understandings of personhood following Mauss' definition, in which a person performs a social role as part of a collective (Mauss, 1985). Working through a Maussian theory of bodily techniques allows an observation of the material cultures of redundancy, power and agency utilised in Hardin's aesthetics of action; in this case, the ways the body and objects are used during sex.

It hardly needs to be stated that social norms are not abstract. A theoretical framework that combines techniques of the body (see also

Warnier, 2001, 2007) with aesthetics of action posits that habituated and naturalised behaviours are not prescriptive, or layered onto individuals in an impositional manner. Schematic forms are, rather, negotiated through embodiment, considered as internalised experiences of a particular group's life world, interacting with and through quotidian practices until they become non-reflective givens, and – along with physio-anatomic qualities – constitute the subject.

The next section charts the above theoretical field within several ethnographic encounters that occurred during interviews and fieldwork with one of my interlocutors, Lisa.

Sucking the strap-on

> The meaning of this butch cock contains and exceeds its phallic potential, it is not the power of the phallus or its ability to structure the sexual dynamic, but the material reality of the penis [...] he had already invested it with sexual significance, as he waits for the femme to name it, assert its worth, and kneel before it.
> (Rodríguez, 2007, p. 287)

At the time of our interview, Lisa is 27 years old; she is a White, cisgender, working-class butch lesbian woman who 'came out' four years ago. This is our first time properly meeting each other but, like many queer people in the UK, we have known about each other through social networks. We are discussing dildos – most specifically strap-on dildos, that can be attached to a harness worn on the hips to act as an implement most usually used to penetrate a partner (typically, vaginally or anally). Made of silicone, Lisa's dildo measures approximately 6.5 inches in length, 1.75 inches in width, and has a purple-white marble effect. Throughout our conversation, such a technical object is interchangeably referred to as a 'strap', a 'dildo', a 'dick' and a 'silicone dick'.

In this section I map out the particularities of Lisa's experience of her strap-on, illustrate the material facet of meaning-making, and dedicate time to exploring further how Lisa's dick illustrates something of the nature of bodily techniques as being crucial to Lisa's process

Techniques of the Body as Techniques of the Self

of emerging, and fully enacting, her 'lesbian self' from a compulsory heterosexuality. In other words, I answer the question posed by Jean-Pierre Warnier: "by what means does material culture embodied in motricity reach the subject in its depths?" (Warnier, 2001, p. 13).

As our conversation together moves on from the topics of vaginal penetration, Lisa recounts the history of her fascination (and satisfaction) with the act of receiving fellatio on her dildo as she wears her strap-on:

> N posted on her [Instagram] accounts [a video] of her with a blue swirl [dildo] just licking and sucking the tip of it [...] the catalyst for how we ended up fucking was that video of her sucking on the end of that dick. It fucked me up on a fundamental level, in a good way! I was like I wanna fuck you, I want you to suck *my* dick. And then she did, and it was fucking great. [...] And then my girlfriend sucked my dick last night [for the first time] and it was fucking incredible [...] It was so good, to such an extent that we did it in every possible situation you could. I was lying down, and then I was standing up with my hand on her head, and then I was lying back down again [...] It was so fucking good! I have no idea how something that you're not feeling can feel so good – well, I mean I do know. So much of sex is like that.
> (Lisa, Interview, 2018)

Butch-femme sexual desire has historically been assigned as morally reprehensible by both heterosexual institutions, and by lesbian feminists in the late 1970s and 1980s, whose ideology believed that any power exchange present within a sexual dynamic was a residue of heterosexuality that must be expunged from the women's movement (Bauer, 2014; Echols, 1989). The act of sucking someone's dick – silicone or otherwise – has typically been constructed as symbolic of a woman's passive (therefore submissive, therefore subjugated) role in sex. Despite the pathologising and silencing of women whose claim to such an act is ingrained in an active, agentic choice (Duggan & Hunter, 2006; Jackson & Scott, 1996; Rubin, 2011), there have been consistent counter-attempts by prominent butch and femme writers to reclaim and name such a sexual and romantic configuration within academia and beyond (Rodríguez, 2007; Hollibaugh, 2000; Cvetkovich, 2003; Newton & Walton, 1984).

I am not interested here in a purely symbolic reading of the reason why that Lisa loves having her dick sucked; rather, I am concerned with how such an analysis can relate to the physical act itself. As such, I attempt to marry a psychoanalytic framework of sexuality with a material culture reading on sexual action in a particular material milieu, contending that the site of sexual pleasure for Lisa rests on what at first appears to be a deeply contradictory reasoning; that the strap-on is *not* part of Lisa's bodily subjectivity, and that it is possible to conceive that in fact, the strap-on *is* part of her bodily subjectivity.

The first part concerns broader questions of where it is assumed that one finds sexual desire in the body. Applying Freud's psychoanalytical framework of 'polymorphous perverse sexuality' (Laplanche, 2011), and most specifically taking into account the additive nature of such a framework (in Irigaray & Burke's terms, 1985), can go some way to justify the particular aesthetics of action and choice of bringing into a sexual performance an external technical object for something other than penetration. The second part concerns the extension of the body's boundaries, and the ways that proprioception and motricity will help us to understand how the self can incorporate external objects into one's subjectivity, via a process of interiorisation. Both components concern wider questions about where the boundaries of the body are drawn. This reading relates to a material culture reading of body techniques and practices. It also avoids simplistic theorisations that the butch woman is typically conceived of as a pathological or inadequate performance of masculinity (Halberstam, 1998) who seeks to dominate and objectify women (in Lisa's case, the women that were performing fellatio on her strap-on dick).

"I have no idea how something that you're not feeling can feel so good"
In an interpretation that understands sexuality to relate intrinsically to the release of sexual tension – what Freudian psychoanalytic

thought places at the phallic/genital stage of a subject's psychosexual development – the sex act of receiving fellatio onto a silicone dick would be constructed as perverse, against the 'instinctual' drive (Hartmann, 1948). This reading asserts that the butch-lesbian wearing her dick and receiving fellatio is a false imitative performance of a heterosexual configuration, in which a biologically male person would receive fellatio from a biologically female person, in order to rectify the phallic fixation brought on by the Electra complex. This analysis is reductive and biologically essentialist, and pathologises butch and femme individuals as at best a ludicrous imitation of 'real' sex and at worst as deviant women that must be 'corrected'.

Once we enter this form of analysis and rely on the idea of sexuality as the pursuit of relieving tension and the satisfaction of a release – in other words, the orgasm (de Lauretis, 2017) – cultural codes of what sex 'is' or is 'not' centre around the pursuit of a (typically male) orgasm. The drive orientated towards pleasure-satisfaction was thought, by Freud, to lead to adult heterosexual behaviours focused on the procreative drive (Klein, 1969). This structurally embedded form of heteronormativity goes some way to explaining modernist notions of homosexuality as illegitimate, as improper, and/or as inappropriate because it is not sex (as defined by the Oedipal stage of sexuality).

I posit that we might achieve an alternative reading by considering Jean Laplanche's elaboration of Freud's second (under-utilised) concept of psychosexual development – polymorphous perverse sexuality – in which it is theorised that desire and erotic pleasure can be attached to any object which may bring pleasure (Stein, 2007). Although not erasing of genital-specific acts (or desires), or specific erogenous zones, polymorphous perverse sexuality can account for a "multiplicity of erogenous zones" (Irigaray & Burke, 1985, p. 64) which can then extend beyond the body's corporeal form. As such, one could consider it an unfixed, or 'without-borders' sexuality, appearing in the developmental stage, according to Freud, before subject differentiation (around five years of age) (Freud, 1962, cited in de Lauretis, 2017, p. 1914), but extending throughout adulthood, evidenced by the fact that it is "forever being condemned, repressed, and denied by adults"(Laplanche, 2015, p. 23).

Polymorphous perverse sexuality has been conceived of under the rubric of Laplanche's reformulation of Freud's psychoanalysis as borderless (1976). Otherwise known as the drive sexuality (Laplanche, 1976), polymorphous perverse sexuality is one in which the increase in tension (rather than the release of sexual tension), constitutes the drive for such stimulus. This sexuality in which the 'pursuit of excitation' (Laplanche, 2011) is the drive for action, has been defined by de Lauretis as "perverse, nonreproductive, anarchic sexuality" (de Lauretis, 2017, p. 1928). A concept of human sexuality that accounts for an expansive orientation towards objects, as opposed to one that conceives sexuality as a drive towards genitalia and reproductive acts, is a means through which we are able to make sense of sex acts performed for the purpose of sexual pleasure, rather than sex acts performed for the purpose of sexual release. This results in a de-centreing of the genitals as the site for sexual pleasure/release and as such, expands the horizons of what acts and affects constitute 'sex'. Following this, a polymorphous perverse sexuality can incorporate a whole milieu of experience, including bodies, fantasies and thoughts that can produce sexual desire for the person, as well as materials and objects separate from the body.

When Lisa proclaims, therefore, that "I want you to suck *my* dick", and that it felt "so good", we have to seriously consider this sexual desire and sexual pleasure as felt inside her body – separate from secondary physiological arousal responses, for example an engorged clitoris, or secretion of fluids from the Bartholin's glands – but *as* sexual excitation *in* and *for* itself.

Being turned on by a strap-on blowjob reveals the failures of Freud's five stages of psychosexual development order, or of a Butlerian reading (focused solely on the discursive) of lesbian mimicking heterosexuality (Butler, 1991). By understanding strap-on fellatio through a polymorphous perverse sexuality, and understanding this framework as only possible to be enacted through a Maussian efficacious technique in the vernacular ontology of lesbianism, we can take seriously the sexual techniques engaged in, and understand the acts in and of themselves as something equally worthy of academic concern, as well as the ways such techniques influence one's subjectivity. My argument here is that it is not enough to conceive of sexuality and psychosexual development as purely a psychic matter; we have to consider the material practices through which such a development occurs and evolves throughout the life course. For example, Laplanche's argument is that "sexuality is 'implanted' in the infant body by the necessary *actions* of maternal care [...] Their *actions* are accompanied by feelings and psychic investments" (de Lauretis, 2017, p. 1921, emphasis mine). Without the actions themselves, the feelings and psychic investments cannot occur.

Working through a psychoanalytic reading of polymorphous perverse sexuality to illustrate how desire can be found outside of bounded genital-erotic zones, also helps us to understand the ways that an external technical object (in this case, the strap-on dildo) can be seen as "incorporated material culture [which] reaches deep into the psyche of the subject because it reaches it not through abstract knowledge, but through sensori-motor experience" (Warnier, 2001, p. 10). What is present for Lisa is a bordered borderlessness of her body; she recognises the material distinction between her groin – where the strap-on rests – and the shaft of the dildo that her partner is sucking. But a polymorphous perverse sexual register allows her to experience the sexual borderlessness of her body, and her sexual satisfaction and pleasure, extending out into the strap-on. A reading such as this circumvents a biologically essentialist view of what bodies 'should' or 'should not' experience.

Wearing and being: Lesbian-with-strap-on

> Consider a blind man with a stick. Where does the blind man's self begin? At the tip of the stick? At the handle of the stick? Or at some point halfway up the stick?
> (Bateson, 1972, p. 318)

Talking Bodies III

The 'blind man and his cane' has been a well-utilised analogy in the philosophical sciences to theorise on the boundaries of the self, and the relationship between one's body and the material culture in which it is localised. Gregory Bateson (1972), Maurice Merleau-Ponty (1962), and Lambros Malafouris (2013), amongst others have applied the relationship a blind person has with their cane, and the ways in which their tactile relationship to the world is facilitated through the incorporation of the cane into their bodily schema, as a means to co-ordinate the world around them into themselves; what Bateson calls the "total system" (1972, p. 317), or what we can understand as somatic habituation. The application of a blind person and their cane as a case study has been heavily criticised by proponents of crip theory/philosophy; for example, Joel Reynolds argues that the "cane is problematic insofar as it omits the social dimensions of disabled experiences, misconstrues the radicality of blindness as a world-creating disability, and operates via an able-bodied simulation that conflates object annexation or extension with incorporation" (2017, p. 421). With that in mind, I have chosen to employ this example because of its proliferation in the literature as a starting point for understanding somatic habituation, and do so with the recognition of its outdated and problematic qualities.

Lisa is trying on her harness as we speak, while I am taking pictures of her body in motion. She conceptualises her strap-on as, when wearing it, a 'fifth limb':

> A dildo is one thing, a dick is another thing, a strap-on is a whole other story, okay? Because there's a certain – I think the word is proprioception? How you have a sense of where all your limbs are? Well in that sense, a strap-on is like a fifth limb, right? As in, it hasn't got any feeling *but I feel one enough with it* to know where it is at all times and what it's doing. It's a certain sense – like, I would know immediately if it had come out, because of the micro-difference in the weighting, on my crotch. Any drop in weight, I feel it immediately.
> (Lisa, Interview, June 2018, emphasis mine)

Techniques of the Body as Techniques of the Self

Let me return, to the title of this section, and my conceptual construction of Lisa as 'lesbian-with-strap-on'. I follow Warnier when he attests that "incorporated material culture reaches deep into the psyche of the subject because it reaches not through abstract knowledge, but through sensori-motor experience" (2001, p. 10), and ergo, "techniques of the body in a given materiality are thus *in fact* techniques of the self" (Warnier, 2001, p. 10, emphasis mine). How, then, does material culture reach the subject's deepest psyche?

    Chemist and philosopher Michael Polanyi attempts to fuse ideas of objective knowledge with *knowing* to make Personal Knowledge. His theory is premised on the idea that 'knowing' is an action, requiring skill, and that personal participation of such knowledge requires clues and tools, which are "made to function as extensions of our bodily equipment [which] involves a certain change of our own being" (Polanyi, 2015, p. v). Such knowledge, Polanyi argues, has no basis in prescription; akin to the Maussian technical notion of traditional, and Warnier's apprenticeship, Polanyi declares that such knowing can only be passed down. This includes both skills, which he takes to be physical practice, and connoisseurship, akin to the diagnostician's skill. In short, there is no precept. I hazard here that Personal Knowledge is why Lisa struggled to explain to me how to use a strap-on, but rather eluded to a connoisseurship skill that indicates a natural ease with strap-on sex, a 'naturalness' that had been developed over the course of her life, particularly during her time living as a heterosexual woman, as is illustrated in this exchange with the interviewer:

> Lisa: when you're being topped by a girl that hasn't slept with many men, and she's topping you with a strap-on *you can just tell.* [...] It's like, you just *don't. Fucking. Know.* You need to have *muscle memory fucking experience* of exactly how to move your body, and –
> Anthropologist: so how exactly do you move your body?
> Lisa: Well, it's like ... I guess, it's just like, *understanding* like, well ... [pause] Okay, it depends on what position you're in, right? So, they're on top of you, and [if you've had a lot of experience of sex with men], you know how to, like, push their body back a little bit,

to make it better for them. Like, it's definitely, you just, *knowing how to fuck them* in a way where you apply pressure to the outside of them and you're now just skimming the edges, you know? (Interview, June 2018, emphasis mine)

What we see in the above quote is the difficulty that Lisa had providing me with an explicit precept – a set of rules – for how to specifically use a strap-on to penetrate someone. Reducing fucking someone with a strap-on to simple bodily motricity misses out all of the nuances, the physiological comportments with the psychological, the cognitive, the sexual, the environmental and circumstantial. It misses out the connoisseurship, a 'you just *know*' sentiment that is bolstered by the socio-material context; in this case, the application of penetrative skills learnt by experiencing such penetration during heterosexual encounters. It is so much more than the rhythmic movement of hips back and forth (and in and out).

Although Polanyi consistently stresses that it is through connoisseurship and apprenticeship in which one learns how to operate a tool unconsciously, he makes a false distinction between the physical act of repetition and the mental processes required to move the action from a conscious process to something unconscious, one which he argues is "accompanied by a newly acquired consciousness of the experience in question, on the operational plane" (2015, p. 64). His argument rests on the view that it is a mistake to understand this process as "the mere result of repetition; it is a structural change achieved by a repeated mental effort aiming at the instrumentalization of certain things and actions in the service of some purpose" (Polanyi, 2015, p. 64). This is an arbitrary distinction, for if we return to the Maussian formula of techniques, the "mere repetition", is indeed constituted by mental processes; for the cognitive, physical and social are indissoluble (Mauss, 1979, p. 74).

Lisa's now-unconscious use of her strap-on during sex is constituted by years of what can be understood as building blocks for her current knowledge, in both hetero- and homo-sexual contexts. It is within the repetitive experiences, however varied, of sexual encounters involving penetration – both receiving and giving – that her capacity to perform such acts is conceptualised and 'felt' by Lisa as 'natural'. Taking from Polanyi again, we must consider how Lisa feels "at one with it enough" (Interview, June 2018) from the lens of considering the "process by which an external thing is given a meaning by being made to form an extension of ourselves", which becomes naturalised and is then "transposed into more active intentions which draw on our whole person" (Polanyi, 2015, p. 63). Although not a permanent extension, during the times in which Lisa is using a strap-on to penetrate a partner, her body is arguably extended *out* and *into* the dildo. Just as her body is brought outwards, the strap-on equally has been brought *into* Lisa's material subjectivity, her self. What is more, this process can only occur through the physical act of wearing and using a strap-on during sex.

Understanding human beings' capacity to *bring in* a material object into one's cognitive fold, allows us to respond to Mauss' original quandary of why a Kabyle man never loses his slippers (Mauss, 1935/1979), how a blind man 'sees' through his cane (Bateson, 1972; Malafouris, 2013), or how Lisa grows a fifth limb during sexual encounters. Through a particular bodily schema, founded on bodily motricity within a given materiality, the Kabyle man is a "man-with-slippers" (Warnier, 2001 p. 7), the blind man is a man-with-cane, and Lisa is a lesbian-with-strap-on. It is *only through* Maussian technique that we arrive at the efficacy of Lisa's fifth limb.

Anxious efficacy

> Anthropologist: So does it ever pop out?
> Lisa: [affronted] what do you mean, pop out?!
> Anthropologist: so, you know when you're fucking, does it sometimes move?
> Lisa: Never. Never happens.
> Anthropologist: really?! That's impressive!
> Lisa: [laughs] It's like you've accused me of erectile dysfunction, and I'm like, "What you on about? Never 'appened, love."
> (Interview, June 2018)

Talking Bodies III

Lisa takes sex very seriously, as indeed did all of my interlocutors. Articulations of anxieties surrounding performance, intimacy and technical proficiency ran throughout all of my interviews. I would suggest that it is possible that Lisa became affronted when I asked her what I deemed to be a mere technical question about whether or not the dildo moved in the harness during sex, because strap-on sex for Lisa is not simply a technical act; it is a defining element of the 'sex she has', and in kind – the sex she *is*. It has become an element of her identity, of her self, producing what she called her 'strap-on complex', both indicative of her frequent use of her strap-on during sex, and damaging stereotypes around butch women:

> [My ex] was an extremely massive power bottom and wanted me to fuck her all the time [with a strap-on], […] it was fucking amazing, but it only added to my strap-on complex, because I came out [of the relationship], like "this is what I do now, and I have to find people to fuck like this! This is who I am and it's my identity, okay?" I couldn't understand, I didn't have this softly, softly, Sapphic sexual coming out […] So yeah, everyone had very big shoes to fill.
> (Interview, June 2018)

Strap-ons, and strap-on sex, became enveloped into her cognitive fold, within her sensory-affectivo-motor medium. During a social evening together, Lisa expressed to me the discomfort and frustration she felt about how some women had perceived her as "just a butch with a dick, […] there to just service you" (Interview, August 2018). As an object that can be 'taken off', one may likely assume that this object has no effect on the core of her subjectivity, her identity. The emergence, however, does not just rest upon her own individual actions as they impact her motricity (which is defined as movement and sensori-postural apparatus, following Warnier (2001, p. 6)). It concerns the normative logic systems within lesbian culture, within the discursive practices and assemblages of other social facts surrounding the word 'lesbian', surrounding the words 'butch lesbian' (Case, 1997; Eves, 2004; Munt, 2001), that make material her identity. What plays out here is the layered complexity of a Maussian efficacy; how the techniques are enacted are governed by socio-cultural notions of a 'correct' and 'satisfactory' performance; of who holds the confirmation of an aesthetic judgement; of which subjects perform which acts with, onto and into other subjects, and the way their partner(s) respond, interact with or reject such acts. Being evaluated by other queer women as 'just a butch with a dick', was an inflammatory, damaging appraisal. The pressure to perform one's identity in a correct manner, as much as it can feel liberating, became constricting, collapsing into and tightly binding Lisa's newfound freedom of finally 'becoming' a lesbian.

Lisa's disidentification process (Muñoz, 1999) with heteronormativity rested on an imperative technical performance of identity in a Maussian sense. It combines both the efficacious nature – she had to create a 'sleeve' of lesbianism in order to see if her performance matched up with her efficacy (that is, her 'true' lesbian self); this efficacy rested on a traditional culture of lesbian – more so, of butch lesbian culture. The way she sat, her posture, ways of eating, whose gaze she sought in public, aesthetics of style, action, language; these idiomatic forms rest upon the norms embedded within the acts themselves. The performance for others in the search for validation – the search to be recognised – required a disidentification process with hetero-norms in order to 'become lesbian', for all of the wealth of positives and ills this position grants you within society. Through this disidentification process, Lisa's identity, her self, became harnessed to her strap-on sex.

Conclusion
Queer subjects have historically been systematically and violently reduced to their genitals, in terms of what they do with them, as well as how they are constituted in relation to normative notions of personhood, gender identity and modernist understandings of sexuality. Queer subjectivity relies upon – and has historically been forced upon – the distinction from their heterosexual counterparts. Expectations of gender identity and presentation, sexuality and desire become conflated with the physical composition of their bodies. Despite this history, the literature on sexuality often lacks an analysis of the

sexual acts themselves. They are regarded as a backdrop to something more important, more discursive. In short, the social nature of sexual practices is missing.

It is through this work that I have argued that we must not treat the subject as a *fait accompli* – an established fact – but rather as one that emerges in continuous dynamism. I have attempted a union of psychoanalysis with an anthropology of techniques in order to grasp the breadth of elements that go into the somatic habituation, or the interiorisation of the material world into our subjectivities and, by extension, collective identity categories.

Engaging the materials of sex highlights the breadth and depth of the materiality of sexual practices. Regarding technical acts as they 'unfold', or materialise, is essential to understand how to produce and reiterate socio-cultural beliefs and traditions (Mauss, 1979). We thus see a co-emergence, a dance of sorts, between both the techniques of the body, and the socio-material relations that guide, alter or refuse these modes.

We need more ethnographic explorations focusing on the sexual techniques themselves. Taking care of and paying attention to sexual practices amongst queer people provides a platform to support understandings of sex that accommodate them, that demystify, and begin to balance once more the power of sex's fallacy of misplaced scale (Sontag, 1969; Rubin, 1984).

Author biography
Chloe Dominique is a PhD researcher in UCL's Anthropology department. Her current work focuses on the material culture practices of LGBTQ+ sex workers in London. She is the founder of the Materialities of Sex Research Group, which invites cross-disciplinary academics, artists and interested persons to explore themes of identity politics, material cultures, ethics, social morality and the legal frameworks of sexual practice.

Techniques of the Body as Techniques of the Self

References

Bateson, G. (1972). *Steps to an ecology of mind*. Ballantine.

Bauer, R. (2014). *Queer BDSM intimacies: Critical consent and pushing boundaries*. Palgrave Macmillan.

Bourdieu, P. (1977). *Outline of a theory of practice*. Cambridge University Press.

Boyle, S. C., & Omoto, A. M. (2014). Lesbian community oughts and ideals: Normative fit, depression, and anxiety among young sexual minority women. *Psychology of Women Quarterly, 38*(1), 33–45. https://doi.org/10.1177/0361684313484900

Butler, J. (1991). Imitation and gender insubordination. In D. Fuss (Ed.), *Inside/out: Lesbian theories, gay theories* (pp. 13–31). Routledge.

Case, S. E. (1997). Toward a butch-feminist retro-future. In D. Heller (Ed.), *Cross-purposes: Lesbians, feminists, and the limits of alliance* (pp. 205–220). Indiana University Press.

Cocks, H. G. (2013). Approaches to the history of sexuality since 1750. In S. Toulalan & K. Fisher (Eds.), *The Routledge history of sex and the body: 1500 to the present* (pp. 38–54). Routledge.

Cvetkovich, A. (2003). *An archive of feelings: Trauma, sexuality, and lesbian public cultures*. Duke University Press.

de Lauretis, T. (2017). The queerness of the drive. *Journal of Homosexuality, 64*(14), 1913–1929. https://doi.org/10.1080/00918369.2017.1289013

Duggan, L., & Hunter, N. D. (2006). *Sex wars: Sexual dissent and political culture*. Taylor & Francis.

Durkheim, E. (2008). *The elementary forms of the religious life*. (J. W. Swain, Trans.). Dover. (Original work published 1915)

Echols, A. (1989). *Daring to be bad: Radical feminism in America, 1967–1975*. University of Minnesota Press.

Evans-Pritchard, E. E. (2003). *Kinship and marriage among the Nuer*. Clarendon Press. (Original work published 1951)

Eves, A. (2004). Queer theory, Butch/Femme identities and lesbian space. *Sexualities, 7*(4), 480–496. https://doi.org/10.1177/1363460704047064

Freud, S. (1962). *Three essays on the theory of sexuality* (J. Strachey, Ed. & Trans.). (Rev. ed.). The International Psycho-Analytical Library; No. 57). Hogarth and the Institute of Psycho-Analysis. (Original work published 1905)

Giddens, A. (1979). *Central problems in social theory: Action, structure, and contradiction in social analysis*. Macmillan.

Green, A. I. (2007). Queer theory and sociology: Locating the subject and the self in sexuality studies. *Sociological Theory, 25*(1), 26-45. https://doi.org/10.1111/j.1467-9558.2007.00296.x

Halberstam, J. (1998). 1. An introduction to female masculinity: Masculinity without men. In J. Halberstam, *Female masculinity* (pp. 1-44). Duke University Press.

Halberstam, J. (2019). *Female masculinity*. Duke University Press.

Hardin, K. L. (1993). *The aesthetics of action: Continuity and change in a West African town*. Smithsonian Institute.

Hartmann, H. (1948). Comments on the psychoanalytic theory of instinctual drives. *The Psychoanalytic Quarterly, 17*(3), 368-388. https://doi.org/10.1080/21674086.1948.11925730

Hollibaugh, A. L. (2000). *My dangerous desires: A queer girl dreaming her way home*. Duke University Press.

Irigaray, L., & Burke, C. (1985). *This sex which is not one* (C. Porter, Trans.). Cornell University Press.

Jackson, S., & Scott, S. (1996). Sexual skirmishes and feminist factions: Twenty-five years of debate on women and sexuality. In S. Jackson & S. Scott (Eds.), *Feminism and sexuality: A reader* (pp. 1-31). Edinburgh University Press.

Klein, G. S. (1969). Freud's two theories of sexuality. In L. Berger (Ed.), *Clinical-Cognitive Psychology* (pp. 136-181). Prentice-Hall.

Kulick, D. (1997). The gender of Brazilian transgendered prostitutes. *American Anthropologist, 99*(3), 574-585. https://doi.org/10.1525/aa.1997.99.3.574

Laplanche, J. (1976). *Life and death in psychoanalysis* (H. Mehlman, Trans.). Johns Hopkins University Press.

Laplanche, J. (2011). *Freud and the sexual: Essays 2000-2006* (J. Fletcher, J. House, & N. Ray, Trans.). The Unconscious in Translation.

Laplanche, J. (2015). *The temptation of biology: Freud's theories of sexuality; followed by, biologism and biology*. The Unconscious in Translation.

Lemonnier, P. (1986). The study of material culture today: Toward an anthropology of technical systems. *Journal of Anthropological Archaeology, 5*(2), 147-186. https://doi.org/10.1016/0278-4165(86)90012-7

Lenay, C. (2018). Leroi-Gourhan: Technical trends and human cognition. In S. Loeve, X. Guchet, & V. B. Bensaude (Eds.), *French philosophy of technology: Classical readings and contemporary approaches* (pp. 209-226). Springer.

Leroi-Gourhan, A. (1993). *Gesture and speech*. MIT Press.

Lienhardt, G. (1961). *Divinity and experience: The religion of the Dinka*. Clarendon.

Techniques of the Body as Techniques of the Self

Malafouris, L. (2013). *How things shape the mind: A theory of material engagement.* MIT Press.

Mauss, M. (1979). *Sociology and psychology: Essays by Marcel Mauss.* Routledge & Kegan Paul. (Original work published 1935)

Mauss, M. (1985). A category of the human mind: The notion of person; the notion of self. In M. Carrithers, S. Collins, & S. Lukes (Eds.), *The category of the person: Anthropology, philosophy, history* (pp. 1–25). Cambridge University Press.

Merleau-Ponty, M. (1962). *Phenomenology of perception.* Routledge.

Muñoz, J. E. (1999). *Disidentifications: Queers of color and the performance of politics.* University of Minnesota Press.

Munt, S. (2001). The butch body. In R. Holliday & J. Hassard (Eds.), *Contested Bodies* (pp. 95–106). Routledge.

Nanda, S. (1999). *Neither man nor woman: The Hijras of India.* Wadsworth Publishing Company.

Newmahr, S. (2011). *Playing on the edge: Sadomasochism, risk, and intimacy.* Indiana University Press.

Newton, E., & Walton, S. (1984). The misunderstanding: Toward a more precise sexual vocabulary. In C. Vance (Ed.), *Pleasure and danger: Exploring female sexuality* (pp. 242–250). Routledge & Kegan Paul.

Parker, R. G. (2009). *Bodies, pleasures, and passions: Sexual culture in contemporary Brazil.* Vanderbilt University Press.

Polanyi, M. (2015). *Personal knowledge: Towards a post-critical philosophy.* University of Chicago Press.

Piontek, T. (2006). *Queering gay and lesbian studies.* University of Illinois Press.

Reynolds, J. M. (2017). Merleau-Ponty, world-creating blindness, and the phenomenology of non-normate bodies. *Chiasmi International, 19,* 419–436. https://doi.org/10.5840/chiasmi20171934

Rodríguez, J. M. (2007). Gesture and utterance fragments from a Butch-Femme archive. In G. E. Haggerty & M. McGarry (Eds.). *A companion to lesbian, gay, bisexual, transgender, and queer studies* (pp. 282–292). John Wiley & Sons.

Rubin, G. (1984). Thinking sex. In C. Vance (Ed.), *Pleasure and danger: Exploring female sexuality* (pp. 267–319). Routledge & Kegan Paul.

Rubin, G. (2011). Blood under the bridge: Reflections on "Thinking Sex". *GLQ: A Journal of Lesbian and Gay Studies, 17*(1), 15–48. https://doi.org/10.1215/9780822394068-009

Seidman, S. (1993). Identity and politics in a "postmodern" gay culture: Some historical and conceptual notes. In M. Warner (Ed.), *Fear of a queer planet: Queer politics and social theory* (pp. 105–142). University of Minnesota Press.

Sontag, S. (1969). *Styles of radical will*. Vintage.

Stein, R. (2007). Moments in Laplanche's Theory of Sexuality. *Studies in Gender and Sexuality, 8*(2), 177–200. https://doi.org/10.1080/15240650701225534

Warner, M. (1993). *Fear of a queer planet: Queer politics and social theory*. University of Minnesota Press.

Warnier, J. P. (2001). A praxeological approach to subjectivation in a material world. *Journal of Material Culture, 6*(1), 5–24. https://doi.org/10.1177/135918350100600101

Warnier, J. P. (2007). *The pot-king: The body and technologies of power*. Brill.

CHAPTER 7:
"OLDER WOMEN MASTURBATE TOO": FEMINISM, SEXUALITY AND THE OLDER WOMAN IN *GRACE AND FRANKIE*

Alice Churm

Abstract

This chapter will examine the theme of the older woman's sexuality and how this intertwines with an underlying feminist politics within the Netflix series *Grace and Frankie* (Kauffman & Morris, 2015–). The series can be placed within a canon of comedy and drama television that is both heavily inspired by feminist politics and brings women's sexuality to the forefront, such as *Girls* (Dunham et al., 2012–2017) and *Broad City* (Glazer et al., 2014–2019). *Grace and Frankie*, however, sets itself apart from this canon through its prioritisation of the older woman and her sexuality. Through this focus on the older woman the series is able to tap into the second-wave feminist politics and history that underpins ideas of woman's sexuality. This chapter aims to explore how older women's sexuality within the narrative is used as a device for presenting second-wave feminist ideas. Through exploring the narrative themes of self sexuality, intimacy and knowledge sharing and plotting these against key second-wave feminist texts the underlying politics of the series is uncovered. *Grace and Frankie*, both the series and the characters, take on the task of educating older women on their own sexualities informed by second-wave feminist politics as a form of feminist activism. This chapter will then explore how the series is able to act as a generational gap between feminist eras, occupying as a contemporary but second-wave feminist series.

Key words: masturbation, older women, sexuality, sexual liberation, second-wave feminism

Television that has feminist politics at its core is not a new phenomenon. Since the 1970s television has regularly engaged with the tropes and themes of feminism, women and female friendships (Brunsdon et al., 1997, p. 1). Television has long provided a space where feminist politics can flourish, giving women a space to present their issues as sitcoms in particular, often present "strong-minded female characters who openly discuss sexuality" (Holbert et al., 2003 p. 49). The 2010s have been no stranger to women-created and women-fronted American television. From television series such as *Broad City* (Glazer et al., 2014–2019) and *Girls* (Dunham et al., 2012–2017), to *Orange is The New Black* (Kohan et al., 2013–2019) and *Inside Amy Schumer* (Schumer et al., 2013–), women have been at the forefront of creating television that articulates their feminist sentiment, and displays a light hearted but honest look at womanhood in the 2010s. Joy Press marks the sudden prevalence of these sorts of shows as a "rise of twenty-first-century female-centric television" (2018, p. 216) and notes that these television shows coincide with a new resurrection of feminism in the twenty-first century. These shows play with what it means to be a feminist in contemporary America, and display "valid representations of female life and often engage with serious issues such as abortion, equal pay, and violence against women" (Press, 2018, p. 223).

One series that Press neglects is the Netflix Original series *Grace and Frankie* (Kauffman & Morris, 2015). *Grace and Frankie* focuses on two women in their seventies who face a radical change in their life when their husbands leave them to get married to each other. The two women are forced into being self-sufficient at this later stage in their lives. This brings the pair together, and enables them to learn from each other what it means to be single women in their seventies. Much like the television shows mentioned previously, feminist politics is at the heart of *Grace and Frankie*, and the themes presented within the series are told through a feminist political lens. What separates *Grace and Frankie* from these other series, which have feminist politics woven throughout, is the focus on the older woman. The ages of Grace and Frankie are essential to the series, its narrative and themes. Their

"Older Women Masturbate Too"

age is also vital for impact of the series in another way: *Grace and Frankie* exemplifies a different approach to ingraining feminist politics throughout the series. By prioritising the older woman, and her stories, an older more second-wave feminist practice and understanding is revealed. Through Grace and Frankie, as women that lived through the second wave, the series utilises an older form of feminist politics; one that echoes the practices of the second wave and acts to educate contemporary audiences of women on what has come before them. In 'The Fall' (Series 1 Episode 5, S1E5), Finnegan & Thomas, 2015) Grace asks Frankie "Where were you, in a bunker in the sixties? That's where the rest of us learnt you don't need a man to define yourself." This line really encapsulates the sentiment of the series, in that for these women it is second-wave feminist politics that defined how they see themselves, and it is this specific feminist politics that is woven throughout the series.

Interestingly, when Press talks about the resurrection of feminism that coincides with feminist politics becoming more prevalent in contemporary American television, she views this as a departure from older forms of feminism, echoing the idea that up until recently feminism was seen as a thing of the past, "seemingly a sour relic from a long-ago liberation movement" (2018, p. 218). For Press, the series she points us to, focus on a new "legit" and "trendy" form of feminism that was on the rise in the 2010s, and this is clear and distinctively of this time (2018, p. 216). *Grace and Frankie*, however, directly challenges this, not viewing older feminism as sour, but a complementary and essential way of viewing feminism that can be vital for the contemporary woman. The second-wave politics woven throughout the contemporary narrative expresses an understanding and appreciation of this relic of second-wave feminism.

One of the main narrative arcs throughout *Grace and Frankie* is the women's exploration and understanding of their sexuality, independent from their ex-husbands. The narrative explores women's sexuality and examines it through age. This honest approach represents older female sexualities, utilising upfront dialogue about older women's sexuality, and the struggles they face in expressing this. Grace and Frankie fight for sexual liberation, and encapsulate the important intersection between women's sexuality and politics. Sexual liberation during the time of second-wave feminism became a contentious issue, and "feminists were divided about the importance of sexual pleasure to women's liberation" (Lieberman, 2017b, p. 87). The way in which sexuality is articulated throughout *Grace and Frankie* resembles a sex-positive second-wave feminism that worked in tandem with the sexual liberation of the 1960s and 1970s. Many theories, debates and campaigns of second-wave feminist and sex-positive activists can be plotted throughout *Grace and Frankie* and the explicit way in which the show deals with themes of ageing women's sexuality, sexual liberation and how these complement feminist politics. Sexual revolution can bring about "attainment of the female sex to freedom and full human status after millennia of deprivation and oppression" (Millet, 1970, p. 112).

'The Sex' (S1E8, Budin et al., 2015) introduces the theme of women's sexuality to *Grace and Frankie*, which then populates the narrative of the show. This episode focuses on Grace's exploration of her sexuality for the first time outside of her marriage to her ex-husband, Robert. Interestingly though, most of the dialogue takes place with Frankie rather than her new partner, Guy. Here, Frankie takes on the role of sexual educator to Grace, teaching her not only about her own body, and her pleasure, but about women's sexuality in general from her own experiences. Frankie attempts to engage a reluctant Grace into a conversation about the idea of sex between Grace and Guy. Although Grace clearly tries to hide from this conversation, Frankie is not embarrassed, and takes an upfront and frank approach to discussing these issues. It is clear that sex does not carry the same shame for Frankie that it does for Grace, and Frankie is positioned as a sexually-liberated woman. Frankie acknowledges Grace's discomfort in the topic, but continues to question her about it. Frankie does not shy away from the specifics, asking Grace if she is worried about vaginal dryness, and offers Grace some of her home-made lubricant. Frankie tells Grace

"Older Women Masturbate Too"

"my gynaecologist says you should not put anything in your vagina that you would not put in your mouth." Frankie's upfront and explicit approach to discussing not just her own sexuality, but Grace's as well, mirrors the ways in which knowledge sharing was an essential feminist practice in the liberation of women's sexualities. The information from Frankie's gynaecologist is passed to Grace, articulating how by sharing what they have learnt about themselves, women as a collective are able to understand their bodies in ways that the patriarchy has always disallowed. This sentiment is particularly visible through the second-wave feminist book *Our Bodies, Ourselves* (Boston Women's Collective, 1973), a feminist collective book first published in 1970 as *Women and Their Bodies*. *Our Bodies, Ourselves* compiles information about women's bodies, and women's sexuality, authored by women. These women have both researched and learnt about their bodies, whilst also sharing their own experiences to enhance other women's understanding of their own bodies. This sentiment is present throughout *Grace and Frankie*, showing that women's experiences of their own bodies are meant to be shared, to enable women as a collective to liberate their sexualities through knowledge and understanding. In 'The Art Show' (S3E1, Kauffman et al., 2017) Frankie makes direct reference to *Our Bodies, Ourselves*. As the loan officer refuses to give Grace and Frankie a loan, Frankie assumes this is because he fears female sexuality. She states, "You are one of those bankers who has never read *Our Bodies, Ourselves*". Frankie situates the importance of reading this book in not only sharing education between women, but also enabling men to not fear women's sexuality. This seemingly offhand reference demonstrates an active awareness in *Grace and Frankie* to this spirit of learning and sharing experiences with a feminist sisterhood, and therefore an awareness of the second-wave feminist practices that are prevalent throughout.

The fight for sexual liberation for women during second-wave feminism must be in part indebted to the work of Betty Dodson. Dodson was a sex-positive feminist activist whose work centred the important role of acceptance and promotion of women's masturbation.

Talking Bodies III

Dodson hosted sexual consciousness-raising 'bodysex' groups in which women were given the rare opportunity to learn about their sexualities, bodies, and orgasms. For Dodson, masturbation was an important aspect of sexuality, not only allowing women to become comfortable with their own bodies and understand their own sexual functions, but also enabling women to create their own pleasure, both alongside, and free from a sexual partner (Dodson, 1974). Due to this, masturbation became a defiance of traditional notions of sexuality, in particular women's sexuality. Dodson notes that women's masturbation is viewed as a direct threat to patriarchy, as if women understanding their own sexuality and how to give themselves orgasms would lead them to "stop putting out for two-minute men, guys who ignore the clitoris and men who are threatened by vibrators" (Dodson, 2004, p. 158). To educate women on their own bodies, their sexualities and their orgasms, was to free them from a reliance on a male orchestrated and phallocentric idea of sexuality. Within the second-wave knowledge sharing, the fundamentals of women's sexuality was essential to achieve women's sexual liberation. Talking at the time, Dodson notes the importance of this shared education, explaining "since present society has a stake in not enlightening women about sex or encouraging them to grow and be independent, women must teach women" (1974, p. 17). *Grace and Frankie* mirrors Dodson's work in the 1970s, as masturbation and women's orgasms becomes a key theme, and the show embodies this second-wave feminist practice of knowledge sharing and community education.

In her sexual consciousness-raising groups, Dodson encouraged women to become more familiar with their own bodies through looking at them. Whilst gathered in a circle she would give women a hand mirror for them to look at their own vulvas and vaginas alongside each other. For many women this was the first time they would properly look at their own vaginas, an act that enabled women to gather a better understanding of their own bodies. Alongside this, Dodson would show her vagina to the group, and give masturbation demonstrations to aid education around women's bodies. Dodson

"Older Women Masturbate Too"

states this was a necessary strategy "since most women have no visual images of sex, I knew one demonstration would be worth a thousand words" (1987, p. 75). Teaching about sexuality through sharing and demonstrating the experience was essential to the sharing of education that came through these 'bodysex' workshops. On the value of showing as learning Dodson states "I knew we were doing first-rate teaching when live masturbation became a regular feature of the Bodysex Groups" (1987, p. 75). These groups also featured show and tell, where all women were invited to show their vaginas to the group and be able to look at those of other women. This breaking down of the boundaries of sexuality enabled women to create a shared sexuality: one of women together. Through sharing these intimate moments, that were usually expected in society to only exist within heterosexual monogamous relationships, these women were able to break down the boundaries of how they expressed their own sexualities. This enabled women not only to share education about their bodies, but share together their sexual liberation. At two points in 'The Sex' Frankie suggests showing Grace her own vagina, as an attempt to teach Grace about her own body. As Grace is reluctant to even say the word clitoris, Frankie states "how about I show you mine?"; breaking down the barriers of the vagina being something that should be hidden, and offering to use her own body as a tool to teach Grace about herself. Frankie embodies the spirit of the 'bodysex' workshops, and uses the methods of sex-positive second-wave feminism.

This knowledge sharing becomes important, allowing women to learn and take control of their own sexuality, and become in themselves sexually-liberated women. 'The Sex' is a particularly important episode for two reasons. It shows Frankie taking on the role of the sexual educator, and Grace's growth in liberating her own sexuality. After probing from Frankie, Grace retells her first sexual experience with Guy. Whilst she is telling Frankie that he is "no slouch in the boudoir", and that it was a "delicate dance", the scene cuts to shots of Grace and Guy together. It is evident that these are not good experiences for Grace. Guy asks "how does that feel?" and

Talking Bodies III

Grace replies, asking "are you doing anything?". Despite Grace clearly not having a good sexual experience, she still does not question Guy, and would lie to cover Guy's sexual inadequacy. Grace willingly casts aside her pleasure to save her partners feelings. Here Grace's pleasure is not central or even necessary to her sexual experiences. In another flashback Guy asks Grace "are you nearly there?" to which Grace responds "where?". Almost mimicking this completely, Frankie asks Grace "tell me, did you finish at least?" to which Grace replies "I'm here right? Of course I finished!" Her disinterest and cluelessness around her own pleasure is evident. The humour here lies in Grace's complete lack of consideration of her own sexual pleasure. For Grace, her own satisfaction is so insignificant that she isn't even aware when she is asked about it directly. The structure of humour in this scene goes directly against Susan Liddy's argument that in culture older female sexuality is often based in humour to make it more palatable for audiences (2017, p. 171). The audience is not directed to laugh at the idea of older women engaging in sexual activities, but rather at the notion that they would not be prioritising, or even aware of their own sexual pleasure. Throughout this episode Grace is taken on a lesson in female sexuality by Frankie. Frankie is her own Betty Dodson, and she shares her sexual knowledge to empower and liberate Grace. Grace learns from these lessons, and the series shows us the power that can come from this community education between women.

When telling Frankie that she and Guy have arranged to meet again, we see Grace become aware of the orgasm disparity that exists between them, stating "Guy and I just made plans for him to have another orgasm tonight". However, it is the final scene in this episode that represents Grace's growth to becoming a sexually-liberated woman, and emphasises the role Frankie had in enabling this change. As Guy takes Grace's hand to lead her upstairs, Grace stops and holds back, hesitant to return to the sexual experience she had earlier where her pleasure and satisfaction was not paramount. She resists Guy, and instead directs him over to the record player. Whilst she selects a record to play, Guy questions "I didn't realise you were a vinyl lover"

"Older Women Masturbate Too"

to which Grace explains "well, they're Frankie's". This sharing of the items of Frankie's pulls her presence into the scene. Grace is utilising Frankie to support her in this intimate moment with Guy. This becomes emblematic of the shared education and empowerment from Frankie that direct Grace throughout this scene. As the music plays Grace asks Guy to dance with her; whilst his reaction is reluctant, she tells him "That's okay. I'll lead." The dance between Grace and Guy acts as a visual representation for their sex, and Grace takes control of this completely. She leads Guy in dancing and tells him exactly what she wants him to do. She tells him where to put his hands, to be closer to her, and to take his time. She is in complete control of the dance and is finally allowing her desires to be paramount in this act. This whole scene is soundtracked by the diegetic sound from Frankie's vinyl. Although not physically in this scene, Frankie's presence is felt through the music that not only creates the sensual mood of the scene, but enables the dance between Grace and Guy. The influence of Frankie has enabled Grace to become a sexually-liberated woman, and Grace is acting on the words of Frankie "you've got to speak up or it will never get any better".

As the series goes on, the focus on shared sexual education for women continues as Grace and Frankie transcend this feminist practice of sexual liberation through community into the creation of their vibrators designed specifically for older women. Taking direct action to criticise commonly accepted truths about women's sexuality is replicated in *Grace and Frankie* through the creation of their vibrator company 'Vybrant'. 'The Coup' (S2E13, Kauffman et al., 2016) ends with Grace and Frankie's revelation to their family that they are going to start a vibrator business for older women with arthritis. Grace declares to a disgusted and unsupportive family "we are making things for people like us, because we are sick and tired of being dismissed by people like you!" This is the ideology that Dodson embodied, that if society would not accept women's sexuality, then women must cater to their own sexuality. Even in the contemporary age women's masturbation in general is still seen as taboo, due to a range of cultural ideologies such as the emphasis on vaginal intercourse, a prioritisation of male pleasure, and a cultural distaste towards vaginas (Kaestle & Allen, 2011, p. 987). Whilst women's masturbation is still not accepted, older women's masturbation is unheard of. Grace and Frankie are using the techniques of the second wave to challenge the issues that exist for older women in contemporary culture.

The creation of 'Vybrant' has impact through the goal of arming women with the tools of their own sexual liberation. This message has been clear throughout *Grace and Frankie* since the first series, with Frankie's creation and mass production of her yam-based lubricant. This goal of providing women with equipment that will aid them sexually is a key narrative arc throughout the series, and the creation of 'Vybrant' emphasises this. From the lube, to the vibrators, these items are not seen as taboo sexual supplements, in the way that sex toys are often viewed in culture, but rather as essential items to allow women to have more agency over their own sexual fulfilment. As Frankie explains to Grace, "it's not a dildo, it's a facilitator, that's all!". In 'The Sex', these become essential items to aid women in putting their own pleasure and comfort as a priority. Throughout her 'bodysex' workshops Dodson would encourage women to experiment with, and buy, their own vibrators. Dodson "introduced the feminist movement to masturbation as a political act, and vibrators as political objects" (Lieberman, 2017b, p. 143). As women were given the tools to allow them to enjoy their sexuality, independent from a male partner, women were no longer constrained to an androcentric view of sexuality. Even more important here is the sharing of these tools. All of the items which Grace is given to guide her into being a sexually-liberated woman were shared with her by the women in her life. Frankie gifted Grace the lubricant, and Babe (Grace and Frankie's long-term friend) gave Grace her first vibrator. Once again, sharing between women becomes the key to enabling each other in their sexual education. Their sexuality does not just belong to themselves, and through educating women on their sexuality, this frees them from a male understanding of sexuality.

"Older Women Masturbate Too"

From Season 3 the narrative moves into the creation and production of vibrators, specifically for the older woman. This narrative arc mimics the work of another second-wave feminist whose focus was the liberation of women's sexuality: Dell Williams. Following her attendance at one of Dodson's bodysex workshops, Williams noted the difficulty for women trying to purchase vibrators in the 1970s. Therefore, Williams did exactly what Grace and Frankie did; she created something for people like her, so she was no longer dismissed by people that weren't. In 1974 Williams set up the first feminist mail order sex store, Eve's Garden, which eventually progressed to become a physical sex store in New York. Lieberman argues that feminist sex-toy shops such as Williams' Eve's Garden adhered to Enke's idea of 'feminist commercial spaces' which were an "integral and constitutive component of feminist emergence ... that popularized a movement" (2017a, p. 101). Grace and Frankie's 'Vybrant' offers somewhere for women to both explore and understand their sexualities and needs whilst also joining a community of sexually-liberated women. 'Vybrant' is not a company made with the desire of commercial gain, but rather political gain through educating women in their own sexualities. Lieberman argues that Eve's Garden created "a nationwide network of feminist commercial spaces through mail-order sales" (Lieberman, 2017a, p. 101). We see this nationwide network represented within *Grace and Frankie*.

Through their online store they are able to create an online and offline network of sexually educated and liberated communities of women. 'The Death Stick' (S4E10, Wied & Whittingham, 2018) introduces 'Vybrant''s number-one fan, Harriet. Harriet is an idealised version of their clientele: the sexually-liberated older woman, who put her own sexuality at the forefront and enjoyed her sexuality right up until the end of her life. Harriet personifies the community that 'Vybrant' has created, and the care that Grace and Frankie show for her is emblematic of the care they have for each woman that they have sexually liberated. Grace and Frankie created a movement of liberating women through their own understanding of their bodies and their sexualities. Williams brought sexual liberation to women through changing commercial sex stores for women, with Eve's Garden providing a much more meaningful, educational and political experience in these sorts of sexual commercial spaces. For Dodson and Williams, sexuality and politics were intrinsically linked. Both Dodson's workshops and Williams' stores were informed by their politics and involvement in feminist spaces, which allowed their own feminist politics to shape their aims and values. When it comes to feminist sex-positive spaces, such as Eve's Garden or Dodson's 'bodysex' workshops, "individual store owners and employees typically determined what feminism or queerness means for a particular business" (Comella, 2017, p. 162). Informed by what their own sexuality, feminism, and queerness meant to them, Dodson and Williams created a sex-positive movement where different ideas of what it meant to be a sexual woman could be explored, and education could be shared within a sisterhood. The role that these women took in liberating female sexuality is reflected within *Grace and Frankie* by the protagonists; Frankie acts as the upfront, sexually-liberated educator who is not afraid to talk about her vagina, and clitoris, ensuring that her sexuality is as important as male sexuality. Grace acts as the newly sexually-liberated woman who aims to create a space where women can buy sex products, such as vibrators, without the shame that she once lived with.

The focus of women's orgasms and women's sexual pleasure throughout *Grace and Frankie* stems from the focus on the clitoris. The product that 'Vybrant' creates and sells is the 'Ménage à Moi' which is a vibrator designed for women with arthritis. The cushioned sleeve allows it to be used for longer without flaring up arthritis; therefore older women would be able to have longer to reach orgasm. The importance here is that the toy created by Grace and Frankie is a vibrator created solely for clitoral stimulation, and not a penetration centred sex toy such as a dildo, or a vibrator that is able to be inserted into the vagina. It is clear that Grace and Frankie prioritise the clitoris as the centre of women's sexual pleasure through the creation of this product. This can be read as an awareness of the critiques of a phallocentric understanding of sexuality that were rife during second-wave feminist criticism of the sexual revolution. Koedt's essay 'The Myth of the Vaginal Orgasm' (1970) offers a second-wave feminist analysis of sex, and argues against the existence of vaginal orgasms. For Koedt, women's sexuality had long been defined in relation to what pleases men, so the acts that give men pleasure become the standard idea of sexuality. Koedt exclaims:

> We must discard the "normal" concepts of sex and create new guidelines which take into account mutual sexual enjoyment [...]. New techniques must be used or devised which transform this particular aspect of our current sexual exploitation. (Koedt, 1970, p. 38).

This call to arms from Koedt can be read throughout *Grace and Frankie*, where their central message is educating women on the importance of their own pleasure, as well as providing women with the tools to allow them to take charge of their own orgasms. The creation of the 'Ménage à Moi', a tool that allows women to define, be in control of, and create their own sexual pleasure could be read as what Koedt argues for as a "new technique" (Koedt, 1970, p. 38). By giving women the tools to achieve sexual pleasure in a way that works for them, and that is considerate of their own needs, *Grace and Frankie* seeks to end the sexual exploitation of women as secondary to male sexuality.

Echoing the sentiment of Dodson earlier, Koedt notes that the myth of the vaginal orgasm is maintained by men, not only because sexual penetration is preferred, but because the vaginal orgasm enables men to avoid their fear of being sexually expendable. If the clitoris, and not the vagina, becomes the centre of sexual pleasure for women, men fear that sexually, women will no longer have sex with them (Koedt, 1970). Koedt also links men's attachment to the vaginal orgasm, and therefore the denial of sexual liberation for women, to the dual desires to both not view the woman as a human in her own right, and to continue to control women. It is "not in the men's interest to have women totally free sexually" (Koedt, 1970, p. 41). As Koedt notes, "society has been a function of male interests, and women were not organized to form even a vocal opposition to the male experts" (p. 40). This sentiment was echoed in the work of Susan Lydon who states "the definition of normal feminine sexuality as vaginal … was a part of keeping women down, of making them sexually, as well as economically, socially, and politically subservient" (1970, p. 201). The dismissal of clitoral orgasms was a political choice to dismiss female pleasure and make women sexually reliant on the man. Dismissing female pleasure allows for the dismissal of female independence. This is where both community education, and the creation of sexually liberating tools for women, is so essential for *Grace and Frankie* in articulating the second-wave feminist message. The goal of freeing women of their sexual ties to the male body and allowing them independence is felt throughout, and through this *Grace and Frankie* challenges a version of sexuality that is focused on male interests. Grace and Frankie become the experts of their own sexuality and share this message to empower other women to do the same.

To return to 'The Sex', whilst Grace is questioning Frankie about her sex with Guy, Frankie openly asks her "were you open with him? Did you tell him what you like?". For Frankie, as a sexually open and liberated woman, ensuring that her needs are catered to is paramount to the sexual experience. Grace responds by stating that what she likes in bed "is for the guy next to her to be the right guy". Grace here was still motivated sexually by the needs of the man she is sleeping with. Koedt notes that, just like Grace, many women continue perpetuating the myth of the vaginal orgasm and remain in a position secondary to the man: "many more women were simply afraid to establish their right to equal enjoyment, seeing the sexual act as being primarily for the man's benefit, and any pleasure that the woman got as an added extra" (Koedt, 1970, p. 40). It's clear that for Grace, her sexual satisfaction was not as important to her, as her male partner(s). Frankie differs from this position, and she forces Grace to think about her clitoris and by extension her own sexual pleasure. Frankie asks Grace "did you

"Older Women Masturbate Too"

remind him that direct clitoral stimulation is essential before, during, and often after stimulation?" Grace's response "No! I'm 70 years old ... Actually I have never once talked about my c-l-i-t-o--" exemplifies how little she takes, not just her own pleasure, but even her own anatomy into consideration in relation to sexuality.

Although Grace and Frankie are similar in age, it is clear that Grace's age is contributing to her discomfort with her own sexual satisfaction. Frankie leads by example, showing Grace that her age should not impact her comfort with her sexuality. It is through Frankie that Grace is able to move away from perpetuating the myth that older women have a lack of interest in their own sexual satisfaction. This idea is revisited in "The Myth of The Vaginal Orgasm". Koedt refers to the work of Freud, as "A Father of the Vaginal Orgasm" (1970, p. 38). Koedt explains how he perpetuated the myth that clitoral stimulation and clitoral orgasms were that of the adolescent woman, and when a woman matures, she is able to achieve orgasm through vaginal penetration, realigning the centre of the orgasm to the vagina. Koedt states that Freud had the belief that "the vagina [...] was able to produce a parallel, but more mature, orgasm than the clitoris" (1970, p. 38). Although Koedt admits Freud's theory was not based "upon a study of woman's anatomy, but rather upon his assumptions of woman as an inferior appendage to man, and her consequent social and psychological role" (Koedt, 1970, p. 38).

Despite this, the myth that clitoral stimulation and therefore sexual satisfaction is not for older women is still maintained throughout, and we can view this through Grace's understanding of her own sexuality. Grace's initial reason for not talking about her own pleasure with her partner is because of her age. Sexually, Grace views herself as "an inferior appendage to man", and it is not until Frankie's intervention that she is able to break free of this. *Grace and Frankie*'s central focus on the sexuality of the older woman acts in a direct challenge to the myths that Freud created. Centreing a specifically clitoral vibrator for the older woman within the narrative *Grace and Frankie* validates older women to not only understand that the centre of their pleasure is within the clitoris, but also creates a version of their own sexuality that is free from a phallocentric definition. Liddy comments that in popular culture older women's sexual relations are almost exclusively represented within the confines of marriage or committed relationships (2017, p. 170), yet *Grace and Frankie* importantly departs from this, and the most important sexual relationships that these women experience are with themselves. The radical act of prioritising masturbation over any other form of sexual connection empowers women to make their own sexual satisfaction the priority.

Koedt's essay refers to another important text in understanding women's, and especially older women's, sexuality. The *Human Sexual Response* (1966), by William H. Masters and Virginia E. Johnson, is a key text in aiding the feminist sexual revolution. Their research explored the location of women's orgasms, finding that although orgasms could be achieved through indirect contact during vaginal penetration, all of women's orgasms were located in the clitoris. It is clitoral stimulation that causes women to orgasm, and the clitoris is the central point of women's sexual pleasure. For Koedt this research proves that the ever-present idea of the vaginal orgasm as a source of pleasure for women is in fact a myth. Alongside this key message of the importance of the clitoris that *Grace and Frankie* also reflects, Masters and Johnson's exploration of human sexual response can be read in the ethos of *Grace and Frankie* through another lens. Their research also looked at the sexual reception of older people to understand if and how they were able to climax. What they found was that sexual climax was possible for older people; however, this took them much longer to achieve. In the creation of the 'Ménage à Moi' this research comes through. This vibrator specifically caters to the older woman and the time it takes for her to reach sexual climax. In 'The Coup', Frankie declares "It takes us a lot longer to get off" and Grace explains "She's right! Our blood doesn't flow as easily and our genital tissue is more delicate." The creation of 'Vybrant' and the 'Ménage à Moi' has been specifically made with the backing of Masters and Johnson's research in mind. By making this toy explicitly and directly for the older women, Grace

"Older Women Masturbate Too"

and Frankie are making the radical choice, not just to fight for female masturbation, but for older female masturbation. Maureen C. McHugh and Camille Interligi (2018) comment on menopause suggesting that it allows "women the opportunity to define their sexuality based on their own desires and needs rather than on the cultural expectation of reproduction or satisfaction of marital duties" (p. 101). This echoes findings in Sarah Jen's study, in which participants claimed that their sexualities became more about their own pleasure than pleasing their partners as they got older (Jen, 2017, p. 93). *Grace and Frankie* once again represents this idea of self-pleasure for the older woman through its upfront discussions of female sexuality and active promotion of masturbation and masturbation tools. Through centreing this in the storyline, the show performs a female sexuality that is expressed completely outside of a male domination of sexuality. Through masturbation, the ageing female is able to present a sexuality that is shaped around her needs.

Once again, thinking about the separation of the clitoris from the vagina in the aim for women's sexual liberation, a key second-wave text is "The Clitoral and the Vaginal Woman" (Lonzi, 1971/1975). Here Carla Lonzi defines the 'clitoral woman' and the 'vaginal woman' as two distinct types of women based on the relationship and understanding they have in relation to men's sexuality. Margrit Brückner explains Lonzi's definition of these two types of women. The vaginal woman must "accept the male definition of sexuality, thereby making her a complementary being" (2014, p. 280). This is a woman that does not see herself or her sexuality as paramount, and becomes an accessory to her male partner. As *Grace and Frankie*'s central narrative surrounds the two women's struggle to separate themselves from their previous relationships, their progression through the series becomes a move away from the positions of 'vaginal women'. Although Frankie does take on the role of a sexually-liberated woman, even alluding to her past relationship with Sol, Grace's sexuality had always been defined in relation to her ex-husband, Robert. It is through the sexual education that she gains from Frankie, from Babe, and through the creation of

'Vybrant' that Grace can move away from her 'vaginal woman' role. Brückner describes Lonzi's clitoral woman as having "found psychic autonomy from the man" which "does not submit to the required vaginal position" (2014, p. 280). By Season 3, it is clear that although Frankie always took up the role of a 'clitoral woman', Grace has indeed joined her there. The acts of not only using, but creating her own vibrators that work specifically for her, exemplifies Grace creating, defining, and empowering her own sexuality. 'Vybrant' is about more than just selling vibrators to older women but giving older women the tools to transform themselves into 'clitoral women'.

Grace and Frankie, a show that so heavily prioritises the experience of the older woman, clearly has second-wave feminist politics at its core. Despite this, "during the second-wave of feminism, the emphasis was on issues that are associated with the earlier years in the life course, with, for example, reproductive rights, child care, and the right to enter certain domains of work" (Woodward, 1999, p. xi). This age disparity is also prevalent in contemporary feminism. Older women of the second wave, much like Grace and Frankie, are thought of as outdated antagonists to the younger, and more culturally relevant, forms of feminism that are occupied by younger women (Jermyn, 2012, p. 2). Yet, the show's very focus on the older woman allows *Grace and Frankie* to offer a good education on the approaches, theories and practices of second-wave feminism. It is vital that *Grace and Frankie* encapsulates the perspective of older women, to allow them to become a portal to a second-wave feminism of the past, and a vital part of retelling feminist history. The community education that exists throughout *Grace and Frankie* is not simply extended to the characters within the series, but to the wider community that make up the audience. The reliance on retelling, knowledge reproduction, and shared experience that *Grace and Frankie* exemplifies through discussions around sexuality, is reflected in the plethora of ways that the series stays indebted to second-wave feminist politics. It is through this that we can reject the notions of second-wave feminism being a "sour relic" (Press, 2018, p. 218), but rather an important precursor to the feminist revival that coincides with Press' "twenty-first-century female-centric television" (2018, p. 216). Placing *Grace and Frankie* within this canon enhances a focus on older women being able to share an understanding of their narratives, told through the lens of their own version of feminist politics.

Grace and Frankie are women of the second wave, who should share space in this television canon that is currently populated by younger women that present a contemporary form of feminist politics. Allowing *Grace and Frankie* to sit side by side with shows of young women acts as a rejection of the mother/daughter tensions that have populated so much of the discourse between second-wave and contemporary feminism. Grace and Frankie are not judgmental mothers, but women, who lived through the second wave, understood its theories, practised its methods, and are continuing to educate women on this history. *Grace and Frankie* does not just exist to educate younger women though. *Grace and Frankie*'s retelling of second-wave feminism allows its older fan base to relive these experiences in a contemporary society that looks more fondly on feminism. *Grace and Frankie* opens up a second-wave feminist approach to life for women that potentially lived through the second wave, but did not adopt these feminist politics at the time. Now that feminism has become slightly more accepted or as Press states "trendy" (2018, p. 216), in many contemporary societies, *Grace and Frankie* can bring forth ideas from the second wave that would have otherwise been lost to a contemporary society that is now more open to this way of thinking.

Author biography

Alice Churm is a Film and TV Master's student at the University of Warwick, who is currently on a sabbatical year at Warwick Student's Union. She previously completed her undergraduate studies at the University of Liverpool in Media and Communications.

References

Boston Women's Collective. (1973). *Our bodies, ourselves* (2nd ed.). Simon & Schuster.

Brunsdon, C., D'Acci, J., & Spigel, L. (1997). *Feminist television criticism: A reader*. Clarendon.

Brückner, M. (2014). On Carla Lonzi: The victory of the clitoris over the vagina as an act of women's liberation. *European Journal of Women's Studies, 21*(3), 279-282. https://doi.org/10.1177/1350506814529900

Budin, D., (Writer), McCarthy, B. (Writer), & Gordon, D. (Director). (2015). The sex [TV series episode]. In M. Kauffman & H. Morris (Executive Producers) *Grace and Frankie*. Okay Goodnight, Skydance Television; Netflix.

Comella, L. (2017). *Vibrator nation*. Duke University Press.

Dodson, B. (1974). *Liberating masturbation: A meditation on self love*. Bodysex Designs.

Dodson, B. (1987). *Sex for one: The joy of self loving*. Random House.

Dodson, B. (2004). We are all quite queer. *Journal of Bisexuality, 4*(3/4), 155-163.

Dunham, L., Apatow, J., Konner, J., Landress, I. S., & Kaplan, B. E. (Executive Producers). (2012-2017) *Girls* [TV series]. Apatow Productions, I am Jenni Konner Productions, HBO Entertainment; HBO.

Finnegan, B. (Writer), & Thomas, B. (Director). (2015). The fall [TV series episode]. In M. Kauffman & H. Morris (Executive Producers), *Grace and Frankie*. Okay Goodnight, Skydance Television; Netflix.

Glazer, I., Jacobson, A., Poehler, A., Becky, D., Hernandez, T. Saifer, S., Downs, P. W., & Aniello, L. (Executive Producers). (2014-2019). *Broad City* [TV series]. Paper Kite Productions, 3 Arts Entertainment, Jax Media, Comedy Partners; CBS.

Holbert, L., Shah, D., & Kwak, N. (2003). Political implications of prime-time drama and sitcom use: Genres of representation and opinions concerning women's rights. *Journal of Communication, 53*(1), 45-60. https://doi.org/10.1111/j.1460-2466.2003.tb03004.x

Jen, S. (2017). Older women and sexuality: Narratives of gender, age and living environment. *Journal of Women & Aging, 29*(1), 87-97. https://doi.org/10.1080/08952841.2015.1065147

Jermyn, D. (2012). "Get a life ladies. Your old one is not coming back": Ageing, ageism and the lifespace of the female celebrity. *Celebrity Studies, 3*(1), 1-12. https://doi.org/10.1080/19392397.2012.644708

Kaestle, C. E., & Allen, K. R. (2011). The role of masturbation in healthy sexual development: Perceptions of young adults. *Archives of Sexual Behavior, 40,* 983–984. https://doi.org/10.1007/s10508-010-9722-0

Kauffman, M., & Morris, H. (Executive Producers). (2015–). *Grace and Frankie.* Okay Goodnight, Skydance Television, Netflix.

Kauffman, M. (Writer), Morris, H. (Writer), & Asher, R. (Director). (2016). The coup [TV series episode]. In M. Kauffman & H. Morris (Executive Producers). *Grace and Frankie.* Okay Goodnight, Skydance Television; Netflix.

Kauffman, M. (Writer), Morris, H. (Writer), & Kauffman, M. (Director). (2017). The art show [TV series episode]. In M. Kauffman & H. Morris (Executive Producers). *Grace and Frankie.* Okay Goodnight, Skydance Television; Netflix.

Koedt, A. (1970). The myth of the vaginal orgasm. In S. Firestone, *Notes from the second year: Women's liberation* (pp. 27–41). New York Radical Women.

Kohan, J., Friedman, L., Hess, S., Herrmann, T., Vinnecour, L., Tannenbaum, N. K., & Burley, M. A. (Executive Producers). (2013–2019). *Orange is the new black* [TV series]. Tilted Productions, Lionsgate Television; Lionsgate.

Liddy, S. (2017). Older women and sexuality on-screen: Euphemism and evasion. In C. McGlynn, M. Schrage-Fruh, & M. O'Neill, *Ageing women in literature and visual culture* (pp. 167–189). Springer International.

Lieberman, H. (2017a). Intimate transactions: Sex tours and the sexual discourse of second-wave feminism. *Sexuality & Culture, 21*(1), 96–120. https://doi.org/10.1007/s12119-016-9383-9

Lieberman, H. (2017b). *Buzz: A stimulating history of the sex toy.* Pegasus.

Lonzi, C. (1975). Die klitoridische und die vaginale Frau [The clitoral and the vaginal woman]. In *Die lust frau zu sein [The Lust of Being a Woman]* (S. Vagt, Trans.). Internationale Marxistische Diskussion 55 (pp. 35–79). Merve. (Original work published 1971)

Lydon, S. (1970). The politics of orgasm. In R. Morgan (Ed.), *Sisterhood is Powerful.* Random House.

Masters, W., & Johnson, V. (1966). *Human sexual response.* Churchill.

McHugh, M., & Interligi, C. (2018). Sexuality and older women: Desirability and Desire. In V. Muhlbauer, J. Chrisler, & F. Denmark (Eds.), *Women and aging* (pp. 89–111). Springer International.

Millet, K. (1970). *Sexual politics: A manifesto for revolution*. In S. Firestone & A. Koedt, *Notes from the second year: Women's liberation* (pp. 37–41). New York Radical Women.

Press, J. (2018). *Stealing the show: How women are revolutionising television* (Kindle Edition). Faber & Faber.

Schumer, A., Posch, B., & Powell, D. (Executive Producers). (2013). *Inside Amy Schumer* [TV series]. It's So Easy Productions, Irony Point, Jax Media; Viacom.

Wied, B. (Writer), & Whittingham, K. (Director). (2018). The death stick [TV series episode]. In M. Kauffman & H. Morris (Executive Producers). *Grace and Frankie*. Okay Goodnight, Skydance Television: Netflix.

Woodward, K. (1999). *Figuring age: Women, bodies, generations*. Indiana University Press.

CHAPTER 8:
FROM LITTLE WOMEN TO THE 'NEW WOMAN': REPRESENTATIONS OF FEMALE ADOLESCENT IDENTITY FORMATION IN THE LATE NINETEENTH CENTURY

Michelle D. Ravenscroft

Abstract
The conflict and crisis involved in the process of adolescent identity formation is linked to the need for the adolescent to identify with a successful role model including manifestations of how a body should be presented. This chapter considers the connection between adolescent development and adult role models during the late nineteenth century. Dubas et al. (2003) argue that "[d]uring the Middle Ages, the idea that adolescence was a unique life phase was overshadowed by the predominant view that children were miniature adults" (p. 376). This view is supported by representations of parents and adolescents in nineteenth-century publications, in particular novels, didactic texts and advice literature. The representation of female adolescents, identifying as a 'junior angel in the house' and adopting the dress and manner of adult women in Louisa May Alcott's *Little Women* (1868), will be explored in relation to the conflict between traditional, established parental role models and attitudes towards shifting gender boundaries. It will be argued that, as the century progresses, the increasing autonomy of women and adolescents and the desire for independence is linked to the threat to the patriarch and social order. The chapter also analyses George Bernard Shaw's *Mrs Warren's Profession* (1893), and how this illustrates family and personal conflict; initiated by the narrowing division between gender roles and the widening gap between generations, through representations of the parental role model and the increasingly influential manifestation of the 'New Woman' identity.

Talking Bodies III

Key words: adolescence, identity formation, nineteenth-century literature, parental role models, 'New Woman'

Introduction

This chapter will explore nineteenth-century literary representations of familial and parental influences on female adolescent identity formation. The questioning of parental roles and identity, within society and the home, increasingly created conflict and instability for adolescents and parents. Discussions relating to the continuing survival of the traditional family unit in the mid nineteenth century, reliant on the division between genders, will be linked to representations of traditional and evolving parental role models and adolescent attitudes towards these identities in Louisa May Alcott's *Little Women* (1868) and George Bernard Shaw's *Mrs Warren's Profession* (1893). The texts consider the viewpoints of parents and adolescent girls during the crisis of adolescent identity formation. *Little Women* illustrates this crisis through the masculine-like behaviour and attitude of the adolescent Jo March. The tension arising between expectations that young adolescent girls would continue to fill established maternal roles and the increasing development of individual identity will be analysed. Consideration is given to why, during the nineteenth century, adolescents began to desire an individual identity that would distinguish and separate them from their parents. As the century progresses, it will be argued that the increasing autonomy of women and adolescents, and the desire for independence, is linked to the threat to the patriarchy and social order. *Mrs Warren's Profession* explores both family and personal conflict, initiated by the narrowing division between gender roles and the widening gap between generations, through representations of the parental role model and the increasingly influential manifestation of the 'New Woman' identity.

Historical views on adolescence and identity

Historically, attitudes towards child development conceded the importance of youth as a developmental stage. However,

From Little Women to the 'New Woman'

representations of adolescent identity formation evolved throughout the nineteenth century in direct relation to the factors that influenced parental identity. Judith Semon Dubas et al. (2003) suggest a historical connection between child and adult identity: "[d]uring the Middle Ages, the idea that adolescence was a unique life phase was overshadowed by the predominant view that children were miniature adults" (p. 376). The dominating effects of parental influences during the nineteenth century can be charted through various representations in literature and art. John Tosh includes images of the evolving family unit in his text *A Man's Place: Masculinity and the Middle-Class Home in Victorian England* (1999) to highlight the changing focus of the child and role of the father. For example, George Morland's late eighteenth-century painting, *The Cottage Door* (1790), depicts a 'child-centred home', a dynamic argued by Tosh to support a "Romantic idea of the child [...] in Victorian England" that is reflective of Jean-Jacques Rousseau's eighteenth-century text about adolescent development, *Émile* (Tosh, 1999, pp. 40–41). Another illustration highlights the apparent contrast half a century later. *Morning Prayer* (1840) depicts the strict, patriarchal influence of Evangelical beliefs relating to control and formation of identity, through the influence of the father (Anonymous, 1840). The authority and power of the father over the family unit is suggested through the male-centred gaze of not only the mother and child, but also the two female adults at the periphery of the image. Despite his physical closeness to the women of the household, the father is somewhat detached; he is seated at the end of the table, with his head tilted downwards to read the Bible or a prayer book. The change in focus suggests a link between the patriarch, authority and power, and underlines how a perceived outward identity can be reinforced or portrayed through behaviour. However, this portrayal of patriarchal power comes into question as the nineteenth century progresses.

Throughout history, the idealised family was not necessarily a solid unit; as Joseph F. Kett (1977) observes in *Rites of Passage: Adolescence in America, 1790 to the Present*, "what strikes most historians about the family in the past is less its strength than its fragility" (p. 4). The increasing instability of the parental role model, both within the family and society, is reflected in the shifting authority and gender boundaries that led to changing identities. The sentiment and importance of family identity during the early nineteenth century is reflected in William L. Burn's comment, "to hear Victorians talk about the family one would suppose that it had been invented in the 1830s" (Burn, 1964, cited in Kett, 1977, p. 79). However, the stability of the family unit was threatened by the shift in parental authority throughout the century, influenced by changes to gender roles that reflected societal issues. John Demos (1988) suggests that, due to economic factors, responsibility for child rearing began to evolve: from the responsibility of the father to the mother (p. 7). By the late nineteenth century the emergence of women's rights and the desire for female autonomy impacted on the control and authority within the family and society, and on established roles and identities. Traditional measures of success were beginning to be undermined and young men and women began to question the success of their parental role models, no longer wanting to adopt the identities provided by their parents. Instead, they increasingly strove for independence and an independent identity, often by developing their education and professions.

When considering how parental identity impacts on adolescent identity formation it is important to understand the internal and external factors that influence both. It was not until the twentieth century that adolescent studies began to increase our understanding of this life-stage. Carol Dyhouse (1981) argues that "[m]uch of the debate over and social concern with 'adolescence' over the last century can be best understood as a concern with questions of autonomy and independence" (p. 119). This experience is reflected in Dyhouse's summary of influential, early twentieth-century psychologist G. Stanley Hall's view: "[f]or the boy it was a time of ambition, growth and challenge. For the girl it was a time of instability; a dangerous phase when she needed protection from society" (p. 122). Twentieth-century theories surrounding identity formation also illustrate the impact and conflict of micro and macro influences. Developmental psychologist, Urie Bronfenbrenner, considers the significance of personal interaction and environmental factors, with a microsystem consisting of 'interpersonal relations' deemed to be the most influential (Bronfenbrenner, 1993, cited in Dubas et al., 2003). However, Erik H. Erikson's seminal text, *Identity: Youth and Crisis* (1968), argues external factors increasingly become more influential than the family: "a larger unit, vague in its outline and yet immediate in its demands, replaces the childhood milieu – 'society'" (p. 128). Conflict between the personal desire to maintain one's own individuality and the impact of social attitudes and conventions is highlighted by Erikson (1968) and how this can impact on the adolescent: "[t]hey are sometimes morbidly, often curiously, preoccupied with what they appear to be in the eyes of others compared with what they feel they are" (p. 128).

It can be argued that during the nineteenth century there was a shift in concern, and therefore control, from the opinion and acceptance of parents to the opinion and acceptance of society, which is supported by the representations of adolescents and their interaction with their parents in nineteenth-century texts and adolescent advice literature. The idea that this change in attitude was connected to the instability of parental roles and the dwindling success of traditional identities in society can also be argued through ideologies in nineteenth-century parental advice literature. Eastwood Atwater (1983) suggests that "[y]outh often adopt a negative identity because they lack positive models" (p. 127). This reflects the adolescent conflict arising out of the desire to become an individual, with the need for guidance from increasingly unstable parental role models.

When linking identity formation and the family, twentieth-century family historian, Demos, considers the three different perspectives used to interpret adolescence: biological, psychological and cultural; with the psychological development of adolescence linked to the "resolution of internal issues around oneself and one's 'significant others'" and the impact of cultural "ideals, values, norms" (Demos, 1988, p. 95). However, upbringing and past experiences remain influential to adolescent identity formation. F. D. Brooks highlights the continuity of adolescent development, suggesting that "[c]hanges do take place and they are of great importance, but life is a continuous function; the youth does not break with his past"(Brooks, 1929, pp. 3-4, cited in Dubas et al., 2003, p. 378). This indicates a strong link between adolescents and their parents. However, the impact of parental influences, that can be argued to represent the bridge between the past and present self, is increasingly questioned in many late nineteenth-century texts.

Questioning the future: The threat to traditional gender roles in the mid nineteenth century

Charles Strickland (1985), writing about the family in Louisa May Alcott's work, suggests that a "'sentimental' revolution" took place during the nineteenth century, whereby "didactic" literature, "concerned with domestic themes", relied on sentiment as the "preferred guide in perceiving reality and acting on it" (p. 4). Strickland notes that "[p]rior to the sentimental revolution, parents were advised to rely on the child's awe of authority or fear of punishment as the principal sanction for discipline" (Strickland, 1985, p. 12). However, as predicted by William Cobbett's *Advice to Young Men* (1829), a moralist manual written to "instruct youth" (p. 3) on the temptations of society, it is external influences and how these impact on not only individual identity, but that of the family, that begin to pose an increasing threat.

The threat to the family ideal and individual identity relied on the guiding influence and authority of the parent. The fear that external influences would destabilise this authority by blurring gender roles and identities is represented by both John Ruskin's essay "Of Queen's Gardens" (1865) and Dinah Maria Mulock's feminist text *A Woman's Thoughts about Women* (1858). The desire to maintain a gender balance is reflected in the way differences between men and women are celebrated and encouraged. Ruskin comments that men and women are "nothing alike" (Ruskin, 1865, cited in Greenblatt et al., 2012, p. 1608), advocating the restriction of opportunities for women to ensure they remain focused on their domestic responsibilities. Mulock takes a different stand, agreeing that "[m]an and woman were made for, and not like one another", yet considering one similarity to be the 'right' to develop as an individual (Mulock, 1858, cited in Greenblatt et al., 2012, p. 1624). This indicates a rebellion against the continuing subordination of women. The difference between parental gender roles and their influence on adolescent identity formation were beginning to be undermined by the 'Woman Question' that debated the imbalance of gender status both in society and the home, and dubbed the "greatest social difficulty in England" by Justin M'Carthy (M'Carthy, 1864, cited in Greenblatt et al., 2012, p. 1607). Debates surrounding women, education and marriage even infiltrated the royal household, with uncertainty and instability reflected in the "mixed opinions of Queen Victoria" regarding support for a women's college, and her marriage advice in letters to her daughter (Greenblatt et al., 2012b, p. 1607). Despite this questioning of gender roles, the iron hand of the patriarch as God's representative in the home was still present by the mid nineteenth century, supported by Queen Victoria's admission that "the woman's devotion is always one of submission [to her husband] [...] though it cannot be otherwise as God has willed it so" (Greenblatt et al., 2012b, p. 1608). This indicates that the survival of the ideal nineteenth-century family relied on the clearly defined, predetermined roles of its members, as highlighted by Demos:

> [T]he "ideal family" [...] comprised of a tightly closed circle of reciprocal obligations [...]. If the family did not function in the expected ways, there were no other institutions to back it up. If one family member fell short of prescribed ways and standards, all the others are placed in jeopardy. (Demos, 1988, p. 34)

The repercussions of failing to adhere to these defined roles are reflected in literature, with "[o]nly the most careful and moral 'rearing'" of parents ensuring they did not "imperil their destiny irrevocably" (Demos, 1988, p. 35). The growing confusion surrounding gender roles affected the stability of parental roles within the family unit, in turn affecting the success of the family and its members. Demos considers how this unsettling of both individual and family identity created a

Talking Bodies III

"'crisis phase'. [...] [that] [a]fter mid-century, popular literature on domestic life poured out a long litany of complaints" relating to the family (Demos, 1988, p. 30). These complaints were often hidden behind the desire to uphold the idealised family described earlier by Demos, and considered to be "a bastion of peace, of orderliness, of unwavering devotion to people and principles beyond the self" (Demos, 1988, p. 30), supported by parental role models in an attempt to preserve the traditional family unit. Valerie Sanders' observation that Prince Albert, a "typical authoritarian father figure", was adored by his daughters (Sanders, 2009, p. 27) indicates the sentimental desire for a traditional patriarchal influence within the family unit. Although her argument that "the culture produced no universally acknowledged ideal father-figure" (Sanders, 2009, p. 27) suggests that no one, single identity was successful.

In Louisa May Alcott's *Little Women* (1868) the instability of traditional roles can be explored through the growing influence and autonomy of the female. Mulock's suggestion that women were voicing a concern relating to wasted opportunities, "'What am I to do with my life?' [...] whether marrying or not, each possesses an individual life, to spend, to use, or to lose" (Mulock, 1858, cited in Greenblatt et al., 2012, p. 1625), links anxiety to the importance of successful identity formation. Atwater argues that for adolescents, the main concern surrounds their future identity: "it is the concern over the 'self I can be' that occasions the most anxiety" (Atwater, 1983, p. 124). This concern over identity formation can be linked to the anxiety around the blurring of gender roles within both society and the home during the mid nineteenth century, and connected to the rebellion against an enforced female identity. Demos considers the impact of this rebellion, suggesting that "organized feminism [...] expressed an anguished cry from the depths of oppression" (Demos, 1988, p. 11), indicating the frustration of wasted opportunities. The rebellious nature of changing gender roles is represented in a shift of autonomy, reflected in *Little Women* under the backdrop of the American Civil War. The roles within the 'family sphere' are destabilised by Mr March's absence.

From Little Women to the 'New Woman'

Lynne Vallone writes that American advice books and novels depict "real womanhood" within the domestic sphere (Vallone, 1995, p. 114), of which *Little Women* is an interesting example. It is in the domestic setting that Mrs March, as the authoritative role model, is able to use her influence within the family to ensure the conflict of adolescence is negotiated.

The growing influence of mothers over their adolescent children's identity is represented by the strong, positive presence of Mrs March, who has been a "good example" (Alcott, 1868/2010, p. 448) to her daughters. Mrs March's reference to their relationship, "I never have to force my children's confidence, and I seldom have to wait for it long" (Alcott, 1868/2010, p. 321), indicates her daughters' trust in her ability to guide them. This supports the idealised version of the mother, described by Demos as the "centrepiece in the developing cult of Home" (Demos, 1988, p. 32). However, although Mrs March assigns much of her time and effort to her daughters' upbringing, she shows a reluctance to advise her daughters to become confined to the domestic sphere. Strickland argues in his analysis of *Little Women* that Mrs March "defied the stigma that convention attached to spinsterhood" (Strickland, 1985, p. 77), reflected in her attitude towards female autonomy. Strickland suggests traditional gender roles are challenged when "Marmee, that embodiment of motherly virtues, advised her daughters [...] [to] remain single [...]: 'Better be happy old maids than unhappy wives'" (Strickland, 1985, p. 77). This encouragement of individuality is in contrast to the long-established acceptance of the invisible, angel-like presence of the mother in the home, marked forever in history by Coventry Patmore's poem, *The Angel in the House*. Criticised for the "sentimentality of its ideal of women and the repressive effect of this ideal on women's lives" (Patmore, 1854–62, cited in Greenblatt et al., 2012, p. 1613), women are represented by the references to their "affecting majesty/so meek" (Patmore, 1854–62, cited in Greenblatt et al., 2012, p. 1614).

In contrast, the debate surrounding the autonomy of women highlights an increasing threat to gender differences in society, often, as suggested by Strickland, brought on by social upheaval linked to social reform: "The decades before the Civil War were marked by a ferment of reform [...] promoting equal rights for women" (Strickland, 1985, p. 4). However, despite this, gender stereotypes became more defined. Demos (1988) argues that increasingly from the 1850s:

> gender created boundaries of difference [...] [g]irls approaching womanhood were seen through a haze of romanticization: to them fell the role of "junior angel in the house", [...]. These images particularly implied suppression of self and suppression of sexuality – key elements, both, in adolescent development.
> (Demos, 1988, p. 103)

Despite Mrs March's endorsement of autonomy and individuality there is still a desire in her daughters to mimic the identity of the successful parent. Beth March imitates her successful mother and represents the 'junior angel in the house', with an "unselfish ambition, to live for others, and make a home happy by exercise of those simple virtues which all may possess" (Alcott, 1868/2010, p. 184). However, her untimely demise indicates that this method of adolescent identity formation is no longer viable in enabling transition into adulthood. The crisis and conflict of adolescence and the fear of an unsuccessful transition is reflected in Jo's reluctance to change: "[d]on't try to make me grow up before my time, [...] let me be a little girl for as long as I can" (Alcott, 1868/2010, p. 153). This desire to remain a child and hold onto the past identity is contrasted by the pressure placed on girls to become women in miniature. A fashion picture from *Godey's Lady's Book* (1864) encourages the adoption of an adult identity, with the adolescent girls mimicking the older female in both dress and demeanour. This is represented in *Little Women* when the March girls dress for a party, attempting to imitate grown women. Meg's desire to look taller, in "high-heeled slippers [that] were dreadfully tight, and hurt her" (Alcott, 1868/2010, p. 25), and Jo's sophisticated hairstyle, made possible by "nineteen hair-pins [that] all stuck straight into her head" (Alcott, 1868/2010, p. 25), were necessary, as they had to "be elegant or die" (Alcott, 1868/2010, p. 26). The ultimatum indicates how important it is for the girls to conform to societal expectations.

It is not only external factors and their maternal role model that influence the decisions of the March girls. Mr March also places pressure on his daughters to conform. Even in his absence during the Civil War he is influential, reminding them of their "duty, [...] [as] little women" (Alcott, 1868/2010, p. 8), highlighting the desire by the patriarch to continue to uphold the idealised version of the family through the traditional division of roles. However, Mrs March concedes that "the secret of our home happiness" (Alcott, 1868/2010, p. 392) depends on partnership: "we work together, always" (Alcott, 1868/2010, p. 392), suggesting a shift in attitude and a shared responsibility. Unlike early nineteenth-century examples, where the patriarch is most authoritative when he assumes a God-like detachment, Mr March prefers to be an approachable parent, like his wife. He is most influential in his study, the "church of one member" (Alcott, 1868/2010, p. 433), when speaking to Jo as an equal: "[s]he gave him entire confidence, – he gave her the help she needed, [...] for the time had come when they could talk together not only as father and daughter, but as man and woman" (Alcott, 1868/2010, p. 433). These representations of equality suggest an increasing connection between mothers and fathers in their roles as parents and the weakening of division between genders. The relationship between Mr March and Jo indicates a shift in dynamics within the home that is becoming apparent within society.

The increasing desire for equality is represented by the female adolescent desire to attain the status of the American version of a 'real woman', defined by the "active, intelligent, playful, and loving tomboy" (Vallone, 1995, p. 119), yet conflicts with the adoption of the motherly role. Vallone suggests that Jo March, "lively, intelligent and charming" is an example of the American tomboy (Vallone, 1995, p. 119). Jo's attitude towards her development suggests the desire to suppress her sexuality. However, rather than remaining in a child-like state by adopting the 'junior angel in the house' role she adopts a boy-like identity. Jo cuts off her hair, her 'one beauty' (Alcott, 1868/2010,

p. 162), to sell, which reduces her femininity, but she is pleased to have the option of "a curly crop, which will be boyish" (Alcott, 1868/2010, p. 162). The referral to the 'boyish' hairstyle suggests that Jo's efforts to adopt a more masculine appearance will never be quite enough to earn her the equal status of a man. Vallone argues that "girls generally could not be trusted with the freedom of boy-life" (Vallone, 1995, p. 120), and highlights the restrictions imposed on their identity: "the tomboy is always measured against a male standard [...]. The possessor of some of his qualities but few of his prerogatives, a tomboy merely plays at being a boy" (Vallone, 1995, p. 120). Jo desires to have the same prerogatives, "in time I may be able to support myself and help the girls" and be "independent, and earn the praise of those she loved", yet understands they may only be "the dearest wishes of her heart" (Alcott, 1868/2010, p. 156). Independence, success and the ability to support others were seen to be adult, masculine attributes. Jo's wishes echo the growing desire for equality of status, independence and responsibility for this new generation of adolescent girls.

Cultural changes further weakened the gender division, but only temporarily. Demos argues that although girls from middle and lower-class homes were encouraged to expand their horizons and work, either in domestic service, factories or schools, and as nurses, it was understood that "marriage would move a woman back to her appropriate domestic "sphere" (Demos, 1988, p. 104). In *Little Women* Jo aspires to be a writer to enable autonomy, so she can "supply her own wants, and need ask no one for a penny" (Alcott, 1868/2010, p. 269). Her younger sister, Amy, also desires to develop, "learning, doing, enjoying", into an "accomplished woman" (Alcott, 1868/2010, p. 257). The girls have followed the advice given by Mrs March, who suggests that the key to a happy, balanced life is through developing as an individual: "Have regular hours for work and play, make each day both useful and pleasant, and prove that you understand the worth of time by employing it well. Then youth will be delightful, old age will bring few regrets, and life becomes a beautiful success" (Alcott, 1868/2010, p. 118).

Despite some success, both sisters return to the domestic sphere, with marriage, "the sweetest chapter in the romance of womanhood" (Alcott, 1868/2010, p. 250), mimicking the successful partnership of their parents and enabling a successful transition into adulthood.

It is not only the young women in the text that have to negotiate the tension and anxiety of identity formation. Although Jo indicates an awareness of the complexities of adolescence, assuming this is particular to girls and that gender equality would solve the dilemma, "why weren't we all boys? Then there wouldn't be any bother!" (Alcott, 1868/2010, p. 203), their neighbour, Laurie, an "accomplished boy" (Alcott, 1868/2010, p. 71), is expected to negotiate adolescence as a "little gentleman" (Alcott, 1868/2010, p. 22). This suggests that the conflict and crisis of adolescence, despite the debate over the 'Woman Question', the desire for individual autonomy, and the blurring of gender boundaries within the home, was increased by the sentimentality connected to traditional, established gender identities.

Late nineteenth-century transitions: *The Awkward Age* of the 'New Woman'

Dyhouse (1981), writing about sexual divisions within late nineteenth-century society, argues that the growing debate surrounding adolescence influenced how this life phase was viewed.

> [a] proliferation of discussion and writing about "youth" from around the 1890s onwards testifies to the increasingly common assumption that *adolescence* as a phase posed developmental problems, while *adolescents* as a group might well constitute something of a social problem. (p. 115)

The fear of adolescents as a group within society capable of causing upheaval led to "a steady stream of literature [...], focusing on the problems of youth and adolescence" (Dyhouse, 1981, p. 115). The desire to analyse adolescence and voice these fears throughout the nineteenth century is apparent in the continuing publication of advice literature, such as Charlotte Mary Yonge's *Womankind* (1890), and the didactic text by Henry James, *The Awkward Age* (1899), which takes its title from a phrase Sarah Bilston suggests was used to define female adolescence (Bilston, 2004, p. 22). In addition, the early twentieth-century psychoanalytical text, *Adolescence*, by G. Stanley Hall (1931) made some bold statements about female adolescent identity formation, as Dyhouse summarises: Hall "argued that women never really outgrew their adolescence – psychologically and emotionally they could best be understood as having their growth arrested in the adolescent phase" (Dyhouse, 1981, p. 118). Despite the intrinsic factors, this stalling of development and the adolescent transition into adulthood is influenced and determined by society. Dyhouse considers how the effects of society create a division of gender identity, with men defined by their "economic and occupational independence", and argues that a society which "discourages women from achieving economic independence *is* effectively condemning women to a permanently *adolescent* state" (Dyhouse, 1981, p. 118). This supports the idea that cultural factors were becoming increasingly influential in both the identity formation of adolescents and their parents throughout the century, and also raises some questions surrounding the stability of gender roles.

Changes to the way women and adolescents viewed their life-options continued to blur gender boundaries both within the home and society. The idea of 'separate spheres' still continued, with men realising their potential within the world of "work, commerce and professional endeavour" (Dyhouse, 1981, p. 139), whilst women were confined to the home. Dyhouse suggests that the feminist fight for independence focused on unmarried women, seeking to "enlarge women's sphere of autonomy" (Dyhouse, 1981, p. 139), which became a feature of feminist literature. The fight to 'enlarge the woman's sphere of autonomy' was taken up in 1876 by Queen Victoria when, following the Royal Titles Bill, Victoria was awarded the title of Empress of India. Miles Taylor argues that Queen Victoria was "less a modern icon of Empire and more a European-style monarch, exercising a considerable sway of personal influence" (Taylor, 2004, p. 266). This public display of female authority to rule autonomously and construct an individual identity reflects the Queen's increasing power and control over her empire and further undermines defined, traditional gender roles and identities.

In her article "The Revolt of the Daughters" (1894) B. A. Crackanthorpe responds to the rebellion driven by the "rights of the individual" (Crackanthorpe, 1894, cited in Nelson, 2000, p. 265), who want to "make their own minor mistakes and not to be strictly limited by unwritten law to produce feeble imitations of their mothers' best copies" (Crackanthorpe, 1894, cited in Nelson, 2000, p. 263). Crackanthorpe also suggests that parents were partly responsible for the growing desire for female autonomy. She argues that conflict arose out of the increasing education of women who were then prevented from accessing opportunities and expected to become 'mothers in miniature':

> These girls are withering because they are not allowed to live their own lives, but are always compelled to live the lives of other people. They have no chance of self-development, no work, no pursuits of their own; [...] "No wonder they wither, and no wonder they revolt."(Crackanthorpe, 1894, cited in Nelson, 2000, p. 270)

In her analysis of female adolescence, Bilston considers how societal concerns, such as the perceived threat posed by the feminist movement, and a change in the traditional gender power balance were in part manifestations of 'New Imperialism' and concerns relating to 'natural' world order' at the *fin de siècle* (Bilston, 2004, p. 131). Legally imposed changes to power affected not only the "'natural world' order", but also threatened the stability of the family. Tosh (1999) suggests that:

> [t]he legislation on wives' property and the rights of custody over children appeared to serve notice that power and privilege in the home, which had hitherto been largely beyond the reach of the law, were now subject to scrutiny and restraint. (p. 168)

In contrast to their mothers, the 'New Woman' also threatened to destabilise the 'natural order' of men and women in society and the home, and offer a different role model in relation to female opportunities in the late nineteenth century.

The destabilisation of gender boundaries within different 'spheres' is supported by Tosh's argument that the "'New Woman [...] a tangible reality, daily encountered in the drawing room, as well as the office' affected '[d]omestic patriarchy'" (Tosh, 1999, p. 153). The increasing autonomy of women and the impact this has on the behaviour and identity of both men and women in the home is depicted in a *Punch* cartoon from 1895. The man of the house is represented by a rather feminine Jack. Standing with his hand on his hip, he is ready to exit the room as he no longer perceives his wife to be a feminine companion. He resorts to self-exclusion from the main household, stating "I'm going for a Cup of Tea in the Servants' Hall"; preferring what he now considers to be the more refined company of the servants: "I can't get on without Female Society" (Du Maurier, 1895, in *Punch*). Jack's comments highlight how the lack of representation of traditional femininity threatened gender differences within the home and society. His wife and her friend, wearing a masculine-looking shirt and tie with their long skirts and pinned-up hairstyle, represent an identity constructed from both male and female signifiers. The image reflects a conflict of 'natural order' for the patriarch within the domestic 'sphere'. Tosh suggests that by the end of the century "there was a sense that an era of stability in domestic life had come to a close" (Tosh, 1999, p. 169). This is supported by the women depicted in the picture as being unconcerned, and displaying a confidence in their growing status, attained by adopting the 'New Woman' role.

Despite changing attitudes towards gender autonomy, the defined roles within the family unit remained generally intact, with Tosh arguing that it "takes more than a few legal changes and an egalitarian tendency in the prescriptive texts to disturb longstanding assumptions about family order" (Tosh, 1999, p. 160). However, the questioning of roles within the family influenced the way adolescent children viewed their parental role models, and their own future prospects. Traditionally the success of a mother relied on her ability to maintain a "'perfect home' [...] [to] an almost impossible standard", and fathers were measured on their "'success' or 'failure'" (Demos, 1988, p. 33) in the world of work or commerce. This is echoed in Bilston's consideration of Norman Keill's 1964 text, *The Universal Experience of Adolescence*, in relation to adolescent identity formation. Bilston highlights Keill's suggestion that the transitional stage of adolescence is directly linked to the identity of role models: "[f]or the adolescent, the question, 'What shall I be?' actually means, 'With whom shall I identify?'" Central to his vocational choice is the problem of identification" (Keill, 1964, p. 657, in Bilston, 2004, p. 63).

The problem of identification and the impact of changing roles on adolescent identity formation are represented in George Bernard Shaw's *Mrs Warren's Profession* (1893). The portrayal of Vivie Warren as a young woman aspiring to independence is reflective of the changing attitude towards female autonomy and how this impacts on family relationships. The opening paragraph describes Vivie surrounded by the objects that came to be associated with a 'New Woman', and illustrates how the female desire for knowledge and autonomy threatens and surrounds the family home:

> A lady's bicycle is propped against the wall, under the window. [...] [and] within reach of her hand, is a common kitchen chair, with a pile of serious-looking books and a supply of writing paper on it. (Shaw, 1905, p. 159)

Tosh argues that "smoking and cycling, [were] the most visible badges of emancipated womanhood", often "applied to the young middle-class women who not only had a job but maintained herself" (Tosh, 1999, p. 152). The fight for female autonomy and independence is explored in *Mrs Warren's Profession*, reflected in the behaviour and "magnificent [educational] achievements" (Shaw, 1905, p. 163) of Vivie Warren. The significance of self-development is reflected in Dyhouse's argument that higher education for women threatened the patriarchal authority within the 'separate sphere' of educational institutions: "[C]lerics in Oxford and Cambridge, already gloomily contemplating the decline of power of the church in universities, saw the 'invasion' of their hallowed male precincts by women as the final desecration" (Dyhouse, 1981, p. 121).

This indicates the further diminishment of the authority and status of men during the latter half of the century, and the increasingly destabilised boundaries of gender role differences.

The importance of the role of the parent in educating adolescents to make important life decisions is suggested in Yonge's *Womankind*. Yonge considers adolescence to be the time when "the maiden of seventeen or eighteen [...] needs the training of home and family life [...] before choosing a profession" (Yonge, 1890, p. 80). However, although Vivie desires autonomy, a "reputation [...] social standing, and [a] profession" (Shaw, 1905, p. 190), her lack of parental influence, "I hardly know my mother" (Shaw, 1905, p. 165), does not threaten her future prospects; instead it threatens the continuation of the 'mother in miniature' identity. Atwater (1983) argues that the division between generations is enhanced by education: "education affects one's personal values, we would expect adolescents' values to change as they acquire greater education" (p. 117). The division between generations is made apparent in *Mrs Warren's Profession* when it is conceded that, unlike Vivie, Mrs Warren was a "very poor woman who had no reasonable choice" (Shaw, 1905, p. 212). Dyhouse highlights how women were "economically dependent on the male breadwinner" (Dyhouse, 1981, p. 4), reflected in Mrs Warren's lack of choice: she was "unable to 'pick and choose [her] own way of life'" (Shaw, 1905, p. 192), leaving her financially dependent on men. Vivie's aspirations do not replicate her mother's enforced dependency. However, Dyhouse argues that by the late nineteenth century maternal influence was still important: "[m]others provided daughters with some image of how their lives might take shape" (Dyhouse, 1981, p. 30). Yet the distance and division between the generations is reflected in the observation of a family friend of the Warrens about Vivie's identity in relation to Mrs Warren's expectations. Praed states, "you are so different from her ideal" (Shaw, 1905, p. 165), indicating that a predetermined identity based on her mother's and society's expectations is used to measure Vivie's success, rather than her own achievements. The text also supports the idea that growing female autonomy and changing gender boundaries destabilises identity, rather than consolidates it, with Praed assuring Vivie of her individuality in behaving "conventionally unconventionally" (Shaw, 1905, p. 162), despite her adoption of the 'New Woman' role.

The widening gap between mothers and daughters in the late nineteenth century is represented in the text by the new generation of women, described as "splendid modern young ladies" (Shaw, 1905, p. 162), in contrast to the growing parental autonomy of their mothers, which is seen as a negative aspect of parenting. The negative impact matriarchal autonomy may have on their daughters' identity formation is suggested by the "anarchist" (Shaw, 1905, p. 162) Praed: "I'm so glad your mother hasnt [sic] spoilt you" (Shaw, 1905, p. 162). This comment hints at the remaining long-held fear surrounding the inadequacy of mothers, supported by his suggestion that Mrs Warren's authority may have been used to ensure the continuation of established female roles: "I was always afraid that your mother would strain her authority to make you conventional" (Shaw, 1905, p. 162) and hinder Vivie's prospects. The threat posed by the increasing autonomy of women is represented when Praed considers how a shift in parental power influences family dynamics: "authority [.][…] spoils the relations between parent and child – even between mother and daughter" (Shaw, 1905, p. 162). This suggests the importance of parental authority and control in a time when the 'New Woman' threatened to both devalue the traditional female identity within the domestic 'sphere' and undermine the patriarch within his work or educational 'sphere'.

Bilston (2004) highlights the threat posed by the autonomous female, arguing that increasingly autonomous adolescent women were "represented as dangerously modern creatures in late Victorian discourse – as very different creatures from their mothers" (p. 172). Vivie considers herself one of a new generation of women, "[t]he sort the world is mostly made of" (Shaw, 1905, p. 192). She is a different 'creature' from her mother, who finds her unidentifiable: "[m]y God, what sort of woman are you?" (Shaw, 1905, p. 192). This suggests a lack of both generational and gender connections, exacerbated by changing attitudes towards the role of women in society. Susan C. Shapiro (1991) argues that the 'New Woman' has been represented in texts for centuries: "[e]ven in 1600 the 'mannish', bold, athletic, ambitious New Woman was old; she had by then been around for at least 250 years" (p. 510), and how the threat to patriarchal power, through their rejection of traditional roles and desire for equality, has been a constantly reinvented and "ridiculed [...] phenomenon of the moment" (p. 510). This is supported by Yonge's suggestion that strong-minded women were a "bad imitation" of men, who "made game of her little affections" (Yonge, 1890, p. 233). Imitating the increasingly unstable male identity seems at odds with the desire to form a successful identity. Yonge (1890) argues that strong-minded women did not strive for men to "tolerate" them, rather:

> [s]he does not want to cease to be a woman, but [...] make out that the woman is physically as well as mentally the superior creature, and [...] be on an equality and perhaps take the lead. (Yonge, 1890, p. 233)

This is represented by Vivie's masculine "resolute and hearty" (Shaw, 1905, p. 160) handshake and her academic success in mathematics. Vivie's desire to succeed in a male-dominated world reflects Yonge's theory surrounding the development of the child, who, striving for autonomy "has the instinct of trying its strength with its keeper, and experimenting how far it can go" (Yonge, 1890, p. 20). This testing of the boundaries of independence and status links with the idea earlier suggested by Dyhouse, that women are continually kept in a state of adolescence by societal expectations and constraints (Dyhouse, 1981, p. 118). Representations in *Mrs Warren's Profession* reflect the desire of women to attain and overshadow an increasingly diminishing male identity, threatening not only gender differences and patriarchal power, but also the mother/child bond.

Conclusion

Nineteenth-century literature reflects the crisis of adolescence through the portrayals of conflict relating to identity formation during this life-stage. The representations not only reflect adolescent stress and turmoil, but also the conflict of parental responsibility and relationships, and the influence of society on parental role models and identity. Due to this conflict, the literature is often didactic, offering advice to both parents and adolescents regarding identity formation. Advice literature focuses on how to nurture or attain an 'ideal' adult identity, representative of established gender roles and societal expectations. Success is not only measured on how well an adolescent or parent meets these expectations, but on how they adhere to the expectations of the adolescent experience. Dyhouse summarises Hall's view of adolescent identity formation in relation to external factors: "[f]or the girl it was a time of instability; a dangerous phase when she needed protection from society" (Dyhouse, 1981, p. 122). This view is reflected, although not always supported, in representations of the adolescent experience in texts throughout the nineteenth century.

Mid nineteenth-century literature reflects the questioning of traditional roles and the increasing awareness of the right to develop as an individual. The increasing awareness of the subordination of women, both in society and the home, is viewed as a rejection of established roles that threaten the continuing success of the family. The questioning of roles was also seen as a threat to the continuing link between the past and present that ensured the success of a patriarchal society. Parental identities both represent and replicate the past, as reflected in *Little Women*, whilst the adolescent protagonists provide the opportunity to recreate these adult identities in miniature. However, the questioning of gender roles and the desire to create an individual identity is in direct conflict with the inability of adolescent girls to utilise their attributes in a society that prevents them from transitioning fully into an independent adult. It was both the desire within society and older generations to retain and uphold the established gender roles, and the increasing rejection of them by younger generations, that increased the crisis of adolescence and the diminishing influence of parents.

By the end of the nineteenth century the combination of increasingly unsuccessful parental role models and the pressure of societal factors increased the desire for adolescents to disassociate themselves from their family identity and strive for individuality. The success of traditional gender roles is questioned by aspiring adolescents, represented by Vivie Warren in *Mrs Warren's Profession*, who desire to distance themselves from their parents both socially and psychologically by adopting a socially constructed, 'New Woman' identity. Even though adolescent identity formation and the influence of parental role models are featured in nineteenth-century literature, the passport to fuller knowledge in relation to this life phase and the influence of parental role models does not begin to manifest itself until the scientific exploration of adolescence at the beginning of the twentieth century. However, despite this increasing knowledge surrounding adolescence and parental influences, it is Cobbett's advice to youth in 1829 that perhaps predicted the key to successful identity formation: "Happiness ought to be your great object, and it is to be found only in *independence*" (Cobbett, 1829, p. 19, emphasis in original). This sentiment is echoed in 1858 by Mulock, who argues for the "'right'" to develop as an individual (Mulock, 1858, in Greenblatt et al., p. 1624). Nineteenth-century representations suggest the role models provided by parents were never completely successful for either generation. Therefore, for the influential parent, as much as the adolescent, it can be argued that success depended on the ability and autonomy to develop an individual identity in a society that valued established and constructed roles and identities.

Author biography
Michelle D. Ravenscroft is a graduate of the University of Chester, where she studied English literature, education, and nineteenth-century literature and culture. This research was undertaken at the University of Chester, and formed part of her Master's dissertation,

From Little Women to the 'New Woman'

"'With whom shall I identify?': Nineteenth-century representations of parental influences and adolescent identity formation". Michelle is an educational consultant working on projects relating to personal and social education and development in the primary and secondary education sectors. She also delivers enrichment sessions in a North Wales primary school. Michelle is currently undertaking doctoral study at Manchester Metropolitan University, researching nineteenth-century and early twentieth-century Northern literature and identity in relation to the Portico Library's collection and archives.

References

Alcott, L. M. (2010). *Little women*, E. Showalter (Ed.). Penguin. (Original work published 1868)

Anonymous. (1840). *Morning prayer* [Painting]. Cited in J. Tosh (1999), *A man's place: Masculinity and the middle-class home in Victorian England* (pp. 40–41). Yale University Press.

Atwater, E. (1983). *Adolescence*. Prentice-Hall.

Bilston, S. (2004). *The awkward age in women's fiction, 1850–1900: Girls and the transition to womanhood*. Oxford University Press.

Bronfenbrenner, U. (1993). The ecology of human development: Research methods and fugitive findings. Cited in J. S. Dubas, K. Miller, & A. C. Petersen (Eds.). (2003), The study of adolescence during the 20th century. *The History of the Family, 8*, 375–397. https://doi.org/10.1016/S1081-602X(03)00043-5

Brooks, F. D. (1929). *The psychology of adolescence* (pp. 3–4). Houghton Mifflin. Cited in J. S. Dubas, K. Miller, & A. C. Petersen (2003), The study of adolescence during the 20th century. *The History of the Family, 8*, 378. https://doi.org/10.1016/S1081-602X(03)00043-5

Burn, W. L. (1964). *The age of equipose: A study of the mid-Victorian generation*. Allen and Unwin. Cited in J. F. Kett (1977), *Rites of passage: Adolescence in America, 1790 to the present* (p. 79). Basic.

Cobbett, W. (1829). *Advice to young men, and (incidentally) young women, in the middle and higher ranks of life*. William Cobbett.

Crackanthorpe, B. A. (1894). The revolt of the daughters. *Nineteenth Century, 35*. Cited in C. C. Nelson, (Ed.), *A new woman reader: Fiction, articles and drama of the 1890s* (pp. 261–276). Broadview.

Demos, J. (1988). *Past, present, and personal: The family and the life course in American history*. Oxford University Press.

Du Maurier, G. (1895). *The New Woman*, in *Punch*. https://punch.photoshelter.com/gallery-image/George-du-Maurier-Cartoons/G0000TU9ZzpotCGc/I0000rc87lkkUS5Y

Dubas, J. S., Miller, K., & Petersen, A. C. (2003). The study of adolescence during the 20th century. *The History of the Family, 8*, 375–397. https://doi.org/10.1016/S1081-602X(03)00043-5

Dyhouse, C. (1981). *Girls growing up in late Victorian and Edwardian England*. Routledge & Kegan Paul.

Erikson, E. H. (1968). *Identity: Youth and crisis*. Faber and Faber.

Godey, L. A., & Hale, S. J. (Eds.). (1864). *Godey's lady's book, 68* (p. 113). Godey Company.

Greenblatt, S., Robson, C., & Christ, C. T. (Eds.). (2012a). Coventry Patmore: The Victorian debate about gender. In *The Norton anthology of English literature: The Victorian age* (pp. 1613–1614). W. W. Norton.

Greenblatt, S., Robson, C., & Christ, C. T. (Eds.). (2012b). The "woman question": The Victorian debate about gender. In *The Norton anthology of English literature: The Victorian age* (pp. 1607–1610). W. W. Norton.

Hall, G. S. (2011). *Adolescence – its psychology and its relations to physiology, anthropology, sociology, sex, crime, and religion*. Hesperides Press. (Original work published 1931)

James, H. (1987). *The awkward age*. Penguin. (Original work published 1899)

Keill, N. (1964). *The universal experience of adolescence*. International Universities Press. Cited in S. Bilston (2004), *The awkward age in women's fiction, 1850–1900: Girls and the transition to womanhood* (p. 63). Oxford University Press.

Kett, J. F. (1977). *Rites of passage: Adolescence in America, 1790 to the present*. Basic.

M'Carthy, J. (1864, July). ART. II. – Novels with a purpose, *Westminster Review, 26*, 40. Cited in S. Greenblatt, C. Robson, & C. T. Christ (Eds.). (2012), The "woman question": The Victorian debate about gender, *The Norton anthology of English literature: The Victorian age* (p. 1607). W. W. Norton.

Morland, G. (1790). *The cottage door* [Painting]. Cited in J. Tosh (1999), *A man's place: Masculinity and the middle-class home in Victorian England* (p. 40). Yale University Press.

From Little Women to the 'New Woman'

Mulock, D. M. (1858). A woman's thoughts about women. Cited in S. Greenblatt, C. Robson, & C. T. Christ (Eds.). (2012), The "woman question": The Victorian debate about gender, *The Norton anthology of English literature: The Victorian age* (pp. 1624–1626). W. W. Norton.

Patmore, C. (1854–62). *The angel in the house.* Cited in S. Greenblatt, C. Robson, & C. T. Christ (Eds.). (2012), The "woman question": The Victorian debate about gender, *The Norton anthology of English literature: The Victorian age* (pp. 1613–1614). W. W. Norton.

Ruskin, J. (1865). "Of Queen's Gardens". Cited in S. Greenblatt, C. Robson, & C. T. Christ (Eds.). (2012), The "woman question": The Victorian debate about gender, *The Norton anthology of English literature: The Victorian age* (p. 1608). W. W. Norton.

Sanders, V. (2009). *The tragi-comedy of Victorian fatherhood.* Cambridge University Press.

Shapiro, S. C. (1991). The mannish new woman: Punch and its precursors. *The Review of English Studies, 32,* 510–522.

Shaw, G. B. (1905). *Mrs Warren's profession; A play in four acts.* Constable. (Original work published 1893)

Strickland, C. (1985). *Victorian domesticity: Families in the life and art of Louisa May Alcott.* University of Alabama Press.

Taylor, M. (2004). Queen Victoria and India, 1837–61. *Victorian Studies, 46*(2), 264–274.

Tosh, J. (1999). *A man's place: Masculinity and the middle-class home in Victorian England.* Yale University Press.

Vallone, L. (1995). *Disciplines of virtue: Girls' culture in the eighteenth and nineteenth centuries.* Yale University Press.

Yonge, C. M. (1890). *Womankind.* Macmillan.

CHAPTER 9
BETWEEN GENDER AND TRADITION: HOW NORMATIVE CRAFTS-MAN-SHIP CAUSES ROLE CONFLICTS FOR TRAVELLING CRAFTSWOMEN

Hannah Rose Bayer

Abstract

Young people in their twenties wearing strange, outdated clothes with crooked walking sticks. Carrying all of their belongings in printed sheets of fabric; not owning any mobile devices; asking strangers for a shelter for the night; hitch-hiking; not being allowed to visit their hometown for at least three years and one day. All this may sound like a weird cult to the unaware, but all the above are regulations of an old crafts-tradition called the *Walz*, or *Tippelei*, which still exists today. This chapter explores the tradition which has a long history in Germany, Austria and Switzerland although, as in many other fields, women have been excluded from the historiography of this tradition. Not only are *Wandergesellinnen* (as these journeying crafts-women are called) excluded from many of the organised, institutionalised groups of this tradition (*Schaechte*), but their existence is often negated even when they are physically present. This research follows journeying crafts-women to explore their potential gender-specific experiences whilst participating in this tradition. Through this research these under-represented crafts-women are given a voice to elicit if there is a connection between choosing to participate in this tradition and a resistance to pressures of performing specific gender roles. As all participants of this tradition spend most of the time on their 'journey' in unfixed environments, travelling and working in different kinds of workspaces with a variety of teams and in a range of circumstances, the *Wandergesellinnen* break with gender norms of care and reproduction work by the very act of leaving their homes. One could argue that they are also 'Un-/doing gender' by the presence of their bodies in a male-dominated (work)space and in public space. This chapter presents a

Between Gender and Tradition

narrative analysis of interviews with seven journeying crafts-women, exploring the similarities and differences in their experiences and if these are in any way gender-marked.

Key words: gender, tradition, travelling, craft, roles, sexism

Introduction

Growing up in Austria, a country with a rich and conflicted history, I have encountered many traditions, customs and rituals that exist, mainly undiscussed, in society. Some of these are exercised nationwide, others are specific to one region and again others are based on Christian or pagan beliefs. As an academic, feminist scholar, I have come to challenge many of these traditions, especially those which inherently exist and consist through restraints and exclusions of female participation. One of these traditions, and its unequal treatment of participants due to their gender categorisation, will be discussed in this chapter. I will first give a short his/herstorical background to the craft-tradition of the *Walz*, as it is lesser-known in non-German-speaking countries. Then I will reveal my research findings, giving excerpts of female narratives inside this tradition.

Tippelei, Gesell_innenwanderschaft or *Walz* are just three terms used in the German language to describe this crafts-tradition. In English the word 'journeying' seems to be used, although I find that it doesn't grasp the intention of this tradition to its full extent, as it excludes the 'work' aspect. Going on the *Walz* is a craft/artisanal tradition that exists in many regions of Austria, Germany and Switzerland, and similar traditions can also be found in Belgium and France. Originating in the thirteenth century, young craftspeople were sent away from home for at least three years and one day to refine their craft, learn new techniques, and become a more versatile artisan (see Bohnenkamp & Möbus, 2012; Vosahlíková, 1994 for further reading on this tradition). This practice also had socio-economic elements. On the one hand, a small village could not provide work for too many craftspeople of the same trade, as these young craftspeople endangered established craft businesses; on the other hand, many underprivileged working-class families were happy to have one less person to feed. The *Walz* was also seen as a kind of 'coming of age' adventure, in which a young person should leave home to become more independent and self-sufficient, and to become 'marriage material' after they had come back home. Interestingly enough the German term *bewandert*, meaning 'skilled', 'experienced' or 'versed', is a direct adaption from the term *Gesell_ innenwanderschaft*, which is one aspect that shows how ingrained this tradition is in the German/Austrian/Swiss culture and terminology. The tradition of the *Walz* has persisted mostly unchanged since its beginnings (Bohnenkamp & Möbus 2012; Vosahlíková, 1994). Today young people who have finished their apprenticeships in specific crafts – mainly those traditional artisans such as carpentry, tailoring and dressmaking, millinery, forging, basket-weaving and many more – can decide to participate in the *Walz* either within the institutionalised frame of a *Schacht* or as a freely travelling craftsperson. *Schaechte* are institutions especially for, and of, travelling craftspeople. They add a framework, camaraderie and guideline to this otherwise relatively free experience of journeying craftsmanship. All *Schaechte* that still exist today were established in the twentieth century (Bohnenkamp & Möbus, 2012, p. 51). They can assist young craftspeople, for example with sleeping and working arrangements, give an institutionalised network of active and already finished (*ausgewanderte* or *einheimische*) travelling craftspeople and also have specific, often secret, rituals and rules which enforce the idea of connection and belonging. The installation of these interpersonal connections (not only in this case, but in many other societal settings) is often (re-)produced by creating exclusive men's societies, which is an evident factor in this tradition, as five of the eight existing *Schaechte* exclude women's participation.

My research shows how this craft tradition has been portrayed as, and is therefore seen as, a male sphere, in which women are the 'outsiders', 'others' or 'intruders'. Not only through male alliances which enforce the exclusion of female participation, but also through the normative traditional craftsman being a physical MAN, therefore creating a role conflict (West & Zimmerman, 1987) between being *female* and being a traditional *Wandergesell_in*.

The tradition of *Walz/Tippelei/Gesell_innenwanderschaft*

Before presenting my research findings I will provide a short his/herstorical review of the most important facts concerning the *Walz*. I have found it hard to describe this tradition in English, as many terms and definitions are only used in the German language. Also the Austrian, German and Swiss educational system, relating to trades and crafts, differs from the British or American system, hence some positions or definitions do not exist.

First, I want to express that this tradition is not unique to Austria, but originated in different countries, even before the current national borders existed. There are regional differences in the beginnings and intricacies of this craft-tradition, and even the name differs from region to region. The *Walz*, *Tippelei*, or *Gesell_innenwanderschaft* are all equally used terms in different regions, to describe this tradition. The term *Gesellin* (female) and *Geselle* (male) describe craftspeople who have finished their (at least) three years of apprenticeship in a specific craft or artisanship, and are now a certified craftsperson (for instance carpenter, tailor/dressmaker or milliner). In this educational system, it is a precondition to be able to open one's own craft business, to participate in the tradition of the *Walz* or to get the award of *Meister* (meaning master craftsperson) which is the highest crafts qualification. The term *Wandergesellin* or *Wandergeselle* describes the travelling craftspeople who are actively participating in the *Walz*. I use *Wandergesell_in* as a gender-equal term, including not only male and female gender, but also non-binary genders through the underline. The exact translation would be journeyman or journeywoman, but I find that this definition does not pay tribute to the artisanry that is essential for this tradition. Thus, I will consequently call the participants travelling craftspeople.

I will now outline the basic points of the *Walz* to provide a framework to people who are unaware of this tradition. Researching in this field is difficult as there is very little accessible documentation about this tradition. This is due to the secrecy that surrounds the *Walz*, and also that it is a tradition deeply ingrained in German, Austrian and Swiss working-class crafts(wo)manship, and has not yet been academically processed or researched. Beginning my research, I noticed that the institutionalised unions of the *Walz* (*Schaechte*) especially, but also many active travelling craftspeople, are not interested in participating in academic research about their tradition. Some information about the rules and regulations inside this tradition can be found in historical books on artisanry, but I derived most of the following information directly from talking to travelling craftspeople whilst undertaking field research.

There are rules, creating boundaries as to who is allowed to participate in this tradition. Any person wanting to engage in it must have successfully completed a craft apprenticeship. But not just any craft will do, only 'old' or 'traditional' crafts are accepted, only those crafts which were already performed in the Middle Ages, for example blacksmith, bookbinder or joiner. When beginning the *Walz* the craftsperson must be under thirty years old, have no previous criminal convictions, and must be unmarried and childless. All these requirements have been passed on since the tradition originated around the thirteenth century. For example, not allowing convicted criminals to participate in this tradition was mainly introduced to maintain the good reputation of the tradition and its participants. This was and is essential for the continuance of the *Walz*, because participants are highly dependent on help from wider society. Travelling craftspeople are not allowed to use their own cars, and are required to travel and sleep without spending money. This means that they mostly hitch-hike or walk and have either to sleep outside, or ask strangers for accommodation. Thus, a bad reputation for its participants would be fatal for the survival of this tradition, as hitch-hiking and sleeping in strangers' houses requires trust, which is mostly given to these young people by their mere appearance as traditionally travelling craftspeople. Because of the *Walz*'s long history, travelling craftspeople are highly respected in the German, Austrian and Swiss crafts society and many people are happy to help preserve this tradition.

The *Walz* consists of leaving the hometown behind and travelling and working away from home, in places and situations that are unknown. This is supposed to make the participants more rounded and versatile craftspeople. In pre-modern times it was especially important to learn different crafts techniques, as they differed from region to region and were not as easily accessible as nowadays. Moreover, the travelling craftspeople would have the chance to get to know new environments, people and cultures, and become mature enough during the process to settle down afterwards, and maybe inherit their family business (Bohnenkamp & Möbus, 2012, p. 16ff.). Participation in this tradition was, and continues to be, seen as a positive qualification for a further career. Success in unfamiliar realms was often, and remains to be, seen as an important life achievement (Bohnenkamp & Möbus, 2012, p. 17f.; Vosahlíková, 1994, p. 22). Today the main reasons for young people to engage in this tradition are the freedom of travelling for work experience, and working for the travelling experience. Also, the prospect of not having any commitments and not being in fixed employment for at least three years seems inviting.

Even though young people participating in the *Walz* have no commitments at home for at least three years and a day, there are many other rules and regulations with which they have to adhere. Participants are obliged to travel without any mobile or Internet-connectable device, only using a map. All luggage must be carried in a big, colourful cloth, which is called a *Charlottenburger*, no modern rucksack or bags are acceptable. Hiding their belongings in cloth is supposed to protect the travelling craftspeople from being robbed, whilst also not showing publicly how many and what belongings they own. It is important to emphasise that these rules and regulations are unwritten, but have been passed down orally within this tradition over decades and centuries. Some regulations may have changed, others adapted or even eliminated, but they are always passed on from more experienced travelling craftspeople to the next generation.

Talking Bodies III

> Yes ... I mean these rules ... in the end, it's not like a system of rules that somebody wrote down. There are these rules ... and ... for some people the most important aspects of the rules are where they came from ... the external effect, so to speak. And some people, I have the feeling, they insist on all the rules so rigidly, that they ... completely forget about the external effects.
> (Cori, joiner and travelling craftswoman)

'Outsiders' (like me) may be told some details, but definitely not every secret of this tradition is shared. There are countless rituals, from specific greetings and drinking rituals to particular songs and even their own language, *Rotwelsch*, which includes an assemblage of some old slang terms thieves and travelling folk used to use. Many of these regulations are put in place to sustain the respectability (*Ehrbarkeit*) of travelling craftspeople in the public sphere, as they are highly dependent on outside support for accommodation, travelling or work arrangements. When travelling within a *Schacht*, violations of these rules can be sanctioned by the institution, in which *einheimische* craftspeople also still have power in the decision-making process. It is astonishing to me as a researcher how these regulations are enforced within the group of freely travelling craftspeople via a mutually agreed form of self-regulation. Even though these are interesting aspects, I will focus on gender in this tradition, and so I will not go into further detail regarding the more complex regulations surrounding the *Walz*.

Nevertheless, one evident characteristic of the *Walz* must be mentioned here: the *Kluft*. To identify young craftspeople as travelling and working traditionally, they wear specific clothes whilst participating in this tradition. The outfit, which is called the *Kluft*, is not a uniform (as I was told explicitly), but more like a symbol of recognition. It unites every active travelling craftsperson, whilst giving distinction between them, and also divides the participants from the 'outer world'. Every travelling craftsperson must wear these clothes when in public. Most *Wandergesell_innen* travel with one outfit for working and a second more elegant *Kluft* which is worn whilst hitch-

Between Gender and Tradition

hiking. This is due to practical reasons rather than aesthetic ones, such as to prevent a stranger's car from getting dirty whilst hitching a ride.

The *Kluft* consists of a white shirt called *Staude*, a vest, and specific trousers which commonly have bell-bottoms and two zips in the front, called *Zunfthose*. It is also possible to wear a skirt (*Zunftrock*), but I observed very few people wearing these, and I assume this is because they are less convenient for working. Over the top the travelling craftspeople wear a jacket, with many large pockets, where they keep their most precious belongings. Every travelling craftsperson wears a hat (*Deckel*) which must be taken special care of and an earring in the left ear, which has to be pierced in a special ritual during the first three months of the *Walz*. These are the aspects of clothing all travelling craftspeople have in common. For outsiders it may seem trivial, but there are different ways of reading information about the specific travelling craftsperson from the *Kluft* they are wearing. Colours and details like buttons or ties differ depending on their craft, or if they are travelling freely or in the institutionalised setting of a *Schacht*. Also specific information can be derived from the earring or belt-buckle worn by the travelling craftspeople. The general public usually has no idea of the symbolic meanings surrounding the *Kluft*.

> Because I am a woman, some people think that my outfit is just a style aspect for me. Ahm, and then when I tell them that I am traditionally travelling, they think: Red because I am a woman. (Christina, milliner and travelling craftswoman)

There are different ways to participate in the *Walz*, one possibility being to travel within a *Schacht*. These are institutionalised groups that organise and connect travelling craftspeople and support them during their time on the road as well as after finishing the *Walz*. The other possibility is to travel freely (*freireisend*) without connecting within a *Schacht*, but for many *Schachtgesell_innen*, this is seen as the less traditional way. Today there are eight of these institutions in German-speaking countries, some of which have a long history, being continuations of old, historical *Schaechte*. Five of these eight *Schaechte* exclude female craftspeople completely, due to gender categorisation.

Thus, another *Schacht* (*Axt & Kelle*) was formed in the 1970s, which was the first one to allow women to travel in an institution. Since then two more *Schaechte* have been formed, that also encourage female craftspeople to follow this tradition. The exclusion of women from these male institutions has never been officially explained, or even mentioned on official *Schacht*-websites, which maintain a masculine ideal of the travelling craftsman.

Much of the written output (by this I mean their websites, flyers, media coverage *if* they have any) of male-only *Schaechte* accentuate brotherhood and the 'hard life on the road'. These ideals are also triggered through other customs that go alongside the *Walz*, and which are often perceived as masculine, like songs about the hard life travelling, beer drinking rituals, and so on. These *Schaechte* have the function of uniting young craftspeople, and helping them with sleeping arrangements as they have their own houses for accommodation. They often organise their own building sites and recommend each other to clients and so on, so travelling within one of these institutions is an advantage for the young people, who are often away from home for the first time. This is a privilege which many women cannot make use of, as there are only three institutions that female craftspeople are permitted to travel within. These are also linked to specific crafts. Depending on which craft a woman performs, she has perhaps only the opportunity to travel in one *Schacht*. This is also one of the reasons why all of my interviewees, except for one, travelled and worked freely as *freireisende Wandergesellinnen*.

Research
Despite its long history, this tradition has seldom been the subject of research in traditional research disciplines such as sociology, ethnography or even history. Due to the semi-secrecy of the *Walz* and its rootedness in working-class culture there has only been limited academic research, and to my knowledge no gender-related research at all. One reason could be the refusal of (especially male-only) *Schaechte* to open up to academic research.

Between Gender and Tradition

My research interest lies in revealing the 'hidden' female, travelling craftspeople participating in this tradition. Not only have women been excised from history, with hardly any mention of women in traditional crafts, or this tradition, but they are still seen by some as imposters in this mainly male-dominated tradition of the *Walz*.

I had some difficulties in finding the first travelling craftswoman, due to the fact that they use mobile phones or the Internet infrequently, and because of the relative secrecy of this tradition. I made contact with one woman through the Internet who would speak to me about her gendered experience in this tradition. We met at a building site in Germany which was organised by freely travelling craftspeople, who were renovating a manor house. Overall, I found seven travelling craftswomen to participate in my research, one of them travelling within the *Schacht Axt & Kelle* and the other six travelling freely.

Of the women I interviewed, three were cabinet-makers, one a brewer, one a milliner, one a dressmaker and one a bookbinder. I tried to get a good cross section of women in different crafts, some of which are explicitly male dominated, while others are more typically perceived as feminine trades. I also paid attention to interviewing some women in the beginning of their *Walz*, some mid-experience and one after she had already finished her *Walz*, all giving different insights into the stages of experiences along the duration of the journey. All of my interview partners were women, as they self-identified as female and were also passing socially as women. Though queerness, transsexuality and intersexuality would be interesting aspects to this topic, especially concerning the procedure of inclusion and exclusion in *Schaechte*, this is beyond the scope of my initial research project.

I adhered to feminist research methodologies (see criticism of androcentrism and objectivity in science by DeVault & Gross, 2012; Althoff et al., 2001; criticism of patriarchy, imperialism, classism and racism by Mies, 1983; Harding, 1991; criticism of hierarchies and colonialism in social sciences by Fonow & Cook, 2005) using reflected interviewing and trying to incorporate the ideas of my research partners in my writing. After posing my prepared questions, I asked my interviewees if there were any other topics they wanted to include in the interview. I also sent the transcription of the narratives I used in my work to each of them, so that they could make changes. My main goal was to give these women a chance to share their gendered experiences in an academic context and help to represent them as female craftspeople in this male-dominated tradition. The experiences and contributions of travelling craftswomen have been hidden and excluded in nearly all historical research or literature about the *Walz*. This has been so pervasive that most people even believe that it is forbidden for women to travel and work within this tradition. Even the physical existence of traditionally travelling craftswomen – seen as a 'wrongly' gendered Crafts*man* – causes discussion in our society. Keeping to the feminist slogan 'the personal is political' (Hanisch, 1969) I wanted to explore if these individual experiences as a female craftsperson in this male-dominated tradition can be explained with other gendered mechanisms that are based on discriminations or stereotypes in our society.

When interviewing I discovered different overlapping issues and I chose six topics emphasising those that I as a researcher found most relevant for my research goals. My research could not represent all the different experiences travelling craftswomen encounter, or all topics they find important and is, thus, one perception of this very broad field of experience.

The six topics that I chose to analyse are the following:

- "Why did I choose to work in this specific craft?";
- "I am treated like everyone else" – Women in crafts;
- "Aren't you afraid?" – Women alone in the public sphere;
- "Freedom isn't a 40h-job" – Capitalism criticism;
- "I just don't have a penis ..." – Structural exclusion from male-alliances;
- "Traditionally travelling craftswomen" – that doesn't work!

For this chapter I took a detailed look at the last two points, as they specifically target the experience of 'being a woman' in this male-dominated tradition, as well as in a sense of bodily experience in a role conflict situation. They also meet the mission of this book, to explore issues of representations and gendered body politics, through exclusion mechanisms and experiences of (biologically framed) structural sexism.

I just don't have a penis ...
The structural exclusion of women from male alliances is a primary topic to consider as a feminist researcher whilst exploring this tradition. Though to me this sexist mechanism seemed relevant, it is interesting that only two women I interviewed talked about it unprompted.

As West and Zimmerman argue in their iconic paper "Doing Gender" (1987), some occasions are organised to routinely display and celebrate behaviours that are conventionally linked to one or the other sex category (West & Zimmerman, 1987, p. 140). For the exclusively male institutionalised *Schaechte* the tradition of the *Walz* seems to be one of these occasions, in which the normative male characteristics are reproduced. It is not coincidental that the mere term craftsMANship contains the masculine form, which underlines the male characteristic of this occupation. Work and occupation are used to define and reproduce normative masculinities or femininities, through exclusion of the 'other' gender. This exclusion mostly happens subliminally through socialised ostracism, but in some cases, as here, can be institutionalised through formal, sexist discrimination (Acker, 1992, p. 568). With the exclusion of women (or all female categorised people) in these exclusively male *Schaechte*, they manage to maintain and reproduce ideals of masculinity in the craft-tradition, whilst the accountability of femininity is also ensured by the exclusion of female craftspeople in these institutions (West & Zimmerman, 1987, p. 140). The discrimination of women through their exclusion from five out of eight existing *Schaechte* strengthens the masculine ideals of the hard-working craftsman, especially of dominant, hegemonic masculinities, which further legitimates the exclusion of female participants (Acker, 1990, p. 153).

Talking Bodies III

The joiner Nala told me that she had already experienced her gender as being a 'problem', even before she started journeying on the *Walz*. While she was still in her apprenticeship, she met two young traditionally-travelling craftsmen, who confronted her with the exclusion of women from the *Schacht* they were travelling within.

> (...) and then I understood, no, they are being serious. They wouldn't take me. I could be the best craftswoman in the world ... I just don't have a penis. And that is apparently important! And with that I really ... I was shocked. And then ... well, I had never been exposed to sexism that hard ... somehow ... and this time I really noticed it strongly.
> (Nala, joiner and travelling craftswoman)

In this narrative, Nala talks about her first conscious experience with sexism. I suppose with that she means structural sexism, as she also told me about other incidents concerning personal experiences of sexism, for example sexual harassment in a workspace. I found it interesting that she detects her gender as being the 'problem', instead of the sexist selection criteria of many *Schaechte*. With this, gender or the lack of having the 'right' gender is seen as problematic, because the ideal of masculinity that is transported and reproduced through the traditional travelling craftsmen is defined only with the exclusion and absence of the female gender in these institutions (Acker, 1992, p. 568; Cyba, 1993, p. 40). Nala names a body part which is not beneficial for performing any kind of craft, as crucial for inclusion or exclusion in these institutions. According to Joan Acker "Women's bodies cannot be adapted to hegemonic masculinity" (Acker, 1990, p. 153), which is exactly what this narrative supports.

Nala is the only travelling craftswoman I interviewed who was travelling inside a *Schacht*, specifically *Axt & Kelle* which was the first one to include female participants and openly present a feminist stance. For Nala travelling within this *Schacht* is a political statement against the discrimination of women in this craft-tradition. Whilst Nala is obviously opposed to the idea of structural sexism, some travelling craftswomen tolerate, excuse or even legitimised this exclusion as a 'natural' or 'historical' and unchangeable fact. The dressmaker Miri, who contributed the next narrative, had travelled and worked freely without the support of a *Schacht*. I asked her why this was.

> (…) at first … ahm, when you, when you are interested then you go to the different associations … take a look at them … and see which one can actually take you in. Because for instance, for a woman, well, half of them drop out already. They don't admit women. Not dramatic … that's just how it is. And … that meant for me, that only two Schaechte were left, within which I could have travelled. (Miri, dressmaker and *einheimische* craftswoman)

Even though three *Schaechte* take in female craftspeople, only two would be open to Miri, a dressmaker, as some of the institutions only take people working in specific crafts (e.g. *Axt & Kelle* only admit people working in building crafts). In this narrative Miri describes the unequal access to support and participation in this tradition as an irreversible fact, even though it is de facto socially constructed. This unequal access not only recreates gendered hierarchies but also creates a minority group, which Miri is a part of. According to Mayer Hacker's (1951) conception, "A person who on the basis of his [sic] group affiliation is denied full participation in (those) opportunities which the value system of his [sic] culture extends to all members of society satisfies the objective criterion" (Mayer Hacker, 1951, p. 60). Though not every person who de facto belongs to a minority group also defines themselves as belonging to one, or feels discriminated. Some members of minority groups, as for example my interview partner Miri, are aware of discrimination towards them but comply with it, because of ascribed differences of genders (Mayer Hacker, 1951, p. 60). Miri's claim, "that's just how it is" signals her disinterest in changing the status quo inside this tradition, concerning the exclusion on the basis of gender ascription. Another travelling craftswoman I spoke to ignored the gendered inequality completely. Even though she compared the tradition with all-male fraternities (*Burschenschaften*) due to their drinking rituals, collective singing and secret ceremonies, she did not mention their similarity in excluding women. To me it seems very unlikely that she had not noticed this overlap. This could be due to not wanting to be cast into the role of the victim (which was a common reason for women *not* wanting to participate in my research, as I found out), or because she (as it seemed to me) was trying to cast a solely positive light on the tradition of the *Walz*.

Nala's engagement with the *Schacht Axt & Kelle* represents a feminist reaction to the exclusion of women in most other institutions of this tradition, as *Axt & Kelle* is known for its feminist agenda. All other travelling craftswomen I interviewed were travelling freely, and with this were not able to benefit from the support that many of their male colleagues have through *Schaechte*. This gives travelling craftsmen an advantage inside this tradition. I noticed during my stay at the building site that many travelling craftspeople were weary of discussing the topic of female exclusion with me. Even though the building site was run by freely travelling craftspeople many *Schachtgesellen* (craftsmen travelling within a male institution) were also present. I did not ask my interviewees specifically about their opinion on the male *Schaechte* (which in hindsight might have been a missed opportunity), but I was curious to see if they would address the subject themselves and in what way. All of my interview partners were aware of my research being inside a gender studies context, so of course some answers could be linked to socially accepted responses.

Besides the structural exclusion that prevents women from participating in male-dominated spheres, mostly there are more subtle, non-institutionalised mechanisms that cause gendered segregation. In the case of the *Walz* I would identify a mixed form. The structural and institutionalised discrimination is only one aspect, the other is the informal understanding in society of *who and what* a traditionally travelling craftsperson *is* – and that is always male.

Traditionally travelling crafts-women – that doesn't work!
Participants in this tradition are commonly thought of as male, as the

whole tradition is perceived as a predominantly male sphere. This is due to different aspects of the *Walz*: the exclusion of women from the long history of this tradition despite historical evidence of women in different travelling crafts and *Zuenfte* (institutions that were replaced by *Schaechte* in the late eighteenth century) (Vosahlíková, 1994; Elkar et al., 2014), the *Walz*'s location in the public sphere which is predominantly seen as a male realm in which women are vulnerable, and the stereotypical norm of a hardworking craftsperson being male. Also, in public, most crafts that are linked to this tradition (as I have mentioned, not all crafts are included) are also linked to masculinity. Joiners, blacksmiths, boat-builders and cabinet-makers are seen as the typical professions that participate in the *Walz*, whilst they are also seen as normatively male-occupied. On the one hand it is unlikely that people link these crafts to female craftspeople, on the other it is not commonly known that more female perceived trades such as dressmakers, milliners or church-painters can participate. This, again, is due to the absence of travelling and working craftswomen in historical records, even though women have been doing this just as long as men have, but mainly outside of institutionalised guidelines, due to their exclusion (Vosahlíková, 1994; Elkar et al., 2014, p. 101). Historically women were especially important workers in textile crafts, and were also members of *Zuenfte* before they were banned from them in around 1500 (Elkar et al., 2014, p. 103). In the narratives below it is easy to see that most members of the public perceive an intrinsic connection between male-dominated crafts, the *Walz* and ideals of masculinity. This further illustrates the invisibility of female craftspeople in this tradition on the one hand, and women in the public sphere on the other hand.

    The tradition of the *Walz* is seen by many in the broader public as a male realm in which women should not or cannot be included. This segregation, based on gender categorisation, seems very evident in the following narrative, as expressed by the beer-brewer Iris.

Talking Bodies III

> Hmm (...) what I find interesting, well especially as a woman ... that is somehow shocking, because some people who are not so familiar with this tradition really just think from the wall to the wallpaper, they generally assume that we're all men ... not everyone, but very many. And one really alarming phenomenon that happened to me was, that I was in the ladies toilets and came out of the cubicle, and another lady came out of another cubicle at the same time ... looked at me and said "Oh, a travelling journeyman! (*Wanderbursch*)" and that was somehow shocking.
> (Iris, beer-brewer and travelling craftswoman)

Here, Iris witnessed a 'wrong' gender categorisation by an 'outsider' of this tradition. Even though Iris, identifying as a cis woman, was met in a physical space that is predominantly frequented by people of female gender, she was categorised wrongly. This was solely due to her appearance, wearing the traditional *Kluft* travelling craftspeople are obliged to wear in public. This outfit is the most prominent symbol of the *Walz*, and the *Walz* again is deeply connected to normative masculinity. So, in conclusion, only a person of male gender could be wearing this outfit, disregarding the female body physically appearing in it, in a gendered physical space predominantly associated with women. The category that *seems* appropriate is used, without needing prior 'evidence' of the person's gender. According to West and Zimmerman only obvious features, or the absence of these, would rule out its use (West & Zimmerman, 1987, p. 133), but in this case even this ascription fails. Another travelling craftswoman I interviewed was not only wrongly identified, but her mere existence was negated.

> (...) well there are very many rumours about the Walz, things that are just wrong. Like, you're travelling for one year, everyone is a carpenter (*Zimmermann*) ... and women aren't allowed to travel traditionally ... that's also one ... I have heard more than once, that someone told me "Oh no, you can't be travelling traditionally, you're a woman."
> (Miri, dressmaker and *einheimische* craftswoman)

Between Gender and Tradition

Miri told me about different rumours, one of them being that female travelling craftspeople do not exist. Even though she is physically present, her existence is erased. She is in the position where she has to legitimise her existence of being both female and traditionally travelling. The role conflict between these identities seems to be so large, that both cannot be united. In both of these narratives it becomes apparent that only one of these two 'clashing' identities can be accepted, either being a woman or being a travelling craftsperson. West and Zimmerman argue that Goffman's 1977 article, "Arrangements between sexes", highlights role conflicts, which they suggest cause troubles for the "out of place" person (West & Zimmerman, 1987, p. 140). Every woman I interviewed experienced that either her gender or her participation in this tradition was challenged. This is probably one of the most apparent differences to the lived reality of their male colleagues, whose gender category fits to the normative ideal of traditionally-travelling craftsmen and thus does not cause role conflicts. This is the result of the normative idealisation of craftsMANship, the public sphere and this tradition being masculine concepts, into which supposed stereotypical female characteristics do not fit (Wharton, 2005; Acker 1990; Hausen, 1976). So, for at least three years and one day of their lives, women who participate in the *Walz* have to account for either their gender category or their participation in this tradition, to nearly everyone they meet.

So, 'doing' or 'undoing' gender?

One question to consider is: with their participation in the *Walz*, are travelling craftswomen *doing* or *undoing* gender and hegemonic gender relations? The accepted gender routine is challenged when a person categorised as belonging to one gender participates in activities that are assumed as belonging to another; defined by West & Zimmerman (1987), with the term "sex category" (West & Zimmerman, 1987, p. 139f.). West and Zimmerman (1987) suggest this can be "achieved through application of the sex criteria", and "sustained by the socially required identificatory displays that proclaim one's membership in one or the other category" (West & Zimmerman, 1987, p. 127). They make the distinction that "Gender [...] is the activity of managing situated conduct in light of normative conceptions of attitudes and activities appropriate for one's sex category" (West & Zimmerman, 1987, p. 127).

So, are these women 'undoing' gender, by the mere presence of their gendered, female bodies in a male-dominated sphere? According to West and Zimmerman "Doing Gender" is not only living up to conceptions of femininity or masculinity, but also the act of non-conforming with these norms at the risk of a 'wrong' gender assessment (West & Zimmerman, 1987, p. 137), as happened to Iris. Humans have many social identities, one of them in this case being a traditionally-travelling craftsperson. But the gendered category, being either male or female is always present, as it is an omnirelevant circumstance that can be used to legitimate or discredit any activity. So also inside this tradition "[W]hat this means is that our identificatory displays will provide an ever-available resource for doing gender under an infinitely diverse set of circumstances" (West & Zimmerman, 1987, p. 139). This omnirelevance of gender ascription, or the necessity of adapting to the norm of always 'doing gender', was also a big concern for my interview partner Cori:

> Well somehow the gender roles are always in the foreground in our society, in every aspect. And I have often come to the point, where I have asked myself: What is happening? And why? And ... just get off my back with all that! (laughing) And somehow for a long time I just claimed that it (the ascribed gender roles) all didn't concern me, it all just flies past me and I don't notice it all. But then I had to realise that one can't just NOT NOTICE! Because it's just omnipresent. Because others make it omnipresent!
> (Cori, joiner and travelling craftsperson)

Cori tried to exclude herself from any gendered behaviour or necessity to 'do gender', but then realised that gender categorisation from the outside is a daily ritual, producing not only hierarchies but also sanctions, if not done correctly. As Judith Butler puts it, Cori was "struggling for autonomy [...] on the basis of denial of this sphere" (Butler, 2004, p. 21f.), then realising that her gendered body is not only

Between Gender and Tradition

'her own' but contextualised in a gender-segregated society, in which she would be held accountable for her gender at all times. We all live in a world in which gender categorisation or the assumption of gender is done irrespective of if we submit to, or revolt against, them. In some situations these ascriptions become more relevant than in others. According to Judith Butler (2004) we are not autonomously in charge of our gender, let alone sex ascription:

> One only determines "one's own" sense of gender to the extent that social norms exist that support and enable that act of claiming gender for oneself. One is dependent on this "outside" to lay claim to what is one's own. The self must, in this way, be dispossessed in sociality in order to take possession of itself.
> (Butler, 2004, p. 7)

For the travelling craftswomen specifically, the gender categorisation seems to happen first and foremost, before they are read as legitimate participants in this tradition, which leaves the women in a constant act of legitimising either their inclusion in this tradition or accounting for their gender.

> I think, ahm, I didn't really ever think about men and women and the differences and that kind of stuff before I started the Walz. I ... in my feeling, men and women could anyway do everything, I mean we're in 2018 ... at that point 2017. But ... now whilst travelling traditionally I realised, that isn't really the case. But before that I never really thought about it.
> (Christina, milliner and travelling craftswoman)

For me, these interview narratives represent how the participation in this masculine perceived tradition had for the first time caused a form of *gender trouble* or *role conflict* in the lives of these young women. These new experiences provoked them to think more about gendered relations, hierarchies and gendered role expectations that had not yet been as relevant in their former lives at home.

Conclusion

In Butler's analysis on regulation in *Undoing Gender* (2004), she asks if gender exists prior to regulations, or if the subjection to these regulations is the process by which gender is produced (Butler, 2004, p. 40f.). I find that many of these narratives suggest the latter, as my interviewees often were not aware of many gendered segregations or hierarchies in their life, prior to travelling within the tradition of the *Walz*. In this tradition, gender therefore is constructed, on the one hand through structural exclusion and on the other hand through gendered norms.

The *Schaechte* which exclude female craftspeople create a hard dividing line, by re-producing the gendered binary and normative masculinity, whilst also re-creating biologistic *femininity* through exclusion, based on assumed sex and gender categorisation. Their stance on non-binary or queer craftspeople is yet to be explored. The travelling craftswomen who were interviewed by me were either appalled by their exclusion from some of the male-alliance *Schaechte*, excusing of their own exclusion, or did not mention the sexist exclusion in the interview at all. The person who was most vocal about sexist structures in this tradition was also the only person who had decided to travel within the *Schacht Axt & Kelle*, which is known for its feminist position within the *Walz*. This was a direct political reaction to her exclusion, to strengthen the countermovement inside this tradition.

As all of my interviewees had experienced, the normative *Wandergesell_in* is perceived as a masculine *Wandergeselle*. Through extensive exclusion of women in all historical narratives of this tradition, and hence the invisibility of women participating in it, the normative stereotype of the adventurous, hard-working, travelling craftsMAN has been further reproduced and is clearly manifested in (especially outsiders') view of the *Walz*. Next to some other falsehoods about the tradition, for instance that the travelling craftspeople work only for food and lodging or that they are all carpenters (*Zimmermaenner*), the idea that women are not allowed to participate in this tradition is one of the most prominent untruths about the *Walz*.

Between Gender and Tradition

I hope that my work in this field can shed some light onto the active participation of women in this old crafts-tradition and their exclusion from all-male alliances and a large part of artisan history. Hopefully, my research can break down some gendered stereotypes concerning travelling craftspeople or at least give some snippets of the realities women on the *Walz* deal with, for at least three years and one day of their lives. My research doesn't end here, this is merely a first delve into the many unexplored depths of this semi-secret tradition. This research will be developed further by attending a symposium organised by freely travelling craftspeople with the focus on *Wanderschaft* und Gender, in which they plan to discuss and deconstruct gender roles and stereotypes within the tradition in which they are participating. It is highly encouraging to see that gender equality and equal chances is also a priority within the group of active, freely travelling craftspeople, and I am more than honoured to be a part of this exchange. I hope to be able to obtain a deeper understanding of gendered issues within the *Walz*, by conducting group discussions and further research.

Author biography

Hannah Rose Bayer, MA, studied interdisciplinary gender studies at the Karl-Franzens-University in Graz. Her Master's thesis dealt with the experiences of travelling craftswomen in the male-dominated crafts-tradition called the *Walz* or *Tippelei*. Outside of the academic field she engages in political activism, is a musician in feminist bands and engages in different DIY groups.

References

Acker, J. (1990). Hierarchies, jobs, bodies: The theory of gendered organisations. *Gender and Society*, 4(2), 139–158. https://doi.org/10.1177/089124390004002002

Acker, J. (1992). Gendered institutions: From sex roles to gendered institutions. *Contemporary Sociology*, 21(5), 565–569. https://doi.org/10.2307/2075528

Althoff, M., Bereswill, M., & Riegraf, B. (2001). *Feministische Methodologie und Methoden. Tradition, Konzepte, Erörterungen.* Leske & Budrich.

Bohnenkamp, A., & Möbus, F. (2012). *Mit Gunst und Verlaub. Wandernde Handwerker: Tradition und alternative.* Erste Auflage 1989. Wallenstein Verlag.
Butler, J. (2004). *Undoing gender.* Routledge.
Cyba, E. (1993). Überlegungen zu einer Theorie Geschlechterspezifischer Ungleichheiten [Reflections on a theory of gender inequalities]. In P. Frerichs & M. Steinrücke (Eds.), *Soziale Ungleichheit und Geschlechterverhältnisse* [*Social inequality and gender relations*] (pp. 33–49). Leske & Budrich.
DeVault, M., & Gross, G. (2012). Feminist qualitative interviewing. Experience, talk, and knowledge. In S. N. Hesse-Biber, *The handbook of feminist research: Theory and praxis* (pp. 206–237). Sage Publications.
Elkar, R. S., Keller, K., & Schneider, H. (2014). *Handwerk. Von den Anfängen bis zur Gegenwart* [*Craft. From the beginning to the present*]. Konrad Theiss.
Fonow, M. M., & Cook, J. A. (2005). Feminist methodology: New applications in the academy and public policy. *Signs: Journal of Women in Culture and Society, 30*(4), 2211–2236.
Goffman, E. (1977). The arrangement between the sexes. *Theory and Society, 4*(3), 301–331.
Hanisch, C. (1969). *The personal is political.* http://www.carolhanisch.org/CHwritings/PIP.html
Harding, S. (1991). *Whose science? Whose knowledge? Thinking from women's lives.* Cornell University Press.
Hausen, K. (1976). Die Polarisierung der "Geschlechtscharaktere": Eine Spiegelung der Dissoziation von. Erwerbs- und Familienleben. In W. Conze (Ed.), *Sozialgeschichte der Familie in der Neuzeit Europas: Forschungen* (pp. 363–393). Klett-Cotta.
Mayer Hacker, H. (1951). Women as a minority group. *Social Forces, 30*(1), 60–69. https://doi.org/10.2307/2571742
Mies, M. (1983) Towards a methodology for feminist research. In G. Bowles & R. D. Klein, *Theories of women's studies* (pp. 117–139). Routledge.
Vosahlíková, P. (Ed.). (1994) *Auf der Walz. Erinnerungen Böhmischer Handwerksgesellen.* Böhlau.
West, C., & Zimmerman, D. H. (1987). Doing gender. *Gender and Society, 1*(2), 125–151.
Wharton, A. S. (2005). *The sociology of gender: An introduction to theory and research* (2nd ed.). Wiley-Blackwell.

CHAPTER 10
"MY BODY IS YOUR VEHICLE": MOTHERING, RELATIONALITY AND THE TRANSGENERATIONAL BOND IN JANINE ANTONI'S EMBODIED ART

Justyna Wierzchowska

Abstract

The chapter presents a study of Janine Antoni's art viewed through the lens of the transgenerational connection between the mother and the daughter. Born in 1964, American visual artist Janine Antoni combines performance art, sculpture and photography to explore the themes of human vulnerability and interconnectedness. In her work she often introduces traces of human bodily presence – typically her own, but also of other people – into received iconographies of Western art to recontextualise them along the lines of a situated, psycho-somatic experience. The chapter will discuss several works by the artist, including *Wean* (1990), *Momme* (1996), *Cradle* (1999), *Umbilical* (2000), *Inhabit* (2009), *Crowned* (2013a), and *Hearth* (2014), focusing on the articulation of the transgenerational bond between the mother and the daughter as defining for the formation and functioning of the female subject. It is argued that in these works, Antoni disrupts the notion of the self-reliant, autonomous and emotionally self-contained neoliberal subjectivity by bringing into light the historically dimmed yet foundational areas of the female identity-making; that is the mother–daughter transgenerational connection. Antoni's pieces are read as regenerative in their potential to enhance a critical discourse, as well as personal reflection that revisits, modifies and expands the ways in which female subjectivity can be thought by emphasising its transgenerational entanglement.

Key words: gender, tradition, travelling, craft, roles, sexism

Talking Bodies III

Introduction

> To be intimate with the object is to touch the viewer. […]
> I make art because it centers me in my body, and by
> doing so I hope to offer that experience to someone else.
> This direct physical experience is one of the rare things that
> art can offer in a culture of mediation. Janine Antoni
> (in conversation with Douglas Dreishpoon, 2009)
>
> The body is only made in relationship.
> Susie Orbach, 2004

This chapter examines selected works by American contemporary visual artist Janine Antoni focusing on the topic of the transgenerational bond. The transgenerational bond is understood as an emotional attachment that a child develops primarily through an embodied interaction with its adult caregivers. The chapter argues that Antoni's works articulate the fact that a nourishing and supportive transgenerational bond may become the bedrock of our self-making and our comfortable inhabiting of our bodies. To advance its claims, the chapter draws on two interrelated schools of developmental psychology: John Bowlby's attachment theory and Donald Woods Winnicott's conceptualisation of good-enough mothering. Attachment theory asserts that "from the beginning of life, the baby human has a primary need to establish an emotional bond with a caregiving adult" (Laschinger, 2004, pp. xviii–xix) and that this bond forms a blueprint of one's future relational pattern. "One of the richest contributions to our understanding of human development is the concept that the quality of relationships we develop in infancy plays a critical role in future relationships throughout the lifespan", observes Bowlby (cited in Talley, 2018, p. 16; see also Hazan & Shaver, 1987). Concurrently, Donald Winnicott has developed an influential theory that spells out the foundational significance of good-enough mothering for the human life.

Despite his awareness that the primary caregiver does not have to be the child's (biological) mother, in his writings he tends to use the

"My body is your vehicle"

term 'mother', for which he has been criticised. In 1967, in response to Lacan's famous essay on the mirror stage, Winnicott (1967) posited that "in individual emotional development the precursor of the mirror is the mother's face" (Winnicott, 1967, p. 149; see also Wierzchowska, 2019). For Winnicott, contrary to Lacan, it is not the mirror but the mother's eyes that form one's initial anchor point in the maze of the primarily undifferentiated experience. Crucially, for Winnicott, with the mother's eyes comes her body; it is the mother's technique "of holding, of bathing, of feeding, everything she [does] for the baby" (Winnicott, 1973, p. 194) that add up to the child's first idea of the other and which form the child's sense of its selfhood (Winnicott, 1973, pp. 191–194). All these activities create in his view a 'holding environment', that is one which facilitates the child's development by gradually lessening the caregiver's adaptation according to the child's "growing ability to account for failure of adaptation and to tolerate the results of frustration" (Winnicott, 1953/2005, pp. 13–14; 1960). For both attachment theory and for Winnicott, the body is the original channel of relation-making since the child's emotional bonding predates the acquisition of language. What is more, the developments within neuropsychology have revealed that, as Allan Schore observes, the child's relational experience contributes to the shaping of its brain (in Laschinger, 2004, p. xx). One's relational history impacts not only one's ability to form meaningful relationships but is also organically imprinted in one's body.

When discussing transgenerationality and the primary bond, this chapter uses the terms 'mothering', 'mothering desire' and 'affects'. The term 'mothering', should not be understood as a skill attributed solely to (biological) mothers. Following Sara Ruddick's observations put forward in her classic *Maternal Thinking* (1989), mothering is discussed here as a *practice* open to anyone who makes a durational commitment to nurture, protect and socialise a child (pp. 61–103). Also, Winnicott (1960), who predominantly writes about the biological mother, remarks that mothering can be carried out by any adult person who makes a long-term commitment to provide a child with a holding environment. The term 'mothering desire' relates to a longing for such a practice of care. Affects are understood as an innate disposition of the body to experience visceral precognitive stirrings in reaction to events and to cause such stirrings in other bodies ('to affect and be affected', Massumi, 1987, 2002; Brennan, 2004). The chapter highlights the fact that an adult's affective make-up is primarily formed by their early mothering experience, or that the type of care one has received in early childhood has a defining impact on one's future sense of one's own embodiment, one's affective economy, and one's relational pattern.

Within the field of cultural studies, there is a relative scarcity of scholarship that approaches the body as extending across the generations not only as a biological composite of its parents and a (biological) provider for its child, but also as a site of relationality the formation of which starts in prelinguistic infancy through an embodied interaction with a caregiver. If authors undertake the topic of the transgenerational transfer of relationality, they usually focus on matters bound to transgenerational trauma (Bakó & Zana, 2020). The output they produce forms a growing volume of scholarship carried out within the fields of memory studies and trauma studies, often inspired by the sombre legacy of the Holocaust. In these studies, transgenerationality is applied as a lens to examine the lives of the descendants of the Holocaust survivors who vicariously participate in their ancestors' trauma. These people often carry an affective burden that is lodged in their bodies. It manifests itself as, for example, their excessive anxiety-proneness, prolonging depression, or emotional withdrawal. Marianne Hirsch's *Family Frames: Photography, Narrative, and Postmemory* or Mikołaj Grynberg's *Oskarżam Auschwitz* [*I Accuse Auschwitz*] are just two autobiographically motivated examples that illustrate the ways in which trauma trickles down across generations, penetrating the deepest corporeal levels of the human self (Hirsch, 1997; Grynberg, 2014).

This chapter proposes to explore the other pole of the transgenerational bond. Contrary to the scholarship on transgenerational trauma, it centres on transgenerationality in its

"My body is your vehicle"

positive dimension. It close-reads selected works by Janine Antoni, focusing on the body as a central locus of relation-making. Like memory studies, attachment theory and Winnicott's conceptualisations, the chapter premises that, throughout our life, our bodies are engaged in transgenerational conversations that shape our personal and social engagements. Thus it reads Antoni's selected installations, sculptures and photographs as articulating relationality formed through a durational process of embodied communication and care. As we will see, some of the analysed works demonstrate the body's indebtedness to another body, others explore the practices of care. Most of them are highly suggestive of the fact that it is thanks to a nourishing primary bond that an adult person can safely enjoy affective mutuality and feel at home in one's body. Finally, the chapter argues that Antoni's works encourage us to peel off the cultural prosthesis of symbolic meanings and reconnect with our body as an irreducible site of communication and (self-)care.

Antoni, born in 1964, has for over thirty years been creating an autobiographically motivated art that uses the trope of the fragile body to recontextualise well-established tropes of Western art along the lines of relationality. Her artistic interventions feature the body not as a perfected (and dead) ideal, but as a vulnerable and mortal site of relation-making. In some of her pieces, it is the artist's own body that comes into contact with "malleable materials and spaces" while "her mouth, tongue, eyelashes and hair [become] evocative replacements for chisels, pencils and brushes" (Horodner, 1999, p. 48). In others, it is not the body, but its traces that form the pivot of the work's scenario. Antoni is well aware of the fact that humans are made at the threshold of the embodied and the symbolised and thus, as Nancy Princenthal (2001) observes, she "intertwines personal history and art history, psychology and biology" (Princenthal, 2001, p. 126). Or, in the words of Sidonie Smith (2002), the artist "confront[s] regimes of visuality" with her "body and autobiographical subjectivity" (Smith, 2002, p. 134). By doing so, she enriches them with an awareness of the human organic and affective interconnectedness. "All my objects mediate our intimate

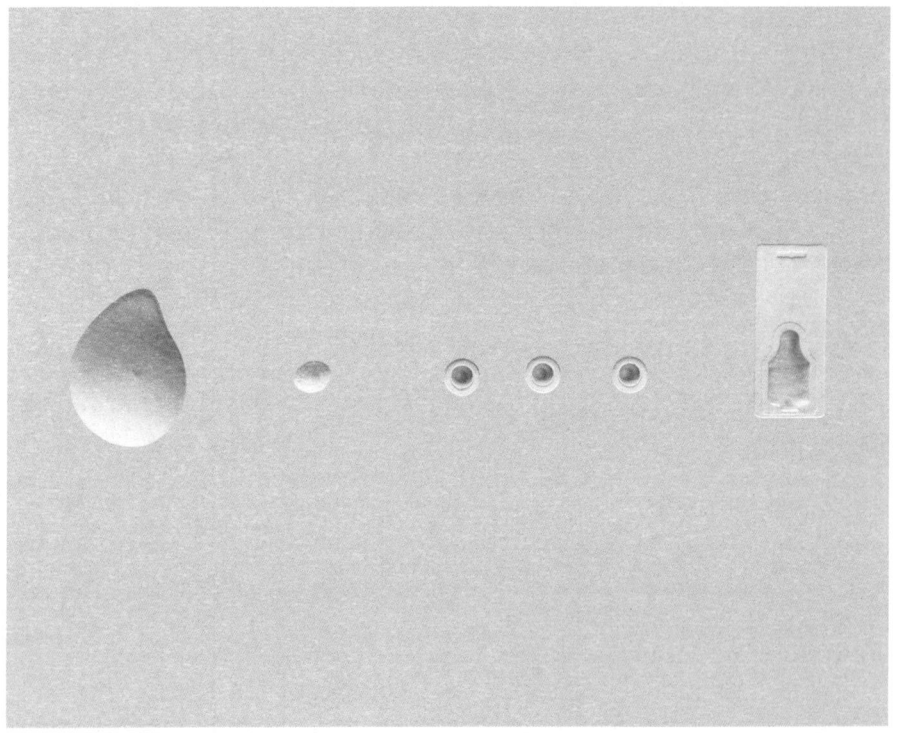

Figure 1: Janine Antoni, *Wean*, 1989/90. Plaster, sheet rock, 12 x 38 x 2 inches (30.48 x 96.52 x 5.08 cm) © Janine Antoni. Courtesy of the artist and Luhring Augustine, New York.

interaction with our bodies", Antoni explains, "or they are objects that replace the body, or that somehow define the body within the culture" (in Enright & Walsh, 2010, p. 40). For Antoni, the legacy of Western art and culture becomes both "a problem and a source of illumination" (Karamitsos, 2006, p. 5), capable of welcoming new meanings that have a potential to advance changes in human sociality. Antoni's early installation *Wean* (Figure 1), created just after graduate school in 1990, quite gingerly beckons towards relationality. Inspired by the child's organic dependency on the primary caregiver, *Wean* consists of six objects associated with the nourishment of the infant which trace the process of weaning. The first object is a plaster cast of Antoni's breast, the second is a cast of her nipple, the next three are latex nipples and the last one is a packaging that latex nipples come in. The arrangement of the objects indexes the disappearance of the maternal body into the field of images and signs, as the breast is gradually replaced by the bottle; the two semantically unified by the word 'nipple'. The piece dialogises with the minimal and conceptual tradition, epitomised by the *oeuvre* of Joseph Kosuth. In his famous piece *One and Three Chairs* (1965), like Antoni, Kosuth plays with the concepts of the signified and signifier. Yet, while Kosuth moves within the symbolic field of the Platonic split between the Idea and the *mimesis*, Antoni brings in the temporal singularity of her own corporeal detail that marks organic relationality (it is capable of feeding a child). *Wean* also references Mary Kelly's seminal *Post-Partum Document* (1973-1979), which documents the first six years of the artist's son through a series of "weanings" (Kelly's term): from the breast, from the holophrase and from the maternal dyad (Kelly, 1983, p. 209). Just like Kelly, in *Wean*, Antoni challenges the alleged disembodiment of the Lacanian Symbolic by demonstrating language's anchorage in the body; the 'nipple' denotes both an anatomical detail of the mother's body and its substitute, a piece of rubber that tops a feeding bottle. Both imply a practice of care that allows for a flow of nutritious fluids from the mother into the baby's body. The rubber nipple is an extension of the corporeal proximity through which the child's affective disposition is initially formed. *Wean* thus supports Kate White's observation (2004) that "affect and meaning-making emerges through relationship" (White, 2004, p. xxiv), highlighting its corporeal, pre-linguistic genealogy. Antoni emphasises *Wean*'s relational dimension: "it's about disconnection and separation from the mother – that's what *Wean* is about. It's wanting to stay connected and be independent at the same time, the lengthening of the umbilical cord" (in Jinker-Lloyd, 1996, p. 5). By emphasising the continuation of the maternal presence in culture, Antoni both challenges the Lacanian tradition (Lacan, 1949; Kristeva,

1987) and asserts that it is the primary bond that forms an irreducible foundation of the developing life (Winnicott, 1953/2005, 1960, 1967, 1973; Bowlby, 1988). Yet, the title and the arrangement of the six objects (the gradual disappearance of the maternal body into language and culture) suggest that *Wean* is more about the mourning of the maternal than about its affirmation, which affiliates the piece with the tradition of the second wave.

The affirmative dominant of relationality becomes ever more pronounced in Antoni's works created since the mid-1990s. In these pieces, the artist explores relationality as closely linked to the matters of the primary bond and the transgenerational transfer of affect. To do so, Antoni uses her own life experience as an attractive, or even seductive, site of enquiry into the foundations of the human condition. She draws from her being a daughter and – later – a mother to a daughter to explore transgenerational bonding as a formative experience that surpasses biological relations and gender. These works seem to announce that it is the *experience* of being mothered (nurtured, protected and socialised), especially in the early, predominantly corporeal phase, that is lived and creatively modified throughout one's adult life. Antoni's works also demonstrate that, as Susan Orbach (2004) puts it, there is "no such thing as a body, there is only a body in relationship with another body" (p. 28), encouraging us to recognise the centrality of bonding and the practice of care for the human life and integrate our body "with the experience of the world" (Antoni in Reiman, 2015, p. 24).

The 1995 photographic piece *Momme* (Figure 2) makes the above claims evident. The picture features a woman serenely sitting by a window, hands resting next to what seems to be her full-term pregnant belly. The image sends messages to the aesthetic of Vermeer, Hopper and to the genre of the portraiture, rendering *Momme* a legitimate participant of the Western canon. "I wanted [*Momme*] to look normal, almost familiar, like a Vermeer painting", says Antoni (in Jinker-Lloyd, 1996, p. 3). Yet, upon closer scrutiny, it becomes clear that *Momme* is a Trojan horse. When analysed closely, the photo becomes intriguing, as there is an additional foot emerging from beneath the mother's gown.

"My body is your vehicle"

Figure 2: Janine Antoni, *Momme*, 1995. C-print, artist's frame, 36 x 29 inches (91.4 x 73.7 cm) © Janine Antoni. Courtesy of the artist and Luhring Augustine, New York.

In fact, the photo features Antoni's mother and a grown-up Antoni hiding between her legs. Unlike Louise Bourgeois' ambivalent *Maman* (a vastly oversized spider sculpture created from bronze, stainless steel and marble), Antoni's *Momme* celebrates mothering in its positive dimensions. On the one hand, the image suggests that the human life is an extension of the organic union during pregnancy. On a deeper level, the mother/daughter hybrid seems to imply that, as Susie Orbach (2004) notes, our body, "like our psychic properties and potentialities, emerges out of the emotional ambience and bodily interaction with our caregivers". What is more, Orbach contends that our "personal body unfolds and develops its individuality in the context of its relationship to and with another and other bodies" (p. 23). Echoing Orbach's observations, *Momme* features mothering as a lifelong desire which, if supportive, can be longed for and safely enjoyed into adulthood.

Figure 3: Janine Antoni, *Coddle*, 1999. C-print, hand-carved frame, 21 1/2 x 16 inches (54.61 x 40.64 cm) © Janine Antoni. Courtesy of the artist and Luhring Augustine, New York.

"My body is your vehicle"

The 1999 *Coddle* (Figure 3) makes the mothering desire similarly pronounced and, in this case, self-referential. This cibachrome print uses the iconic image of the Virgin Mary and child to probe the topic of how the mothering desire continues throughout one's life. This image features a seated Antoni, tenderly embracing her own shin reminiscent of baby Jesus at his mother's breast. The piece visualises mothering as a capacity that can be both internalised and acted out in a gesture of self-care. The artist comments on the making of *Coddle* in the following way: "I am struck by two simultaneous desires: to hold and to be held. I see my foot as other because it is the furthest point from my heart. To bring my leg back up into my chest not only brings me back to the fetal position, but also to a loving encounter, an opportunity to remother myself" (Antoni, n.d.a). Antoni's words describe the mothering desire in a way that carries far-reaching philosophical and psychological implications, put forward by Julia Kristeva (1987) in reference to Freud's famous question. Instead of asking "What does the woman want?" Kristeva asks: "What does the mother want?" (p. 41). The answer is both straightforward and profound: she wants her mother. Antoni articulates this exact condition reminiscing on da Vinci's drawing titled *Saint Anne and the Virgin*. In this image, Antoni notes, da Vinci captures "the poignant moment of a mother relating to her daughter as a mother. ... Mary is both mother and child" (in Princenthal, 2001, p. 128). This transgenerational character of the human condition emerges as the core of Antoni's artistic practice, as the objects of art become "surrogates for [her] own body and [her] desire to be in contact"(in Reiman, 2015, p. 24).

The theme of the transgenerational bond is further brought forward in a sculptural object created in 1999 and titled *Cradle* (Figure 4, overleaf). Executed in a cool minimalistic format of a metal sculpture, the piece shares with *Coddle* the trope of holding oneself; stretched in this case across many generations. The piece features eight diminishing in size spoon-objects, cradled one inside another, creating one object that is holding itself. The smallest object is a baby loop spoon, the largest – a rusty bulldozer scoop, and in between them

Figure 4: Janine Antoni, *Cradle,* 1999 (detail). Two tons of steel, 59 x 58 x 60.5 inches (149.9 x 147.3 x 153.7 cm). Photographed by Larry Lamay. © Janine Antoni. Courtesy of the artist and Luhring Augustine, New York.

there are a teaspoon, tablespoon, ash scoop, two diminishing in size shovels and a digger scoop. All the spoons originate from the rear half of the bulldozer bucket which encapsulates all the spoon-objects inside. With their common material origin and the nestling structure, *Cradle* can be read as transgenerationally connected. The spoons form a Matryoshka-like structure, where the smallest baby-spoon is cradled by a bigger one, which in its turn is cradled by another. The biggest spoon embraces all of them; a playful metaphor of the Primordial Mother conjured up in the era of technology. Just like the Primordial Mother, a digger scoop has the ability to create and destroy and relates to earth.

"My body is your vehicle"

What is more, *Cradle* breaches the gap between nature, technology and domesticity, since the spoons take on a multiple meaning of baby-spoon, baby-cot and building equipment, one nestled within the other. The piece clashes the connotative fields of the cradle and of heavy-duty machinery and brings them together by a gradual transformation of the digger-spoon into a baby-spoon that the piece features. As Amy Cappellazzo (2000) notes:

> If English were a gendered language, the words for bucket, shovel and spoon would all be female. There is a seeming matrilineage to these forms – each is a vessel of one sort or another. Their respective jobs are to carry, hold, give, serve and feed. The function of these tools closely parallels the role of the female body during motherhood – to carry, hold, give, serve and feed. (p. 114)

However, contrary to Cappellazzo, I would argue that *Cradle* bridges biological and gender divides by suggesting that mothering is a practice open to all. The piece may cause an initial epistemic shock, since it combines childcare and the construction industry, which are two spheres of human activity that are traditionally heavily gendered. The dissonance with childcare is strengthened by the piece's minimal-conceptual aesthetic and material (metal), epitomising emotional detachment, durability and the masculine character of Western art. What is more, the bulldozer bucket suggests excruciating physical work, something that many may not associate with taking care of children. Yet, the transgenerational cuddling of the consecutive spoons – the bulldozer bucket included – overcomes this cultural disjunction, suggests that mothering is a heavy-duty job and recognises a systemic significance of the original bond which stretches across generations and genders.

Additionally, even though Antoni maintains that the baby spoon at the centre of *Cradle* "exposes the tension between the need for separation and the need to be held" (in Princenthal, 2001, p. 128), I would take the interpretation further. The fact that the loop spoon, designed for the baby to begin feeding itself, is transgenerationally 'held' by the remaining seven spoon-objects, makes *Cradle* Winnicottian. The sculpture makes a point about the significance of a supporting environment in advancing the child's exploration of the world and mastering survival skills. Viewed this way, *Cradle* exposes a critical fact that our bodies are enveloped in an affectivity handed down to us by our predecessors. Building on Winnicott's famous statement that "there is no such thing as a baby" (Winnicott, 1960, p. 587), we can revisit Susie Orbach's (2004) suggestion that there is "no such thing as a body, there is only a body in relationship with another body"

Figure 5: Janine Antoni, *Umbilical*, 2000. Cast sterling silver of family silverware and negative impressions of artist's mouth and mother's hand, 8 x 3 x 3 inches (20.32 x 7.62 x 7.62 cm). Photographed by John Bessler. © Janine Antoni. Courtesy of the artist and Luhring Augustine, New York.

"My body is your vehicle"

(Orbach, 2004, p. 28). *Cradle* poignantly illustrates the transgenerational dimension of this claim. The fact that all the objects are reminiscent of one another and originate from one piece of metal underscores their interconnectedness and transgenerational support.

Transgenerationality is also central in another spoon-themed sculptural piece, the small object *Umbilical* of 2000 (Figure 5). Like *Momme*, *Umbilical* directly derives from Antoni's biographical experience. This "embodied sculptural autobiography", to use Sidonie Smith's term (Smith, 2002, p. 151), consists of a casting in silver of the inside of the artist's mouth (like a dental mould) and the space inside her mother's hand, linked by a cast replica of a silver spoon. This spoon, however, is different from the spoon-objects in *Cradle*. In Western culture, the silver spoon, through the genre of the still life and the aristocratic connotations of the silverware, is a very much clichéd image of cultural sophistication and inherited affluence, expressed in the phrase of 'having been born with a silver spoon in one's mouth'. *Umbilical* both recognises this genealogy and puts it to a novel task. Featuring anatomical details of Antoni and her mother, and tellingly titled *Umbilical*, the piece follows a maternal, not paternal orientation. By representing the mother–daughter bond in the negative (the silver casting renders their bodies vicariously present, but materially absent), *Umbilical* recognises Luce Irigaray's (1991) argument of the mother–daughter relation constituting the "silent substratum of the social order" (Irigaray, 1991, pp. 47–52; see also Hirsch, 1981, 1989; Braidotti & Camponi, 1982). At the same time, like *Wean*, the piece can be viewed as a metaphor of the ongoing maternal nourishment that stems from the early mother–child transfer of nutritive fluids and which is later extended via the use of culturally sanctioned prostheses that form a build-up on the organic origin. *Umbilical* expresses the value of such nourishment not in economic terms, but in terms of a transgenerational transfer of care, which, even though little visible in culture (the casts are negatives of the actual bodies and the silver spoon has economic value), remains solidly and permanently welded into the material structure of the object. As such, the piece showcases "the critical role of physical interactions between care-giver and child in feeding, soothing, and handling in shaping the experience of self and other" (Laschinger, 2004, p. xvii) and welcomes us to, as Joshua Reiman (2015) beautifully put it, "understand where [our] body is in relation to gestures frozen into forms of loving care" (Reiman, 2015, p. 23).

Like the previously discussed works, *Umbilical* references past art to widen the spectrum of representation and stir social awareness. The piece replicates the gesture of Mary Kelly (1983) who, in *Post-Partum Document*, displayed a series of eight photos of her baby son's hand cast in plaster (Kelly, 1983, pp. 97–108). Yet, by structuring *Umbilical* around the silver spoon, Antoni not only publicises lived mothering, but also challenges the dominant understanding of what it means to inherit. This piece temporalises the silverware, as the silver spoon not only indexes inherited wealth, but becomes an instrument of care that is both essential (the baby existentially depends on its caregiver) and temporarily ephemeral (the baby eventually learns how to feed itself). The two bodies whose details *Umbilical* preserves go on evolving, connected by a nutritious relationship, Antoni seems to suggest, their warmth uncannily encapsulated in the cold metal moulds. This interpretation harmonises with Antoni's more general observation on the warmth of the human bodies: "It's always a profound experience for me to sit down in the subway and feel the warmth of the person who sat there before me. Some people might be repelled, but for me, it's really comforting that, on some basic level, we all produce warmth" (in Dreishpoon, 2009, p. 124). Sidonie Smith (2002) picks up on the ambiguity of the void created by a vanished bodily presence noting in the context of other Antoni's works, that the bodies disappear "only to reemerge as bodily processes worked through the psychic mechanisms of desire" (Smith, 2002, p. 151). David Rau (2001) similarly writes of *Cradle* that it is "the seemingly tangible presence of what is missing that is the most revealing" (Rau, 2001, p. 58). Both *Umbilical* and *Cradle*, by featuring the bodily presence through objects that emblematise the mothering connection, illustrate the transgenerational relay of self-making. In that, the pieces analogise Nancy Chodorow's

"My body is your vehicle"

(1978) important observation that "mothering is reproduced across generations" (Chodorow, 1978, p. 3).

Two more photographic pieces are more unambivalently celebratory of the transgenerational connection. *Mom and Dad* (1994) features Antoni's parents photographed in the convention of the family album photo. The piece consists of three images, reminiscent of the triptych, where each image presents a double portrait and uses prosthetic make-up to play with gender. On the left-hand side, both Antoni's parents pose as her Dad, the centre piece reverses their genders, and on the right-hand side they are both turned into the artist's Mom. Additionally, *Mom and Dad* radicalises the assertion of the transgenerational foundation of the human self by Antoni claiming the piece to be her "self-portrait" (in Jinker-Lloyd, 1996, p. 3). The piece traverses gender divides and suggests that mothering care is an egalitarian practice, sanctified by the religious connotations of the triptych. The other photograph, *One Another* (2008), which features Antoni's little daughter holding a plastic spoon and feeding her mother's belly button, also recognises transgenerationality as an inherent element of the self. In a 2010 interview, Antoni describes her belly button as her daughter's transitional object in the Winnicottian sense: "She [Antoni's daughter] calls my belly her belly. 'Give me my belly,' she says." The artist also remembers the circumstances of how *One Another* was made:

> One time when I was feeding [my daughter] she wanted to feed my belly button. I was struck by the spirit of reciprocity in her gesture. ... Also, she was making my work. I can't claim that piece. Somehow she becomes the mother and her gesture, like an umbilical cord, turns me into a fetus. Certainly having a child has made me grateful to my own mother because you don't know what it takes until you do it.
> (Antoni in Enright & Walsh, 2010, p. 41)

Mothering thus is both a creative exercise in repetition and an opportunity to use the newly acquired mothering skills as an act of self-care, since, as Winnicott maintains "mothering your child is an

Talking Bodies III

Figure 6 (left): Janine Antoni, *Crowned*, 2013. Plaster molding with plaster pelvic bones. Dimensions variable, site-transferrable installation. Installation view at Anthony Meier Fine Arts, San Francisco, 2015. © Janine Antoni. Courtesy of the artist, Luhring Augustine, New York and Anthony Meier Fine Arts, San Francisco.

Figure 7 (right): Janine Antoni, *Rosa*, 2014. Pit fired ceramic, 18.5 x 13.5 x in. (46.99 x 34.29 cm). © Janine Antoni. Courtesy of the artist and Luhring Augustine, New York.

opportunity to re-mother yourself" (Antoni in Enright & Walsh, 2010, p. 41).

The more recent sculptural art works, *Crowned* (2013a) and a set of three similar sculptures, *Martha* (2013b), *Hearth* (2014) and *Rosa* (2014) demonstrate, arguably more than other Antoni's pieces, the fact that

"My body is your vehicle"

"two persons in relation are two bodies in relation" (Laschinger, 2004, p. xx). These sculptures (Figures 6 and 7) imprint material objects – clay and plaster – with the corporeality of the mother and the child during giving birth/being born. Until today in Western culture, this central experience in the human life remains both tabooed and strongly medicalised, which are defensive mechanisms against the realm of the body. In *Maternal Thinking*, Sara Ruddick (1989) writes:

> the idealization of reason in Western philosophy may be in part a defensive reaction to the troubling complexities of birthing labor, that Western conceptions of what it is to be reasonable are intertwined with a fear and resentment of birthing female bodies. ... [T]he Man of Reason is nearly the opposite of a birthing woman-infant couple.
> (Ruddick, 1989, p. 195)

Unlike the Man of Reason, Antoni does not shy away from the concreteness of birth. She closely focuses on the topography of the bone movement, as the two bodies co-operate during the birthing effort. *Martha*, *Hearth* and *Rosa* universalise the birthing experience by being shaped like vessels typical of various cultures and times (*Martha* is a Greek amphora, *Rosa* a Chinese Ding dish and *Hearth* is a set of three culturally indistinct interconnected bowls). All these vessels bear a material imprint of the bones which are key in labour: the pelvic bones, the sacrum, the coccyx. The vessels have been shaped by dragging a bone through the wet clay as the moulded vessel rotated on the wheel. The three bowls in *Hearth*, additionally, present the temporality of the birthing process, as they trace the sequence of the bones' movements when the mother's sacrum moves back to allow the baby's head to pass through the birth canal. In *Martha*, *Hearth* and *Rosa*, it is the labour of the bones that gives the vessel its final form, complete with handles shaped like the bones that have produced that form. These 'pelvic vessels', which, as Stephanie Ann Karamitsos (2006) aptly puts it, "leave in their wake the mute traces of the laboring body" (Karamitsos, 2006, p. 90), constitute material metaphors of a relationality that gives birth: two bodies must collaborate for the child to be born. This natal collaboration may be thought as prototypical for relationality as such, which often involves pain and commitment, yet is transformative.

Crowned forms a conspicuous appendix to the pelvic vessels. It uses a pair of plaster hipbones to form an architectural moulding that encircles the room. Antoni replicates here the historical technique of making plaster moulding, which involved pulling a tool along wet plaster until it acquired a smooth surface and the desired shape. Yet, instead of using traditional tools and aiming at a flawless form, Antoni uses a pair of hipbones, lets the plaster spill and splatter, and renders the tools-bones an integral part of the moulding. What is more, the position of the bones captures a defining moment during childbirth called crowning when "two forms, the baby's head and the mother's hips, negotiate one another for a successful birth" (Antoni in Vogel, 2016, p. 44). At that moment, she notes, the mother's pelvic bones resemble a crown encircling the baby's head (in Belcove, 2015). Antoni thus intervenes into aristocratic tropes and crafts with a messy presence of the birthing body, integrating its trace into traditionally aristocratic architecture. At the same time, this messiness is intertwined with the durational: Antoni notes that the "sacrum is the root of your spine. It's the thickest bone in your body, and it's the last bone to disintegrate" (in Reiman, 2015, p. 24). Just like in *Umbilical*, she claims a different heritage for the human body and validates it with royal signifiers that are culturally far removed from it or even hostile.

This intervention is further strengthened by Antoni's teasing linguistic signification. The sacrum, the crowning, the coccyx (a vestige of the primordial tail) send messages that recast religious, monarchic and phallic signifiers in a new light, opening them to new and possibly liberating interpretations. *Crowned* seems to remind us that it is the womb that is our first form of architecture (Antoni, n.d.b.), while *Martha*, *Rosa* and *Hearth*'s hybridity connects the fragility of the bones with the classical status of the vessel shapes. Antoni artistically turns the birthing negotiation between the child's and the mother's bodies into a visual prompt that boldly introduces the bodies in relation as a prototype of art making: "Because I'm a sculptor, I think of crowning

"My body is your vehicle"

as a sculptural moment of compromise" (Antoni in Vogel, 2016, p. 44). Antoni approaches relationality as what predates the culturally constructed idea of the self or subject, as the mutual effort of the mother and the baby becomes her primary metaphor of sculpture. Antoni follows Ruddick's (1989) observation that "birth implies life-shaping responsibilities to particular vulnerable others", while "reason enables people to ... contemplate without responsibility in rooms of their own" (Ruddick, 1989, p. 195). Stretching this connectivity onto a human lifespan, as numerous Antoni works indicate, the pelvic sculptures are then illustrative of Winnicott's (1958) claim that the "ego-supportive environment is introjected and built into the individual's personality" (Winnicott, 1958, p. 35) and the body is experienced as "the place wherein one securely lives" (Winnicott, 1973, p. 194). In light of Ruddick's and Winnicott's words, Antoni's recent pieces seem like manifestos for a more ready recognition of the culturally dimmed areas of human vulnerability, relationality and capacity for mutual commitment.

Conclusion
Antoni's gesture to stamp objects with her own bodily presence lends them a sense of temporality, intimacy, relationality and human co-dependence, all integral elements of her artistic practice. Martha Buskirk (2003) provides a meaningful perspective on Antoni's embodied art: "The touch or mark is not simply a vehicle for creating an aesthetic effect; rather, recognition of the mark itself and its relation to the body of the artist is central to the message of the work" (Buskirk, 2003, p. 7). Antoni's fusing of the public/permanent with the personal/ephemeral has not been the main currency in Western art and thus expands the horizon of the artistic practice, art discourse and, more broadly, the conceptualisation of the human self. Antoni's works, through the artist's engagement with her singular, embodied experience, such as the transgenerational connection with her mother, interrogate the neoliberal notion of subjectivity as self-reliant, autonomous and emotionally self-contained. Antoni's art is strategically informed by

the iconography of Western art and culture to enhance a shift in our thinking that revisits, modifies and expands the ways in which selfhood and relationality can be theorised. Returning to Susie Orbach's (2004) statement, Antoni's art reminds us that:

> Our body, like our psychic properties and potentialities, emerges out of the emotional ambience and bodily interaction with our caregivers. Our personal body unfolds and develops its individuality in the context of its relationship to and with an other and other bodies. (p. 23)

Antoni's pieces do more than present, as Sidonie Smith (2002) puts it, a "cultural critique through self-referential display" (Smith, 2002, p. 134). In *Coddle*, *Cradle* and *Umbilical*, Antoni enriches the efforts, covertly present in Schneemann's and Mendieta's *oeuvre*, to assert the significance of the primary bond. In a truly transgenerational gesture, the pieces vocalise what the second-wave feminist artists pioneered yet did not not fully articulate, that is the topic of a transgenerational transmission of affect and relational bond, formed through the labour of care, that is a practice of durational commitment that includes nurturance, protection and socialising (Ruddick, 1989). Antoni's works demonstrate that we can – and, in fact, should – think the body transgenerationally, not only because of the crude fact of its being a composite of people who came before it, but also because of the continuous emotional and social support that delivers the body into the place the body occupies and, rudimentarily, makes it what it is.

Antoni's works, most prominently exhibited in *Cradle*, celebrate "the strength and resilience of intergenerational solidarity over time", reminding us that "parenting goes across several generations" (Bengtson, 2001, pp. 1, 6). Some of her most intimate pieces articulate Jung's (1969) belief that "Every mother contains her daughter within herself, and every daughter her mother. [...] Every woman extends backwards into her mother and forwards into her daughter" (in Hirsch, 1981, p. 209). In short, Antoni's art probes the potentiality of the aesthetic field to bridge the gap between the mind and the body and promote human connectedness and interdependence.

"My body is your vehicle"

Author biography

Justyna Wierzchowska is Associate Professor at the Institute of English Studies, University of Warsaw. She holds MA degrees in American Studies and Philosophy, and a PhD in American Studies. She combines psychoanalysis and affect theory to explore the relational and affective dimensions of subjectivity that are manifested in contemporary European and American visual art and culture. Dr Wierzchowska is a recipient of the Fulbright Commission Senior Scholar Award to conduct research at New York University for the academic year 2019–2020. She is the author of *The Absolute and the Cold War: Discourses of Abstract Expressionism* (2011), co-editor of *In Other Words: Dialogizing Postcoloniality, Race, and Ethnicity* (2012) and of the special issue *On Uses of Black Camp* (2018). She also authors numerous academic articles published in Poland and abroad that focus on the manifestations of the mothering function in contemporary visual art. She teaches courses in philosophy, American art history, art theory, feminist art and cultural studies. She translates into Polish American modern fiction and art-related books.

References

Antoni, J. (1989/90) *Wean* [Plaster, sheet rock]. *Janine Antoni official website* janineantoni.net/#/wean/

Antoni, J. (1994). *Mom and Dad*. [Cibachrome triptych, artist's frames]. *Janine Antoni official website*. http://www.janineantoni.net/#/new-page-1/

Antoni, J. (1995). *Momme* [C-print, artist's frame]. *Janine Antoni official website*. http://www.janineantoni.net/#/momme/

Antoni, J. (1999a). *Coddle* [C-print]. *Janine Antoni official website*. http://www.janineantoni.net/#/coddle/

Antoni, J. (1999b). *Cradle* [Steel]. *Janine Antoni official website*. http://www.janineantoni.net/#/cradle/

Antoni, J. (2000). *Umbilical* [Cast sterling silver of family silverware and negative impressions of artist's mouth and mother's hand]. *Janine Antoni official website*. http://www.janineantoni.net/#/umbilical/

Antoni, J. (1994). *One another*. [C-print, artist's frame]. *Janine Antoni official website*. http://www.janineantoni.net/#/one-another/

Antoni, J. (2009). *Inhabit* [Digital C-print, artist's frame]. *Janine Antoni official website*. http://www.janineantoni.net/#/inhabit/
Antoni, J. (2013a). *Crowned* [Plaster molding]. *Janine Antoni official website*. http://www.janineantoni.net/#/crowned/
Antoni, J. (2013b). *Martha* [Pit fired ceramic]. *Janine Antoni official website*. http://www.janineantoni.net/#/martha/
Antoni, J. (2014). *Hearth* [Set of three pit fired ceramic vessels]. *Janine Antoni official website*. http://www.janineantoni.net/#/hearth/
Bakó, T., & Zana, K. (2020). *Transgenerational trauma and therapy: The transgenerational atmosphere*. Taylor & Francis.
Belcove, J. L. (2015, 27 February). Artist Janine Antoni takes on childbirth and the female body in two new shows. *The Cut*. https://www.thecut.com/2015/02/veteran-feminist-artist-takes-on-childbirth.html
Bengtson, V. L. (2001, February). Beyond the nuclear family: The increasing importance of multigenerational bonds. *Journal of Marriage and Family, 63*, 1–16.
Bowlby, J. (1988). *A secure base: Parent-child attachment and healthy human development*. Tavistock.
Braidotti, R., & Camponi, M. (1982). Mothers/daughters/feminists: The darkest continent. *Refractory Girl, 23*, 9–12.
Brennan, T. (2004). *The transmission of affect*. Cornell University Press.
Buskirk, M. (2003). *The contingent object of contemporary art*. MIT Press.
Cappellazzo, A. (2000). Mother lode. In J. Antoni, N. Spector, D. Cameron, E. Lajer-Burcharth, M. Warner, A. Cappellazzo, & R. Martinez (Eds.), *Janine Antoni* (pp. 102–121). Ink Tree.
Chodorow, N. J. (1978). *The reproduction of mothering: Psychoanalysis and the sociology of gender*. University of California Press.
Dreishpoon, D. (2009, October). Janine Antoni in conversation, *Art in America*, 122–128.
Enright, R., & Walsh, M. (2010, March). The beautiful trap: Janine Antoni's body art. *Border Crossings, 113*, 38–54.
Grynberg, M. (2014). *Oskarżam Auschwitz. Opowieści rodzinne*. Wydawnictwo Czarne.
Hazan, C., & Shaver, P. (1987). Romantic love conceptualized as an attachment process. *Journal of Personality and Social Psychology, 52*, 511–524.
Hirsch, M. (1981). Mothers and daughters. *Signs, 7*(1), 200–222. http://dx.doi.org/10.1086/493870

"My body is your vehicle"

Hirsch, M. (1989). *The mother/daughter plot: Narrative, psychoanalysis, feminism*. Indiana University Press.
Hirsch, M. (1997). *Family frames: Photography, narrative, and postmemory*. Harvard University Press.
Horodner, S., & Antoni, J. (1999). Janine Antoni. *BOMB, 66*, 48–54.
Irigaray, L. (1991). Women-mothers, the silent substratum of the social order (David Macey, Trans.). In M. Whitford (Ed.), *The Irigaray reader* (pp. 47–52). Blackwell.
Jinker-Lloyd, A. (1996, March/April). Chewing the fat with Janine Antoni, *Art Papers, 19*, 2–7.
Jung, C. G. (1969). The psychological aspects of the Kore (R. F. C. Hull, Trans.). In C. G. Jung & C. Kerényi, *Essays on a science of mythology: The myths of the divine child and the mysteries of Eleusis* (pp. 156–177). Princeton University Press.
Karamitsos, S. A. (2006). *The art of Janine Antoni: Labor, gender and the object of performance* [Unpublished doctoral thesis]. Northwest University.
Kelly, M. (1983). *Post-partum document*. Routledge.
Kosuth, J. (1965) *One and three chairs* [Wood folding chair, mounted photograph of a chair, and mounted photographic enlargement of the dictionary definition of "chair". *MoMA Learning*. https://www.moma.org/learn/moma_learning/joseph-kosuth-one-and-three-chairs-1965/
Kristeva, J. (1987). *Tales of love* (L. S. Roudiez, Trans.). Columbia University Press.
Lacan, J. (1949). The mirror stage as formative of the function of the I as revealed in psychoanalytic experience (B. Fink, Trans.). In B. Fink (Ed.), *Écrits* (pp. 75–81). W. W. Norton.
Laschinger, B. (2004). Attachment theory and the John Bowlby Memorial Lecture: A short history. In K. White (Ed.). *Touch: Attachment and the Body* (pp. xvii–xxi). Routledge.
Massumi, B. (1987). Notes on the translation and acknowledgments (B. Massumi, Trans.). In G. Deleuze & F. Guattari, *A Thousand plateaus: Capitalism and schizophrenia* (pp. xvi–xix), Minnesota University Press.
Massumi, B. (2002). *Parables for the virtual: Movement, affect, sensation*. Duke University Press.
Orbach, S. (2004). The body in clinical practice, part one: There's no such thing as a body. In K. White (Ed.), *Touch: Attachment and the body* (pp. 17–34). Karnac.

Princenthal, N. (2001, September). Janine Antoni: Mother's milk. *Art in America*, 124–129.
Rau, D. J. (2001). Janine Antoni: Aldrich Museum of Contemporary Art. A review. *New Art Examiner, 28*(7), 57–58.
Reiman, J. (2015). My body is your vehicle. A conversation with Janine Antoni. *Sculpture, 34*(3), 22–29.
Ruddick, S. (1989). *Maternal thinking: Toward a politics of peace*. Beacon.
Smith, S. (2002). Bodies of evidence. In S. Smith & J. Watson, *Interfaces: Women, autobiography, image, performance* (pp. 132–159). University of Michigan Press.
Talley, S. D. (2018). Healing trauma through intergenerational bonds in attachment. *Journal of Family & Consumer Sciences, 110*(4), 14–21. https://doi.org/10.14307/JFCS110.4.14
Vogel, W. (2016, March). Turning inside out: Janine Antoni's new perspective on sculpture and dance. *Modern painters*, 42–45.
White, K. (2004). Introduction to the John Bowlby Memorial Conference 2003. Touch: Attachment and the body. In K. White (Ed.), *Touch: Attachment and the body* (pp. xxii–xv). Routledge.
White, K. (Ed.). (2014). *Talking bodies: How do we integrate working with the body in psychotherapy from an attachment and relational perspective?* Karnac.
Wierzchowska, J. (2019). Motherless subjects and mothered selves: The implications of Jacques Lacan's and Donald Winnicott's writings on the formation of the 'I' for American studies. *Comparative American Studies: An International Journal, 16*(1–2), 1–17. https://doi.org/10.1080/14775700.2019.1617518
Winnicott, D. W. (1958). *The maturational processes and the facilitating environment* (p. 33). Routledge.
Winnicott, D. W. (1960). The theory of the parent-infant relationship. *The International Journal of Psychoanalysis, 41*, 585–595.
Winnicott, D. W. (1967). Mirror-role of mother and family in child development. In D. W. Winnicott, *Playing and reality* (pp. 149–159). Tavistock.
Winnicott, D. W. (1973). *The child, the family, and the outside world*. Penguin.
Winnicott, D. W. (2005). Transitional objects and transitional phenomena. In D. W. Winnicott, *Playing and reality* (pp. 1–34). Tavistock. (Original work published 1953)

CHAPTER 11
"SPEAK OF ME AS I AM": REGENDERING OTHELLO

Beth Flanagan

Abstract

In some academic literature, women actors' performances of Shakespeare's male characters are homogenised under a single heading, often this is 'cross-gendering'. In this context, this chapter draws on examples of women's performances of Othello and applies a new taxonomy to differentiate them: 'cross-gendering' to define when women play Shakespeare's male characters as male and 'regendering' to denote when women actors play Shakespeare's male characters *as if they are female*. Some find the notion of classifying such performances contentious as they often challenge, appropriate or interrogate stereotypical and essential constructions of femininity and masculinity and thus resist fixity in their embodiment. However, using the terms 'regendering' and 'cross-gendering' to differentiate women's theatrical practices does not fix or confine a character or actor: it instead opens up new ways of understanding the dynamics and meanings created when 'different' people speak the same words and do the same actions. Modern female actors' performances of Othello are shown to destabilise essentialist tropes often ascribed to women and such productions privilege under-represented voices and explore discrimination in their mimesis. The utterances and actions of a regendered Othello show how the arguably 'masculine' aspects of each character become adopted into femininity or reinvent which traits are deemed 'feminine'. Regendering thus reduces the essentialist stereotypes that are often used to limit women's actions and opportunities, whereas cross-gendered Othellos expose, interrogate and reinvent the constructions of masculinity.

Key words: regendering, cross-gendered, performances, masculinity, femininity

Talking Bodies III

Introduction

In 2017, I was teaching Shakespeare's *The Tempest* to thirty Year 8 girls. When we first started reading it, most of them did not enjoy it very much. Understandably, they found the language difficult and the play's magical concepts hard to grasp. Some pupils were disgruntled to learn that Ariel was, perhaps, supposed to be a male character when they had pictured 'him' as female in their heads. However, these pupils were happy to learn that between the beginning of the Restoration and 1930, Ariel was mostly played by women on the professional stage. Though why since this time the casting of Ariel has been restricted almost entirely to male actors, I could not answer them (Button, 2008, p. 14).

For this group of young women, the genders of Shakespeare's characters mattered. That a character could conceivably be male or female or ambiguous in different productions of the same play was quite fascinating to them. Or maybe they realised that the more they could get me to talk about the genders of Shakespeare's characters, the less writing they would have to do. When the end of term came, I showed them Julie Taymor's (2010) version of *The Tempest*, which not only has a woman (Helen Mirren) playing Prospero, it also reinvents the character *as female* ('Prospera'). As the film began, the girls were following the dialogue and they noticed immediately: "Miss, Miss, is that Prospero being played by a woman?" Before I could answer, one of my pupils said: "Prospero *is* a woman, Miranda just called her '*mother*'." Then, this group of young women started to cheer and applaud the screen because of the audacious fact that a traditionally male role had been recreated as female. In my head, I was cheering and applauding them.

Opportunities for female actors specifically to explore Shakespeare's roles have not always existed. In Shakespeare's day and prior to 1660, Shakespeare's female characters were probably exclusively played by adolescent males and boys (Wells, 2009). Aside from the breeches roles, where a female character dons male clothing to disguise herself, the first time a female actor played a male Shakespeare character was in the 1730s. This was Charlotte Charke as Hamlet (Howard, 2007, p. 36). While many women actors' performances of Shakespeare's male characters endured criticism until the late twentieth century (Russell, 1996), recently, such practices are increasingly celebrated. Many notable productions featuring women playing the traditionally male roles have taken place in Britain (and globally) over the last two decades. However, this practice has also diversified, and actors and directors now decide whether the female actor will play a male character *as male*, or whether the traditional gender of the character should be changed and played *as female*. Beyond an enjoyable experience in the classroom or at the theatre, what do such performances achieve in the context of modern feminist and Shakespearean drama? And do these performances have nuanced meanings depending on how a character's gender is represented? I explore recent women's performances of one character (Othello) to answer these questions and my findings can also be applied to other performances of Shakespearean characters.

However, the premise of such questions requires a consideration of language used to describe such phenomena. What words are used by the public, reviewers, and academics to represent when women actors play male Shakespeare characters? And do these words reflect the complexity and diversity of such performances? Elizabeth Klett (2009) argues there is no "common language" (p. 3) to denote these practices:

> The performances have been variously described as "androgynous", "butch", "cross-cast", "cross-dressed", "cross-gendered", "effeminate", "gender-bending", "in drag", "sexless", "transgendered", "transsexual", "transvestite" and "unisex", among others. Such terms are often used interchangeably by reviewers and scholars with little or no attention to the differences between them. (pp. 3-4)

I agree with Klett that such proliferation of titles makes these practices hard to conceptualise (2009, p. 4). However, my concern is not that "'little […] attention' is paid 'to the differences between [the terms]'", but that little to no criticism explores how the practices themselves have diversified. In academic literature, women actors' performances of male characters are often referred to as 'cross-gendering'. For example, Catherine Silverstone (2007) uses 'cross-gendering' to encompass the "'diverse ways' performances of Shakespeare 'interrogate dominant representations'" of gender (p. 199). Terri Power uses "cross-gender performance as an umbrella term to indicate any performance of gender that crosses from one 'normative' gender performance to another" (2016, pp. 7–8). I suggest there are two ways female actors perform Shakespeare's male characters and they should be understood as theoretically divergent:

1. Regendering: when self-identifying female actors play a male Shakespeare character as if they *are female*. The 'original' pronouns are changed for the production to make sense (for example, Prince Hamlet becomes Princess Hamlet). The extent to which the feminised character appears 'feminine' is dependent on production choices and the subjective interpretation of spectators.

2. Cross-gendering: when self-identifying female actors play a male Shakespeare character *as male* and the 'original' pronouns remain unchanged. The extent to which the female actor appropriates maleness or masculinity depends on production choices; how far the character appears 'masculine' is dependent on the subjective interpretation of spectators.

I accept the term 'cross-gendering' for the second practice as the prefix 'cross' connotes the action of swapping from one gender to another. However, I choose 'regendering' for the first practice as the prefix 're' connotes adding to something already in existence, as opposed to removing something from a complete whole. 'Regendering' is already being used to describe changing the traditional genders of characters in fanfiction and television series, but the term is yet to take root in Shakespearean criticism and discourses (Baker, 2017).

Other than the meanings created by regendering and cross-gendering Shakespeare's male characters, Shakespearean authenticity

"Speak of me as I am"

is another factor prompting this exploration. Because young men and boys played female characters in Shakespeare's time, some people see it as more socio-culturally acceptable for this to happen today than the other way around (Hutchinson, 2016). However, Carol Chillington Rutter (2001) argues that some 'cross-casting experiments' with adult male actors have erroneously happened in "the name of authenticity" (p. 88). Rutter continues to suggest that "authenticity is [...] a tactic of legitimisation whose end is political and leaves Shakespeare in the sole possession of white male actors" (2001, pp. 88–89). By exploring the cross-gendered and regendered male character, this reflects my stance on the ontology of performances of Shakespeare's characters – that they can and should be performed in a variety of ways by different people. No one can ever truly know what Shakespeare's intentions were. The 'original' ways of performing his plays become irrelevant when they are appropriated and understood in different cultures and contexts, performed by actors who each have their own experiences to bring to a role, and watched by audiences where each member responds to them subjectively. Dispelling 'authenticity' (whatever that might be) creates material employment opportunities for female actors, intersex and transgender actors, and actors of colour, but it also leaves space for new meanings to be generated by Shakespeare's works.

I begin by considering the implications of a female Othello, before examining Golda Rosheuvel's regendered Othello (Bodinetz, 2018). I then compare this to Anita-Joy Uwajeh's cross-gendered Othello (Al-Shaater, 2015) and explore Debra Ann Byrd's experience of playing Othello as male from a semi-structured interview I conducted with her (Byrd, 2019).

Othello is a masculine character, or to put it more tentatively, Othello's character has stereotypically masculine attributes by both modern and Renaissance standards. Othello is a 'valiant' war general; a 'brave' warrior who 'won' the love of a coveted woman of wealth and status and married her in secret. A character who transgresses from a doting spouse to an abusive murderer. Perhaps Othello's 'masculine' form is the reason so few cross-gendered or regendered Othellos have existed in the last century (University of Warwick, 2016). If Othello's character exhibits behaviours that might be associated with hegemonic masculinity (Connell, 1987; Connell & Messerschmidt, 2005) and this is often linked to maleness (Paechter, 2006), then what language is appropriate to speak of a female Othello? It is too simplistic to say that a regendered Othello exhibits masculinity and femininity, because this does not account for the complexities in her interrogation and reproduction of both.

In *Female Masculinity* (1998), Jack Halberstam is clear that masculinity does not have a stable definition; he identifies masculinity as a separate construct to the male body and seeks to recognise "alternative masculinities" when they occur (p. 2). The notion that women might possess or have access to masculinity provides a good theoretical basis for analysing the regendered Othello's behaviours and attributes because it posits that masculinity is not restricted to men.

However, Carrie Paechter takes issue with the concept of 'female masculinity' for two pertinent reasons. First, that the syntax of the phrase ('female masculinity') posits masculinity as a stable homogenous construct that is fixed, with the person's gender identity ('female') as the modifier (Paechter, 2006). She argues that there is a multiplicity of femininities and masculinities that a person may access in different situations and it is the person's gender identity that does not change (2006, p. 259). Second, Paechter critiques Halberstam for "treating gender as fundamentally about how one is recognised by others, as opposed to [how] one experiences oneself [...] to be" (p. 258). Paechter's argument is logical: the way we use language to denote and attach meaning to gender and identity is one of the most important considerations for modern feminism. Equally, the notion that individuals can choose and control their gender and identity is powerful. Paechter considers these concepts through subjective reality; she draws on sociological and educational examples and her self-perception to form her conclusions. This approach is rooted in 'real life' and the 'real world'. But theatre, however it may or may not reflect reality, is not real. I therefore adapt

"Speak of me as I am"

these ideas into my theoretical approach to the regendered Othello's 'masculinity'.

How the character of Othello may perceive herself or construct her identity is relevant to her actions and relationships with other characters on the stage; an analysis of this can be used to understand which new meanings regendering may bring to Shakespeare's 'original' text. However, the audience members are actively engaging with the performance and construct Othello's identity subjectively. Unlike Halberstam (1998) and Paechter (2006), I suggest that both the subject (Othello and the actor who plays her) and others (other characters and audiences) interact in constructing and reading Othello's gender and identity and each has equal importance.

Significantly, when Shakespeare's male characters are regendered by female actors and perhaps act in ways that are deemed stereotypically masculine, this is not the same as when women actors deliberately appropriate aspects of masculinity when they act as if they *are* male (cross-gendering). Regendering makes it problematic to categorise some behaviours as masculine and some as feminine. For example, when Rosheuvel's regendered Othello (2018) held Desdemona (Emily Hughes) to their bed with her hands wrapped around Desdemona's throat, she was sobbing. This conflation of (albeit hyper-stereotypical) masculine and feminine cues, sometimes within the same action or utterance makes it difficult, if not impossible, to conceptualise Othello's masculinities and femininities or to distinguish between them.

In some societies and cultures, women exhibiting stereotypically 'masculine' behaviours and men exhibiting stereotypically 'feminine' behaviours are, to an extent, accepted. However, I think there could be tragic consequences (no pun intended) in reproducing associations between certain behaviours and specific genders. Paechter (2006) calls for a separation between how individuals categorise themselves ("male or female (or something else entirely)" (p. 262)) from how an individual may enact or construct their 'masculinities' and 'femininities'. While this notion has merit in the sense that it discourages strong associations between femaleness and femininities and maleness and masculinities, the examples she uses to explain them are troubling. She states:

> [T]he various femininities I construct [...] in different circumstances all involve significant masculine attributes (such as my combative style of argument) and more feminine ones (such as the major role in the care of the children I have [...]). (Paechter, 2006, p. 262)

The ability to argue and defend one's views and caring for others are, arguably, skills many human beings have. Why is 'argumentative' a masculine trait? If this attribute is a part of masculinity, does this construct its antonyms (such as 'compliant') as feminine? It is perhaps easy for academics to say that we see masculinity and femininity and their implied attributes as a separate entity from maleness, femaleness or something else, but this does not translate to something that the rest of the world easily understands. Fine's (2017) analogy explains: "There's a reason they're called 'social constructions' rather than, say, 'social Legos'." Social constructions are robustly built: you can pull out bricks here and there, but the others continue to hold everything in place (p. 191). If we continue to categorise some traits as masculine or feminine in the usual stereotypical ways, then we are reproducing a hierarchical binary wherein femininity constitutes the subordinate negation of masculinity. And whether this is connected to one's sex category or not, it is wrong. It is perhaps ethically unsuitable to label a regendered male character as exhibiting masculinities. Something far more exciting happens when Othello is regendered.

Brave new world

> [C]an I tell you that I'm not represented? Yes, I can. Because I don't see stories about gay women, I don't see the stories that have the lead protagonist as female and black and gay.
> (Golda Rosheuvel, cited in Catherine Jones, 2018)

When I watched Rosheuvel play Othello *as* a woman at the Liverpool Everyman Theatre in 2018 (directed by Gemma Bodinetz), the play spoke to me in an entirely new way. Words 400 years old, albeit

"Speak of me as I am"

transported into a modern setting with changes to the 'original' pronouns, became relatable and relevant. Before we meet the female Othello, the audience members are drawn into the world she inhabits: a world which is not only spiked with racism, classism and sexism, but which is overtly homophobic too.

Regendering necessitates changes to gendered pronouns and determiners for the play to make sense. However, once this is done, Iago's (Patrick Brennan) and Roderigo's (Marc Elliot) defamations convey a multitude of hate:

> RODERIGO
> What a full fortune does the thicklips owe
> If [s]he can carry't thus!
>
> IAGO
> Call up her father,
> Rouse [her], make after [her], poison [her] delight,
> Proclaim [her] in the streets. Incense her kinsmen,
> And, though [she] in a fertile climate dwell,
> Plague [her] with flies
> (2006, 1.1: 65–70)

Roderigo's lines here express that if Othello manages to "carry't thus" (overcome Iago's purposes: "peculiar end" (1.1: 52)), she will do so because she is lucky, as opposed to because of her skill or intelligence. Perhaps this implies Roderigo's sexist belief that Othello has also achieved her position and rank in the army through 'fortune' and not through her abilities. Additionally, the metonymy of 'thicklips' objectifies Othello as being restricted by her phenotype, reflecting how a person's race may cause them to experience social barriers and discrimination. Lips connote sexuality and pleasure and are literally an erogenous zone; women have two types of lips which both link to sex and desire. This adds a homophobic tenor to Roderigo's line. As we learn that Roderigo sexually desires Desdemona, this adds a motive for his indignation, which manifests as homophobia directed at lesbian sexualities.

Talking Bodies III

Iago already has a motive to hate Othello: he has been passed over for Lieutenant and this job has been given to Cassio (Cerith Flinn) at Othello's insistence ("'Certes', says [s]he,/ I have already chose my officer" (1.1: 15-16)). Yet Iago's first act of revenge focuses on alerting Brabantio to Othello's union with Desdemona, with the hope this will ruin their happiness ("Call up her father" (1.1: 66)). There is nothing new here. There is both much theory and clear textual evidence of Iago's multifaceted hatred of Othello: Iago's racist beliefs, jealousy of Othello and possibly latent desire for Othello are some of the well-documented motives. However, Iago's language here suggests that sexism and homophobia should be added to this list.

The metaphor, "poison her delight" (1.1: 67), associates Iago with infection and disease, preparing the audience for his corruption of Othello's mind. This reveals Iago's intention to destroy Othello's happiness and the ease with which he believes he can do so. Implicitly, Iago suggests that Othello's position as a general and marriage to a woman of status is both unlikely and unstable. Iago's use of "fertile climate" (1.1: 69) to describe Othello's situation further enforces this idea as climates and weather systems are changeable and unfixed. This suggests he believes Desdemona's and Othello's relationship to be so too, presenting sexist beliefs: Iago believes that a woman's – specifically Othello's – status and position is unsteady. If "fertile climate" is a direct, albeit metaphorical, reference to Othello's and Desdemona's relationship, then "Plague [her] with flies!" (1.1: 70) creates the notion that flies are figuratively attracted to it. Flies buzzing around something usually conjures images of rotting food, corpses, or sewage. Perhaps Iago is equating lesbian relationships with such things, which suggests his homophobic attitudes.

A minute or two has passed since the play's opening, and the audience is asked to confront the possibility that the regendered Othello broadens the levels of discrimination the 'original' or cross-gendered Othello receives. Othello remains Black and the subject of Iago's contention, but her sex and sexuality become additional vehicles of hate. However, not all audience members may necessarily notice

"Speak of me as I am"

this; it is only with knowledge of the text and analysis that I arrive at such conclusions for these examples. The production team may have had similar thoughts and granted Brennan's Iago a paralinguistic gesture to make his position clear. When conveying to Brabantio (Paul Duckworth) that Desdemona and "the Moor are now making the beast with two backs" (1.1: 115), Iago accentuates this line by separating his index and middle fingers and thrusts them on to each other in a scissor motion. By doing this, he is simulating and mocking lesbian sex and using a known hand gesture to do so. If the nuanced homophobic meanings in the language are missed, they are cemented with this action.

Later, when Iago explains to Brabantio why he is disturbing him, the 'original' text uses the racist line: "An old black ram is tupping your white ewe" (1.1: 87–88). This production changed this line, presumably to make it more applicable to a woman: "An old black [d]am is tupping your white ewe." Further to the homophobia and sexism evident in earlier lines, the many other aspects of Othello's identity which are later used as tools to manipulate her are clear here. Her age, her race, her social status and how each of these are distanced from Desdemona's. The first scene presents how aspects of a person's identity can cause them to face social, workplace and structural barriers.

While I am not what is considered old, neither am I Black, and nor do I identify as lesbian, I felt an affinity with Othello before she had entered the stage at this point in the play because this story suddenly felt very real. In an interview with Lyn Gardner, Bodinetz articulates how regendering Othello gives a fresh realism to the play: "I wanted to make a modern audience […] feel something of what a Jacobean audience must have felt at seeing a black man commanding an army […] I wanted to make the play feel electric again" (Bodinetz in Gardner, 2018a, para. 5).

Even if we step away from the structural limitations of the plot – out of a fictional war zone – is it realistic to view the way Othello is treated simply because of who she is? The tragic protagonist is mimetic of modern reality when her identity and the way she is discriminated against are somewhat mirrored by the experiences of the actor playing the role. Gardner (2018a) asks: "Why might it be that the widely admired Rosheuvel is, at the age of 47, only now taking a lead role?" Rosheuvel's words which open this section state that she does not know whether she is discriminated against, but she is aware of a cycle of under-representation and oppression (in Jones, 2018). If there are few plays where the protagonist is a Black woman, there will be few Black women actors employed, therefore fewer Black women may seek such opportunities, thus fewer roles are written for or given to Black women.

It is simultaneously simplistic yet a profound conclusion that regendering traditional male Shakespeare roles can highlight modern discriminative issues and privilege under-represented voices. The voices represented through this regendering belong to women – lesbian women, older women, Black women, authoritative women, brave women, so it is important to recognise the new meanings generated by Othello's 'masculinity' and their theoretical differences to *cross*-gendering.

In following her I follow but myself
The first scene portrays Othello as a victim of social prejudices, but Othello's entrance subverts any preconceived notions of what a victim looks like. The masculinist ideal of the tragic hero is nowhere to be found. While other regenderings of Shakespeare's male characters portray a sense of androgyny or have a childlike aura, Rosheuvel's Othello is unquestionably female. She enters wearing a flowing skirt which accentuates her waist and a headdress, the pattern of which resembles women's Nigerian cultural dress. She carries herself with stoicism and her voice is rich and authoritative. If I were to attach the adjectives 'masculine' and 'feminine' to Othello's attributes in these early scenes in the usual stereotypical ways, I might say that visually she is feminine, but she is aurally and physically masculine. But to consider these aspects of Othello in isolation is to look past the character as a whole: Othello is a woman who *has* what might be

deemed stereotypical attributes of masculinity in her identity – they are a part of her and thus they are a part of her femaleness.

While I have suggested that some of the regendered Othello's experiences are realistic or relatable for a modern audience, certain production choices also aid the audience to understand the performance as set in modern times. The costumes are modern: Brabantio wears a flannel dressing gown in scene one, the army uniforms are like current British army field uniforms and security lanyards are worn by actors in the scenes at the Venetian and Cypriot army bases. The characters carry camera phones and text and take pictures of each other. Each of these choices allows the audience to position themselves to understand the plot as if it is happening now, and not as a depiction of something which may have happened in the distant past.

This modern setting is instrumental in affecting how the audience construct their views of the racist, sexist and abusive male characters. Brabantio accuses Othello of witchcraft and mirrors Iago's racism:

> If she in chains of magic were not bound,
> [...] Would ever have
> [...] Run from her guardage to the sooty bosom
> Of such a thing as thou?
> (1.2: 65-71)

While his lines here are provocative and uttered to abuse Othello, most modern Western cultures no longer believe in witchcraft, or find the supernatural terrifying. The emptiness of the unspecific noun 'thing' reflects that Brabantio has no basis to slander Othello, presenting his abuse as ignorant and unfounded. Alternatively, this could be interpreted to mean Brabantio feels homophobia so strongly he does not wish even to say the word 'lesbian'. Bringing this play into a modern context gives an immediacy to the prejudice and discrimination observed, which asks spectators to empathise with Othello.

Othello's response defuses Brabantio and maintains her composure:

Talking Bodies III

> Hold your hands,
> Both of you my inclining and the rest:
> Were it my cue to fight, I should have known it
> Without a prompter
> (1.2: 81–83)

The imperative, "hold ...", undermines Brabantio's command to "subdue [her]" (1.2: 81) and demonstrates her authority over other characters on the stage. Othello indicates her refusal to submit to the wills of others ("I should have known it without a prompter"), which shows assertiveness under pressure. Rosheuvel remains almost expressionless and inanimate during this speech which gives her words a tone of coldness and ridicule. Her question mocks Brabantio, as it is clear he has no authority or real control over the situation. This positions the femininely dressed female character as holding authority over the male, provocative and aggressive Brabantio. Although she is threatened by violence, she does not falter and rebuffs the accusations made of her. Moments like this distance the regendered Othello from the harmful essentialist stereotypes often ascribed to women such as being passive or over-emotional. Additionally, they begin to place a more feminine stamp on attributes that are often attached to masculinity – such as being controlling, emotionless or authoritative. How might this affect audiences? How might they engage with such moments?

Jill Dolan's *Utopia in Performance* (2005) searches for moments in theatre that engage with utopic ideals and the promise of a better future. Dolan's book does not seek to establish a proforma for prescriptively utopic settings or didactically utopic moments. Instead, she defines a "utopian performative" (2005, p. 7) as something that is understood or felt subjectively by an audience member. It is a moment which may or may not reflect reality, but may make audience members imagine and create better realities: Utopian performatives persuade us that beyond this "now" of material pressure and unequal power relations lives a future that might be different (2005, p. 7). This theory may be applied to some moments in this production, specifically regarding the

"Speak of me as I am"

regendered Othello and the concept that regendering adopts aspects of masculinity into femininity.

The audience sees a woman (Othello) occupying a position of influence in fields which are known to be patriarchal and led by men (the military and its governance). This is a given in the world of this performance. In the first act, Othello's occupation is never questioned by the characters, she is already embodying and enforcing power, and this inverts the patriarchal structure one might expect. Audience members may engage with these moments in an uncomplicated way: watching women who *have* power and authority in nominally patriarchal fields satisfies the equality feminist in our heads. Yet, if art or cultural media represents our desires and influences our actions, then stories like this might encourage women audience members to aspire to positions of this ilk across a range of fields and industries.

Could more stories about women like Othello in popular cultural media prompt social change or encourage others to be proactive in making change? Gardner (2018b) emphasises in her review how the story reminds audiences that "the advances made by women are [easily] lost" and that the production (Bodinetz, 2018) depicts "present-day workplace politics". Although the plot ultimately shows Othello losing her status and authority, the early scenes contain moments where audience members may imagine themselves in a powerful position or envision themselves and others exercising their status with integrity. By adopting aspects of masculinity into femininity, regendering allows audiences to experience utopian performatives (Dolan, 2005) which are mimetic of a reality that may be.

Can an audience member envision the potential and promise of a different future (Dolan, 2005) if the female actor is cross-gendering as opposed to regendering a traditionally male character? Klett (2009) suggests that cross-gendering "disrupt[s] mimetic theatrical production by rejecting the concept of theatre as a mirror that represents reality" (2009, p. 4). The idea that cross-gendering is not mimetic of reality can be said of Anita-Joy Uwajeh's cross-gendered Othello (Almeida-Amir, 2015). If it is visually apparent or known prior to purchasing a ticket that Othello (a male character) is being played by a woman and the audience willingly partake in this illusion, then in that sense theatrical mimesis is absent. This is typified by Dawn Kofie's (2015) review which notes that it is possible to forget that Othello is being played by a woman and concentrate on the drama itself:

The cast provide a convincing portrayal of masculinity without ever feeling the need to reach into 'The Big Bag of Social Stereotypes'. And, although you're aware of their gender, there's no sense of it 'getting in the way'.

Cross-gendering is achieving two things here. First, gender can be denaturalised and becomes of less importance to the production. I expect some audience members may enjoy cross-gendered Shakespeare performances because the actor's sex is rendered of no significance to the fictitious plot. This allows the actors and the audience an evening off from socially constructed and essentialist gender stereotypes, which are harmful to all genders. Second, cross-gendering allows actors to challenge themselves by playing a different gender; Harriet Walter (2016) particularly notes the enjoyment she experienced when trying to walk, talk and fight 'like a man'.

However, Klett (2009) also suggests that when women actors play men, they not only access masculinity, they show it to be artificial: "in contemplating [cross-gender] performances, the spectator becomes aware of the construction of masculinity" (p. 19). As Kofie's (2015) review intimated, Anita-Joy Uwajeh's Othello exhibits raucous violence and uncontrollable rage that is highly physical. 'He' smacks Desdemona; hits the set; screams with 'his' hands covering his face and has a jealousy-induced violent breakdown. Unlike Kofie (2015), who suggested the production did not draw from 'The Big Bag of Social Stereotypes', I suggest that at least some parts of the performance could be characterised as appropriating hypermasculinity. Considering the long history of criticism of women's cross-gender performances, I think Kofie's language choices reflect a wish to convey that the masculine aspects of the characters were not tongue-in-cheek or in the style of pantomime. She is not suggesting there is nothing stereotypically masculine about the performance. Surely, the way some men may 'demonstrate status' and 'occupy space' are part of the social construction of masculinity and thus the 'Big Bag of Social Stereotypes' (Kofie, 2015). Maia Almeida-Amir's (2015) review qualifies this: "having women expressing traditionally masculine sentiments, such as the jealousy of a spurned suitor, made the words far more poignant and somewhat eerie." I wonder if this Othello was 'eerie' *because* the performance was a convincing portrayal of masculinity and maleness? For audiences, this fact overlays the knowledge that a woman is playing the role.

Judith Butler argues that: "in imitating gender, drag reveals the imitative structure of gender itself" (1990, p. 137), thereby, an actor successfully parodying masculinity shows that its implied attributes are not enforced by biological sex. Equally, this can be said of femininity. Therefore, the cross-gendered Othello arguably exposes the fictive and parodic (Butler, 1990) aspects of socially constructed and essentialist gender identities and the possible pitfalls of reproducing them. Where regendering might cause some audience members to envision a future free from the prescriptive binaries of masculinity and femininity, cross-gendering mimics them in full view. By exposing them, the audiences are invited to question their understanding of gender or how far they (un)consciously 'perform' behaviours due to their sex. I think a moment like this is utopic too.

I'll tear her all to pieces
There is an 'eerie' dichotomy emerging here. In one sense, Uwajeh's cross-gendered Othello (Al-Shaater, 2015) successfully mimics masculinity. This performance reveals masculinity to be somewhat artificial (Klett, 2009), and a social construction. This practice encourages the audience to question their understanding of gender and its relationship to sex and identity. However, this production also nullifies gender and renders it of little importance (there is 'no sense of it getting in the way' (Kofie, 2015)). In some ways this is good; it represents a hopeful future for humanity where gender, sex and

identity no longer matter because human beings are treated equally, and people are *really* free to make certain choices about how they behave, what they look like, and which genders they have sex with, for example. Yet such a future can only be reached if we recognise, appreciate, and celebrate difference of people. A regendered Othello (such as Rosheuvel's) is powerful because she is exactly a celebration of difference. Uwajeh's cross-gendered Othello neutralises the power that comes from the celebration of difference in regendering – the reviews attest this. So, what dynamics and meanings are created when a female actor goes beyond parodying masculinity and acting *like* a male Othello and instead becomes and behaves as if they *are* male?

Debra Ann Byrd is the founder of the Harlem Shakespeare Festival and of Take a Wing and Soar Productions. She founded both theatre companies to give actors of colour more opportunities to play classical roles. Byrd was inspired to do this because whilst she was studying acting, she was told by a teacher that she should not expect a career in the classics, because, as an actor of colour, she would not be cast in the roles (Alberge, 2017). Byrd first played Othello *as* male in New York in 2013 and is due to publish a memoir entitled *Becoming Othello: A Black Girl's Journey* in 2020. I had the pleasure of participating in a semi-structured interview with Byrd where she shared her experiences and thoughts about playing Othello:

> I wanted […] to see if I could convincingly and logistically play this role [as male]. [Make] audience members really believe that I can *be* him. I was also thinking about how female audience members could be affected. I usually like to make change by [acting].
> (Byrd, 2019)

For Byrd, playing Othello as male was to challenge herself as an actor and to test the limits of subversion and transformation: she was able to play a classical role convincingly as male and be taken seriously by audiences and reviewers. Her cross-gendered Othello is quite unique, both in the context of my research and in a wider socio-

"Speak of me as I am"

cultural context. Primarily, this is because Byrd chose to live as male during the rehearsal process and for the duration of the performances:

> I began to watch men. How they [...] walked, ran to the train, ate food, held onto women, [...] how they spoke. [...] I began to walk with a smooth kind of gait. One that made you know I was confident and in charge. (Byrd, 2019)

Byrd's Othello also wore a beard in performance, which is almost antithetical to other modern cross-genderings of male Shakespeare characters. For example, Maxine Peake's cross-gendered Hamlet (Frankcom, 2015), although sporting a short haircut still wore rouge blusher, eye shadow and had dramatically curled feminine eyelashes. Walter's cross-gendered Prospero's costume (Donmar Warehouse, (Lloyd, 2016)), which although was prison clothing and could be described as unisex, did not attempt to conceal her body. While many cross-genderings of Shakespeare's male characters create a conflation of masculine and feminine cues, Byrd did her "best to erase [her] feminine self" (2019). This cross-gendered Othello negates the notion that cross-gendering disrupts mimetic realism (Klett, 2009, p. 4). While Byrd's female body was underneath Othello's beard and manly persona, I suggest that a male person was at the centre of this representation. This 'act' of becoming and embodying a man links to Butler's notion that if gender acts

> are performative, then there is no pre-existing identity by which an act or attribute might be measured; there would be no true or false, real or distorted acts of gender, and the postulation of a true gender identity would be revealed as regulatory fiction. (1990, p. 141)

Byrd's cross-gendered Othello might be read as a performance of the performance of gender. Her performance is paradoxically truthful and false at the same time: convincingly representing a male Othello with a woman's body establishes gender identity as fictional. While adjectives such as 'eerie' (Almeida-Amir, 2015) and oxymorons such as 'delicately ferocious' (Clapp, 2014) have been used by reviewers to capture the gendered ambiguity of other cross-gendered male characters, there is a distinct absence of such terms to describe Byrd's Othello. Instead, women audience members reported they felt 'empowered' by her performance (Byrd, 2019) and some male spectators suggested they had not realised Byrd was female: "I thought you said this was all female" (Byrd, reporting the comments of a male spectator, 2019). Byrd states that the closest the production came to criticism was comments which suggested the company was 'brave' and that they 'had the audacity to put on some pants' (Byrd, 2019). Although women have been historically criticised for deliberately appropriating or failing to appropriate maleness and masculinity (Howard, 2007; Russell, 1996), the reception to Byrd's Othello celebrates a female actor's ability to transform and transcend the limitations that sex places upon gender.

I now examine how each practice affects the dynamics of the relationships in Othello and specifically how genders are stereotyped in the context of romantic relationships in modern culture. If Rosheuvel's Othello and her Desdemona are lesbian women and Byrd's Othello is a heterosexual man, which new meanings might this generate for Shakespeare's tragically unconventional couple?

Performance choices regarding Rosheuvel's regendered Othello and Byrd's cross-gendered Othello encourage the audience to view Othello in a more sympathetic light than an androgynously cross-gendered Othello. This is possibly to mitigate Othello's behaviours to Desdemona. I recall a conversation I had when studying *Othello* with my all-female A-Level English class: they had some pity for Othello for falling victim to Iago's machinations, but once Othello casts Desdemona to be so excessively whorish that astronomical bodies turn away from her ("heaven stops the nose at it, and the moon winks" (4.2: 76)), they concluded he had gone too far. My students held the view that even if Desdemona had 'cheated on' Othello, this gave him no excuse to abuse her verbally and physically and they vehemently disliked him for this.

Although they are foils in the 'original' text, Gemma Bodinetz's (2018) production works to present the regendered Othello and her Desdemona as two polarised versions of femininity. Desdemona wears

"Speak of me as I am"

heels most of the time with low-cut, skin-tight dresses; in one scene she has bare feet with a swimming costume. While such clothing and several costume changes helps to create a sense of realism and femininity, it also sexualises her. When Othello and Iago enter the stage in act three, they see Desdemona promising to "talk [Othello] out of patience" (3.3: 23) with Cassio's grievance about being dismissed:

> CASSIO
> Madam, I'll take my leave.
> DESDEMONA
> Why, stay and hear me speak.
> CASSIO
> Madam, not now: I am very ill at ease.
> (3.3: 30–33)

This Desdemona spoke these lines with playfulness and a flirtatious air; she touches Cassio's arm. Each choice works to mitigate Othello's culpability for her actions to some extent and encourage the audience to empathise with Othello:

> OTHELLO
> Are you not a strumpet?
> DESDEMONA
> No, as I am a Christian (…)
> OTHELLO
> What, not a whore?
> DESDEMONA
> No, as I shall be saved. (…)
> OTHELLO
> I cry you mercy then:
> I took you for that cunning whore of Venice
> That married with Othello
> (4.2: 81–89)

When Othello spoke these lines to Desdemona, I felt as if I understood better (compared to the 'original' text) why Othello suspects Desdemona of being unfaithful. Othello's leap from devoted wife to jealous tyrant seemed more plausible than the 'original' text. Why did I feel like this?

Does a woman expressing misogynistic jealousy add more veracity to such words than if they are said by a man?

Howard (2007) also questions whether a woman's voice gives misogyny "spurious authority" (p. 25). Judging a woman to be unfaithful or a 'whore' based on the provocative clothing she wears is wrong, regardless of who does the judging. However, these words expose and interrogate cultural notions about misogyny. This is because the concept of misogyny is arguably usually associated with hegemonic masculinity; prejudice against women as a social group is often stereotypically perceived as being perpetrated by patriarchal ideologies, and often by men. However, the independent 'think tank' Demos (2016) found that half of misogynistic language on Twitter (specifically the words 'slut' and 'whore'), is used by women. Therefore, a 'regendered' Othello may destabilise this stereotype, which is harmful to men, showing that some women can be misogynistic, perhaps as often as some men. The regendered Othello exposes how sexism can be endorsed and produced by all genders. While it could be said that this is reductive in that it presents the female Othello as internalising misogyny, in another sense, this portrayal is robustly feminist and powerful because it negates harmful male stereotypes.

If the regendered Othello's abuse of Desdemona highlights that misogyny is not restricted to men, what can a cross-gendered Othello contribute to this discussion? For Byrd (2019), when delivering the misogynistic lines, she states that she did not see herself as a woman who was playing a man who was abusing another woman, because she was "steadfast in erasing" her womanliness. Instead, she focused these lines so they came from a "person to a person" (2019); the words came from a man whose life and future (as far as he knew) had been destroyed: "[My words] came from a space of I'm a man, you've broken my heart, you'll never give me children, you've ruined my life for ever, my legacy is gone – you ho. I can call you anything beastly in the world because you've destroyed me" (Byrd, 2019). Byrd used these lines to express how Othello was experiencing shattering emotional anguish: 'he' delivered them as almost a consequence of the emotions

"Speak of me as I am"

'he' felt, as opposed to an attack on women as a social group. Byrd (2019) also commented that she foregrounded Othello's brokenness and vulnerability, so the audience could see this in her performance:

> I was a broken man; a man who [was] disappointed. I wasn't just a stupid man who was jealous. [The audience] see the soldier guy, but then they see a man who is a human, not a monster.

Byrd's performance constructed misogyny as an effect of emotional turmoil. It could be said that this aspect of the performance lacks resonance because it channels an existing harmful stereotype: that some men become angry and abusive when they feel threatened. However, it also identifies with the notion that some men have been enculturated to mask such sorrow or fear with anger: "countless men deal with their vulnerability by transferring vulnerable feelings to feelings of anger" (Katz, 2006, p. 212). Kate Manne suggests the cause of violence and misogyny in some cases is because the male perpetrator has been made to feel shame (2018, p. 289). Byrd, by cross-gendering Othello as male, was able to interrogate aspects of maleness and masculinity – specifically, drawing attention to the ways in which some men have been enculturated to perform anger. By using theatre to convincingly *represent* maleness and masculinity, this foregrounds its artificiality for the audiences. The stage becomes a metaphor for the 'real world': some men are victims of enculturation, and some women internalise misogyny. Each pertains to material reality, however, as Byrd is female *performing* maleness. As a result, this Othello allows the audience to engage with the notion that some men have also been thwarted by social constructionism. Both Byrd's cross-gendered and Rosheuvel's regendered performances are highly powerful in the way they interrogate masculine stereotypes. There is power in subversion and transformation. Power in simultaneously being a part of two apparently binary categories thus falsifies such categories. These Othellos are 'different' people who say the same words and do the same actions, but what they do might be interpreted differently based on their gender. If this asks audiences to question and understand why, more productions like this might negate some harmful or misunderstood constructions of masculinity.

All gender's staged
Both regendered and cross-gendered Othellos can destabilise gender stereotypes, resist essentialism, ask the spectator to question their understanding of gender and highlight the constructivist and performative (Butler, 1990) nature of gender. However, these effects and how they are achieved are nuanced for each practice and performance, which supports the notion that 'regendering' is an appropriate term to denote changing the traditional gender of a Shakespearean character. Rosheuvel's regendered Othello adopts some masculine facets of Othello's character (such as authority) into a feminine characterisation. This traditionally male character becomes a woman who flouts stereotypes, who reinvents what it means to be 'feminine' in the world of the performance. This different, reified version of femininity engages with the promise and potential of a better future for some women (Dolan, 2005).

The regendered Othello's sexual and occupational identities are used to discriminate against and manipulate her. Unquestionably, this makes her character realistic and easy to identify with. Equally, representing the diverse ways in which an individual may face barriers and discrimination brings greater collective awareness to such things. This textual shift, which affects the fulcrum of the plot, represents some aspects of 'real' modern women or what some 'real' modern women endure. Her relatability might bring audience members to a greater awareness of how gender roles are constructed and how these might be changed.

Perhaps more significantly, the regendered Othello reinvents this character to be understood in new ways. Shakespeare will not remain part of British culture and the literary canon in the centuries to follow if there is nothing new to be gained from watching and studying his texts. Regendering opens space where new meanings can be created and some of these meanings are female-centric. This is inherently satisfying to watch and to be a part of; there needs to be more regenderings.

Cross-gendering Othello eradicates strong associations between maleness and masculinity, utilising theatrical convention to expose some of the fictitious constructions of masculinity. Where Uwajeh's cross-gendered Othello was unconcerned with mimetic realism (unlike Rosheuvel's regendering where the audience are encouraged to identify with Othello), Byrd's cross-gendering was both 'real' and 'false' at the same time because she was convincingly *being* a man (Butler, 1990). Beyond the vulnerability Byrd brought to Othello and how her performance drew attention to the ways some men are stereotyped or enculturated, she achieved a wonderful feat of transformation in acting. This can empower others to realise that they can change – if they want to; they can be who they want to be; they can "stretch [their] wings further than normally allowed" (Byrd, 2019).

Using the terms 'regendering' and 'cross-gendering' to differentiate these practices does not fix or confine a character or actor, it opens ways to understand the dynamics and meanings created when Shakespeare's traditional genders are changed, interrogated or embodied. If a variety of genders and identities playing traditional roles are represented on the stage and the screen and revered by its audiences, can it be so in the 'real world'? Although cross-gendering has been happening for centuries, the recent influx of professional regendered performances in England (Lucy Ellinson's female Macbeth (Haydon, 2019); Justin Audibert's production of *The Taming of the Shrew* where all characters were regendered (2019); Tessa Parr's female Hamlet (Leach, 2019)) suggest the practice is here to stay. Aside from the ramifications of regendering in terms of social change, we can all, at least, delight in hearing Shakespeare's verse sound brand new. Our revels have only just begun.

Author biography
Beth's passion for everything Shakespearean and feminist grew from acting in amateur theatre productions. Her research into modern regenderings of Shakespeare's tragic 'heroes' was completed as part of a Master's by Research at the University of Chester in 2019. Beth has previously worked as an A-Level English teacher, but is pursuing a career in academic research and lecturing. She is currently researching women's performances of Shakespeare in the eighteenth century at doctoral level at The Shakespeare Institute (University of Birmingham). Beth's other writing and research areas include science and dystopian fiction and semi-autobiographical literature.

References
Alberge, D. (2017, 28 October). Black Shakespeare champion working to change views on "colour-blind" casting. *The Guardian*. https://www.theguardian.com/world/2017/oct/28/theatre-company-boss-there-is-no-such-thing-as-colour-blind-casting
Almeida-Amir, M. (2015, 19 August). Maia reviews: Smooth Faced Gent's *Othello*. https://icarusinvictus.wordpress.com/2015/08/19/maia-reviews-the-smooth-faced-gents-othello/
Al-Shaater, Y. (Director). (2015). *Othello* by W. Shakespeare. [Play]. Edinburgh Fringe Festival.
Audibert, J. (Director). (2019). *The taming of the shrew* (by W. Shakespeare [Play]. The Royal Shakespeare Company, Stratford-upon-Avon.
Baker, L. (2017). *What does gender mean in regendered characters* (Unpublished doctoral thesis). Griffith University.
Bodinetz, G. (Director). (2018). *Othello* by W. Shakespeare [Play]. Liverpool Everyman Theatre.
Butler, J. (1990). *Gender trouble*. Routledge.
Button, A. (2008). Ariel. In M. Dobson & S. Wells (Eds.), *The Oxford companion to Shakespeare* (2nd ed.). Oxford University Press.
Byrd, D. A. (2019, 9 February). Interviewed by author.
Chillington Rutter, C. (2001). *Enter the body*. Routledge.

"Speak of me as I am"

Clapp, S. (2014, 20 September). Hamlet review – Maxine Peake is a delicately ferocious Prince of Denmark. *The Guardian*. https://www.theguardian.com/stage/2014/sep/21/hamlet-maxine-peake-royal-exchange-review-delicate-ferocity

Connell, R. W. (1987). *Gender and power: Society, the person and sexual politics*. Polity & Blackwell.

Connell, R. W., & Messerschmidt, J. (2005). Hegemonic masculinity: Thinking the concept. *Gender & Society, 19*(6), 829–859.

Demos. (2016). The use of misogynistic terms on Twitter. https://www.demos.co.uk/wp-content/uploads/2016/05/Misogyny-online.pdf

Dolan, J. (2005). *Utopia in performance*. University of Michigan Press.

Fine, C. (2017). *Testosterone Rex: Unmaking the myths of our gendered minds*. Icon.

Frankcom, S. (Director). (2015). *Hamlet* by W. Shakespeare [DVD]. Royal Exchange Theatre, Manchester.

Gardner, L. (2018a, 3 April). Othello as an out lesbian: Why Golda Rosheuvel's time is now. *The Guardian*. https://www.theguardian.com/stage/2018/apr/03/othello-as-an-out-lesbian-why-golda-rosheuvels-time-is-now

Gardner, L. (2018b, 4 May). Othello review – lesbian Moor boldly puts gender under microscope. *The Guardian*. https://www.theguardian.com/stage/2018/may/04/othello-review-golda-rosheuvel-everyman-liverpool

Halberstam, J. (1998). *Female masculinity*. Duke University Press.

Haydon, C. (Director). *Macbeth* by W. Shakespeare [Play]. The Royal Exchange Theatre, Manchester.

Howard, T. (2007). *Women as Hamlet*. Cambridge University Press.

Hutchinson, D. (2016, 6 April). Half of Brits don't want female Hamlets, claims research. *The Stage*. https://www.thestage.co.uk/news/half-of-brits-dont-want-female-hamlets-claims-research

Katz, J. (2006). *The macho paradox*. Sourcebooks.

Klett, E. (2009). *Cross-gender Shakespeare and English national identity*. Palgrave Macmillan.

Kofie, D. (2015). Othello: An all-female production, *Broadway Baby*. https://broadwaybaby.com/shows/othello-an-all-female-production/708764

Jones, C. (2018, 23 April). Golda Rosheuvel: "I'm interested in the normality of playing a lesbian Othello". *The Stage*. https://www.thestage.co.uk/features/golda-rosheuvel-im-interested-in-the-normality-of-playing-a-lesbian-othello

Leach, A. (Director). (2019). *Hamlet* by W. Shakespeare [Play]. Leeds Playhouse Theatre.

Lloyd, P. (Director). 2016). *The tempest* by W. Shakespeare [Play]. Donmar Warehouse, London.

Manne, K. (2018). *Down girl: The logic of misogyny*. Penguin.

Paechter, C. (2006). Masculine femininities/feminine masculinities: Power, identities and gender. *Gender and Education, 18*(3), 253–263.

Power, T. (2016). *Shakespeare and gender in practice*. Palgrave.

Russell, A. (1996). Tragedy, gender, performance: Women as tragic heroes on the nineteenth-century stage. *Comparative Drama, 30*(2), 135–157.

Shakespeare, W. (2006). *Othello*. (E. A. J. Honigmann, Ed.). Arden Shakespeare. (Original work published 1621)

Silverstone, C. (2007). "It's not about gender": Cross-gendered casting in Deborah Warner's Richard II. *Women: A Cultural Review, 18*(2), 199–212.

Taymor, J. (Director). (2010). *The tempest* by W. Shakespeare [DVD]. Walt Disney Studios Motion Pictures.

University of Warwick. (2016). British Black and Asian Shakespeare Performance Database. https://bbashakespeare.warwick.ac.uk/roles/Othello

Walter, H. (2016). *Brutus and other heroines*. Nick Hern.

Wells, S. (2009). Boys should be girls: Shakespeare's female roles and the boy players. *New Theatre Quarterly, 25*(2), 172.

CHAPTER 12
CONCLUSION:
BRINGING IT ALL TOGETHER

*Michelle D. Ravenscroft, Bee Hughes,
Charlotte Dann and Paul G. Nixon*

Throughout this collection drawn from the conference proceedings of the 2019 Talking Bodies conference, held at the University of Chester in the United Kingdom, we have sought to unpack notions of body image, understandings of sex and sexuality, and consider how art is expressed not just in the material, but through the body as well. 'Talking Bodies', as a series of conferences and ongoing academic and practitioner discourses, has historically been an inclusive, diverse, and thought-expanding space. This is the very essence of the conference and the contributions we have brought forth in this edited collection as a snapshot of the wide-ranging, challenging and engaging discourses enabled by that discursive space. Through the chapters of this book we as an editorial team have sought to present the diversity and the delicacy of the ways in which we view, interact, acknowledge, and interpret 'bodies' in a multi-faceted, yet, often, complimentary way. Whilst the collection presented here is varied, there are commonalities in focus, in exploration, and in the vision created for future research and pedagogy to occupy and enhance.

In producing transformations, we see the value in uncomfortable conversations. Not only will they hopefully lead us to a more nuanced understanding of the present but also allow us to develop and transform our perceptions in the future. There are, almost inevitably, tensions that are navigated when learning about any issue through experience and this also holds true for the consideration of thought centred on the transformations of or enabled by bodies, whilst also using that experience as a starting point to go back and relearn in response to our ever-changing world and indeed to our ever-changing bodies. In a number of chapters, the themes of discomfort and disorientation were drawn on as ways of enabling transformation not just in personal experiences, but also in the production of research and how those two are often interdependent. This collection of work provides us with examples of how to lean into discomfort as a way to move forward more inclusively with a broader knowledge base, rather than resisting it. It is through an acceptance of the challenging nature of our considerations that we begin to accept transformation and change as an imperative part of our being. It is through the uncomfortable and often challenging conversations that we can question our own knowledge, experiences, and actions – and realise the impact of our reactions to these; they are, as this collection has shown, transformative.

Picking up on the notion of resistance, as addressed in some of the contributions here we see extensions of the body, as well as re-inscribing the body, as developing ideas of expression. Whether this be through a querying of bodily borders, or being mindful of the outline of the body that academia has traditionally drawn on – here, this is the body, but not as we have come to know it. Research and pedagogy that provides in-depth exploration of LGBTQ+ spaces, from outside of the standard heteronormative lens, give all of us the opportunity to push boundaries and demystify areas that have not been given enough thought. Equally, discourse that highlights the importance of overcoming institutional and societal barriers to enabling the study, debate and expression of body image is immensely impactful. This collection validates the ways in which through expression, we can make sense of power, agency, and structure as situated within our social, cultural, historical, and political contexts.

Following from this, an intersectional consideration for visibility/ invisibility as well as inclusion/exclusion informs our understandings of movement. The collection presented here demonstrates the interconnectedness of research topics across disciplinary boundaries, not just as applied to the topics themselves, but also to the global research community. Being an insider or an outsider of communities, from travelling craftswomen to travelling migrants, provides us with stories to share and consider from multiple perspectives, whether that

Conclusion

be sociologically, psychologically, historically and so on. It is not so much about the topics individually, but more about the ways that they intersect with other key areas of interest – it is these crossover narratives that often get lost. If we can transfer this into a global research community, we will have access to a larger repertoire of communities and experiences than our Western society lends to us. It is through this consideration and contemplation of differing and sometimes seemingly contradictory narratives that we can truly push the boundaries of our own approaches and research agendas.

Bringing all of this together, it is within the range of research and pedagogical focus that we see the goal – resistance and awareness. Throughout the chapters in this book, we see a resistance against patriarchal traditions and discourse, as well as resistance against White Supremacy and heteronormativity. Those challenges pervade our society and are being discussed and debated in a myriad of ways. It is through this resistance that we challenge and disrupt academic and other spaces. Through awareness, we can make sense of our experiences and those of others and re-evaluate, refresh and relocate our research – culturally, societally, politically – to understand how we can move forward. At the time of writing, we stand at an interesting point in global history that has inevitably impacted our own research practices and pedagogical skills. In this context, we have been forced to think outside of the box, to expand our understandings of what is possible and how we can reorientate ourselves, all of which has created new landscapes for us to work from (however that work may look for each of us). Whilst the Talking Bodies conference from which these contributions were drawn may have occurred pre-pandemic, the themes presented throughout provide us with points for moving forward in the world we find ourselves in. Cross-disciplinary edited collections such as this have never been more relevant for our developing research and pedagogical practices. The value of diversity and the benefits of bringing this range of approaches together – with a clear critical lens – are illustrated through the important themes of transformation, movement and expression.

INDEX

ableism, 35, 37–38, 40–41
action, 11–12, 25, 34, 61, 69, 98–102, 104, 106–107, 109–110, 112–113, 127, 215, 218, 221, 225, 229, 235, 237, 244
actors, 215–219, 221, 226–227, 230, 232
adolescence, 141–145, 149–150, 153–155, 157, 160, 161, 162
adolescent identity formation, 141–145, 147, 150, 154, 157, 161, 162
aesthetics, 2, 37, 97–102, 104, 113, 173, 196, 201, 209–210
affect(s), 191–193, 195–196, 202, 210–211, 227–228, 232, 234, 238
    affective economy, 192
    affective make-up, 192
age(ing), 3, 36, 120–122, 133, 135, 136
agency, 3, 60, 97, 99, 101, 128, 244
Ahmed, Sara, 2, 3, 12, 15, 18–19, 21, 24
Antoni, Janine 4, Chapter 10
armed conflict, 34
art, 4, 229, 243, Chapter 10
    artistic gesture, 199, 204–205, 209–210
    autobiographical, 192–193, 203
    bones in, 207–208
    -making, 208
    as mediator, 193
    non-art, 99
artisan, 167–169, 170, 187
attachment theory, 190, 191, 193
audience, 52–55, 57, 69–70, 121, 126, 136, 219, 221, 223–225, 227–232, 234–235, 237–239
authenticity, 67, 218–219
authority, 77, 85, 143–144, 146, 154, 157, 158–159, 228–229, 236, 238
autobiography, 88–89
autonomy, 136, 141–142, 144, 148–150, 152–160, 162, 184–185, 189, 209
awareness, 8, 10, 15–17, 22, 24, 43, 123, 131, 153, 161, 190, 193, 204, 238, 245

behaviour, 2, 12, 59–61, 65, 80, 99, 102, 105, 142–143, 156–157, 177, 184, 220–221, 231, 234
    deviant 12, 105

Index

belonging, 128, 168, 179, 183, 226
biological determinism, 97
birth/ing, 4, 39, 207, Chapter 2
   as collaborative, 207–208
   crowning, 20, 208
   homebirth, 13
   pleasure, 20
   workers, 13, 18, 20
Black/Blackness, 4, 15, 222, 224–226, 232, Chapter 4
   #BlackLivesMatter, 4, 51, 68
   bodies, 4, 53, 54, 56, 58, 61, Chapter 4
   community, 63, 66, 52–53
   Harlem Renaissance, 57, 61, 62, 66, 67
   hero, 54, 69
   men, 51, 55–62, 64–66, 70, 225
   stereotype, 57, 59, 60, 66
   superhero, Chapter 4
   women, 60, 61, 226
Black Panther, 54–55
bodily motricity, 98, 103–104, 110–112
bodily techniques, 96, 98, 101–102, 109, 110
body, the, 2, 4–5, 7, 14, 19, 22, 24, 26, 38, 85, 96–97, 101, 104–106, 109, 114, 190–195, 209–110, 243–244
   ideal, 4, 193
   images, 1, 52, 56–57, 66, 77, 89, 196–210, 243–244
   in art, Chapter 10
   as intergenerational, 210
   and language, 17–19, 22–24, 77–78, 82, 113, 196, 201, 217–218
   as medicalised, 4, 8–9, 13, 35, 41, 85, 207
   as mortal, 193
   as tool, 56, 125, 201
bodysex, 124–125, 128–130
   groups, 124–125
   workshops, 128–130
bodywork, 12–15, 17–19
bonding, 191, 196

Talking Bodies III

boundary/ies, 1, 2, 6, 20, 104, 108, 125, 141, 144, 150, 153–154, 156, 158–160, 170, 244–245
    breaking, 125
boundaries of
    erogenous zones, 105, 223
Bourgeois, Louise, 197
Bowlby, John, *see* attachment theory
breast(s), 22, 195, 199
    in art, 195, 199
breastfeeding, *see* chestfeeding
Broad City, 119, 120
Byrd, Debra Ann, 219, 232–234, 236–237, 239

Canadian Immigration and Refugee Act, 42
care, 8–11, 13–22, 24–26, 37–44, 61, 85, 107, 114, 129, 136, 147, 166, 190–198, 201–205, 210, 222
    self-, 193, 199, 205
caregiver/giving, 13, 26, 85, 190–192, 194, 198, 204, 210
    intimate, 8–11, 14, 17, 19
    primary caregiver, 190, 194
    provider(s), 10, 17
characters, 51–59, 61, 63, 66–67, 69–70, 119–120, 136, 177, 183, 199, 215, 216–222, 226, 234, 238–239
chestfeeding, 16, 22, 89
childcare, 201
cisgender, 24, 102
    women, 102
class, 58, 60–61, 65–68, 76, 81, 83, 102, 143, 152, 157, 167, 170, 174
    working-class, 58, 66–67, 102, 152, 167, 170, 174
clitoris, 106, 124–125, 130–135
    clitoral woman, 136
comedy, 119
coming out, 22, 112
conflict zones, 35
contingent/cy, 12, 24–25
control, 13–14, 57–59, 63–66, 77, 80, 88, 125, 127, 131, 143–145, 159, 220, 228, 230
corporeal(ity), 87, 105, 192, 195–196, 207
craft, 3, Chapter 9, 208

Index

craftswomen, 3, Chapter 9, 244
cross-disciplinary, 4–6, 245
cross-gendering, Chapter 11
cultural practices, 101

Demos, John, 144–145, 147–150, 152, 157
development
    child, 142
    human, 190
dildos, 102–103, 107, 108, 111–112, 128, 130
disability, Chapter 3
    access, 39–40, 40
    acquisition of, 34, 36, 43
    costs of, 37, 41
    and COVID-19, 36
    deaths from, 36
    discrimination, 34, 36–37, 39
    protocols, 36, 40
disabled
    bodies as having magical powers, 37
    children, 39, 41
    experiences, 108
    health status, 41–42
    marginalisation of, 37, 39, 42
    persons, Chapter 3
    value as individuals, 38–39, 41–42
disaster preparedness, 36
discomfort, 17, 20, 23–24, 26, 44, 87, 112, 122, 133, 243–244
discourse, 1–2, 12, 19, 75, 78, 80–81, 137, 159, 189, 209, 218, 243–245
disorientation, 18–19, 24–26, 243
displacement, 33, 35
    lack of resources, 36, 41
    life experience of, 40
    living conditions, 36
    medicalisation of, 35, 41
    policy, 44
diversity, 54, 70, 83, 97, 243, 245
Dodson, Betty, 123–124, 126–131

domesticity, 146, 148–149, 152–153, 156, 159, 201
domestic sphere, 148–149, 152–159
Dyhouse, Carol, 144, 153, 154, 157, 158, 160, 161

embodiment, 89, 102, 192, 215
emotional detachment, 201
empowerment, 52, 61, 68, 127
equal pay, 120
Erikson, Erik H., 145, 164
ethnography, 3, 89, 174
    auto-, 3, 89
Eve's Garden, 129–130
exclusion, Chapter 3, 156, 166–168, 173–184, 186–187, 244

family, 34, 37, 41–42, 67, 76, 84, 127, Chapter 8, 171, 192, 204
famine, 34
fat, 3, 10, Chapter 5
    activists, 75, 81, 86
    cultural capital, 76
    obesity, 75–79, 81–83, 88
    pedagogy, 80, 83, 85
    studies, Chapter 5
father(s), 59, Chapter 8, 223–224
fatphobia, 84–86, 88
fellatio, 103–106
feminine, 132, 156, 175, 215, 218, 221–222, 226, 228, 233, 238
femininity, 152, 156, 177, 184, 186, 215, 220, 222, 229, 231, 234–235, 238
feminism/feminist, 70, 79, 87, 89, 103, 148, 220, 229, 236, Chapter 7
    contemporary, 136–137
    history, 136
    methodologies, 175
    politics, 119–122, 130, 136–137
    resurrection of, 120–121
    second-wave, 119, 121–125, 129, 131–132, 135–137, 210
    sisterhood, 123, 130
    television, 119–121, 137
fin de siècle, 155

Index

focus group, 11–12, 15–16, 21, 25–26
Freud, Sigmund, 104–106, 133, 199

gender
    doing, 166, 177, 184
    -ed language, 201
    identity, 15, 22, 96, 113, 154, 220, 223
    neutral, 10, 21
    non-binary, 169, 186
    normative, 25, 168, 177, 181, 182, 183, 186, 218
    roles, 60, Chapter 8, 166, 184, 187, 238
genitalia, 106
girls, 216, Chapter 8
Girls 119, 120,
Grace and Frankie, 3, Chapter 7
Grynberg, Mikołaj, 192

Hall, G. Stanley, 144, 154, 161
healthcare, 5, 40, 42, 44, Chapter 2
    in the community, 16, 38
    curricula, 8–10, 25
    in hospital(s), 13, 16, 35
    institutions, 15
    providers, 17
    spaces, 18
heteronormativity, 2–3, 12, 18, 21, 96, 100, 105, 245
heterosexuality, 2, 18, 21, 96, 103, 105–106, 109–110, 113, 125, 234
higher education, 5, 157
Higher Education Funding Council for England (HEFCE), 5–6
Hirsch, Marianne, 192, 203, 210
Holocaust, 192
homophobia, 18, 223–225, 227
homosexuality, 10, 21, 105
human condition, 196, 199
humour, 126

identity
    -making, Chapters 8 and 11, 189

251

immigration, Chapter 3
  history of, Chapter 3
  legislation, 35–37
inclusion, Chapters 2 and 3, 54, 175, 178, 185, 244
independence, 132, 141–142, 144, 152, 154, 157, 160, 162
influences, 142–144, 146, 229
infrastructure, 35, 39, 42, 62
  fractured, 42
Inside Amy Schumer, 120
institutional barriers, 9, 225, 238
interdisciplinary, 5, 6
intersecting, 15, 66, 76, 122, 244–245
  identity/ies, 15, 122
  politics, 15, 122
intimacy, 15, 19–24, 86, 112, 119, 209
intuition, 14
invisibility, 38–39, 41, 44, 51, 64, 69, 71, 88, 149, 181, 186, 244
Irigaray, Luce, 104–105, 203

Jessica Jones, 55–56

Kelly, Mary, 195, 204
Kluft, 172–173, 182
knowledge, 5–6, 10–11, 13, 14, 16, 21, 25, 39, 80, 107, 109–110, 119, 123–125, 126, 136, 157, 162, 225, 231, 244
  personal, 109
  sharing, 119, 123–125
Kosuth, Joseph, 195
Kristeva, Julia, 196, 199

labour *see* birth(ing)
Lacan, Jacques, 191, 195
leakage, 13
lesbian, 10, 21, 23–24, Chapter 6, 97, 106–107, 109, 223–227, 234
  butch, 102–105, 112–113, 217
  couple(s), 11, 21
  desire, 241,
  femme, 102–105, 105

Index

LGBTQ+, Chapter 2, 37, 42, 44, 85, 87, 244
   awareness, Chapter 2
   desires, 8, 9, 18, 105
   maternity care, 9–11, 21
   needs, 8–10, 23
Little Women, 141–142, 148–152, 161
lubricant, 122, 128
Luke Cage, Chapter 4

male pleasure, 128
masculine, 142, 152, 156, 160, 174, 177, 183, 185–186, 201, 215, 218–219, 221–222, 226, 230, 231, 233, 237–238
masculinity, 56, 58–60, 65–67, 104, 143, 177–178, 181–182, 184, 186, 215, 218, 220–222, 226–239
Masters and Johnson, 134
masturbation, Chapter 7
   demonstrations, 124–125
   as political, Chapter 7
   promotion of, 135
   as taboo, Chapter 7
material, Chapters 6 and 10
   culture, 96, 101, 103–104, 107–109
   objects, 201, 203, 207
maternal, Chapter 10
   body, 195–196
   presence, 195
maternity, Chapter 2
   care, 9–11, 21, 27
   services, 8
memory studies, 192–193
Mendieta, Ana, 210
menopause, 135
microaggressions, 85
midwife/midwives 4, Chapter 2
   bodies of, 9, 11, 13, 15, 17, 22–26
   education, 8–9
   emotions, 14, 17

midwife/midwives 4, Chapter 2 (continued)
    etymology, 24
    physical needs, 8–9, 11–26
    sexuality of, 22–23
    student(s), 8, 10–12, 15–16, 19, 22–25
midwifery, Chapter 2
    curriculum, 8, 10, 17, 26
    as physical, 4, 14, 17
migrants, 33–35, 40, 42, 244
migration, 33–34, 36, 42
    reasons for, 34
misogyny, 236–237
monarchy/monarchic, 154, 208
    signifiers, 208
monogamy, 125
morals, 52, 60, 70, 97, 103, 114, 146–147
mother(s), 13, 20, 23, 58–59, 63, 78, 85, 88, 137, 143–144, 149–151, 155–156, 158–160, Chapter 10, 216
    biological, 190–192, 196, 201
    and creativity, 205
motherhood, 20, 201
mothering, 20, 189–192, 197–199, 201, 204–205
    desire, 191–192, 199
    'good-enough' mothering, 190
    as a practice, 191
    The Primordial, 200
mother/daughter, 137
    hybrid, 198
    relationship, 198, 210
mourning, 196
Mrs Warren's Profession, 141–142, 157–160, 162
muscle memory, 109

nature, 11, 56–57, 89, 96, 98, 102, 104, 113–114, 148, 201, 238, 244
neoliberal(ism), 4, 189, 209
    subjectivity, 189, 209
Netflix, 51, 53, 55–56, 61, 65, 67, 69–70, 119–120

Index

'New Imperialism', 155
'New Woman', 144, 142, 155-157, 159-160, 162
nineteenth century, 3, 37, Chapter 8
nipple(s), 195
normative, 2, 4, 60, 96, 112, 113, 168, 177
    non-, 2
nurses/nursing, 11, 13, 22-23, 25
NVivo, 16

Orange is the New Black, 120
Orbach, Susie, 190, 196, 198, 202-203, 210
orgasm, 105, 124, 126, 130-134
    vaginal, 131-134
orientation, Chapter 2, 100, 106, 203
Othello, Chapter 11
Our Bodies, Ourselves, 123
outsider, 76-77, 168, 173, 182, 186, 244

pandemic, 36, 245
parental, 10, 78, 84-85, Chapter 8, 175, 225
    influences, 142, 143, 146, 147-148, 151, 156-157, 159-162, 175, 225
    role models, 141-148, 156, 161-162
Patmore, Coventry, 149
patriarchy/patriarchal, 123-124, 141-143, 147-148, 151, 156-157, 159-161, 175, 229, 236, 245
pedagogical skills, 245
pedagogy, 22, 24-25, 75, 78-80, 85, 243-245
penetration, 103-104, 110-111, 130-131, 133-134
penis, 102, 176-178,
performance/s, 4, 60-61, 89, 104-105, 112-113, 215, 217-219, 221, 227, 229-231, 233-231, 237-239
    art, 189
    of gender, Chapter 11
phallic signifiers, 208
phallocentric, 124, 131, 134
phenomenology, 11-12, 15
    queer, 12, 15
photograph(y), 189, 193, 196, 205

political unrest, 34
politics, 51, 52, 54, 55, 58, 60–62, 65–68, 79, 119–122, 130–137, 177, 229
    of privilege, 2, 12, 35, 43, 51, 54–55, 60, 68, 155, 174, 215, 226
    of respectability, 51–52, 60–62, 65–68
    of Whiteness, 51, 68
portraiture, 196
power, 12–13, 51, 54, 63–65, 68, 83, 97, 99, 101–103, 114, 126, 143, 155, 158, 160, 172, 220, 228–229, 232, 236–237, 239, 244
pregnancy, Chapter 2, 196–197
    discourses of, 12
    images of, Chapter 10
    medicalised model of
        and sexuality, Chapter 2
'pregnant Dad', 10
privilege, 2, 12, 35, 43, 51, 54–55, 60, 68, 155, 174, 215, 226
professionalism, 21–22
pronouns, 16–17, 218, 223

queer, 3, 12, 15, 18, 22, 87, 89, 96–97, 100, 102, 113–114, 130, 175, 186

race, 7, 15, Chapter 4, 81, 88, 223, 225
refugee camps, 36
refugees, 33–36, 39, 44
regendering, Chapter 11
relationality, 192–196, 207–210
relationships, 2, 11, 14, 23, 26, 85, 100, 125, 134–135, 157, 161, 190–191, 221, 224, 234
    relational history, 191
religious, 205, 208
    signifiers, 208
repetition, 16, 100, 110, 205
reproductive justice, 20
research practices, 5–6, 245
resistance, 52, 75, 81–84, 166, 244–245
Rosheuvel, Golda, 219, 221–222, 226, 228, 232, 234, 237–239
Ruddick, Sara, 191, 207, 209–210

Sanders, Valerie, 148
Schacht, Chapter 9

Index

Schneemann, Carolee, 210
sculpture, Chapter 10
   embodied, Chapter 10
   spoon(s), 199–205
self, 4, 78, 87, 97, 99, 104, 107, 108, 111–113, 146, 148, 150, 185, 192, 204–205, 209, 233
   -image, 3
   -making, 190, 204
sex, Chapter 6
   acts, 106
   hierarchy, 2
   -positive, 122–125, 130
   products, 130
   stores, 130
sexism, Chapter 9, 177–178, Chapter 10
sexual
   consciousness-raising, 124
   diversity, 10, 15–18, 97
   education, 123–128, 130, 132, 135–136, 144
   experience(s), 106–107, 122–123, 125–126, 132
   function(s), 111, 124
   healthcare, Chapter 2
   liberation, Chapter 7, including 122–125, 127–131, 135
   orientation(s), 15, 18, 21–23, 106
   passiveness, 103, 223
   pleasure, 3, 104–106, 122, 124, 126, 128, 130–135
   positions, 97, 109
   practices, 2–3, 19, 24, 96, 97, 98, 100–101, 114
   psychosexual development, 105–107
   relationships, 2, 125, 134
   reliance, 124, 132, 136
   revolution, 122, 131, 134
   satisfaction, 103, 105, 107, 126, 132–134
   shame, 122, 130
   socio-sexual, 97–98, 110
   subjectivity, 2, 96, 98, Chapter 6
   techniques, 96, 97, 106, 107, 114, 131

sexuality
  androcentric, 128
  as changing, Chapter 2, Chapter 6, Chapter 7
  discourses of, 12, 19
  and educating, 119, 123–125, 127–129, 131, 136
  exploration of, 121–122, 134
  expression of, 8, 9, 121–122
  male, 56–57, 124, 128, 130–132, 135
  as shared, 125
  polymorphous perverse sexuality, 104–107
sexually transmitted infections, 19–20
Smith, Sidonie, 193, 203–204, 210
social constructions, 222, 231, 237
social barriers, 223, 224, 225, 244
society, 1, 3, 4, 7, 101, 113, 124–125, 127, 132, 137, 142, 144–151, 153–156, 158, 160, 161, 167, 170, 176, 179, 180, 184, 185, 245
stigma, 1, 3–4, 38, 77, 78, 80, 85, 86, 127
strap-on, 2, 102–113
structural invisibility, 38
structurally embedded, 105
subjectivity, 75, 96, 98–100, 104, 107, 111–113, 189, 193, 209
  female, 111–112, 189
  queer, 96, 100, 113
superhero, Chapter 4
  costume, Chapter 4
  masculinity, Chapter 4
Syrian conflict, 34–35

Talking Bodies conference, ix, 6, 243, 245
Talking Bodies: Interdisciplinary Perspectives on Embodiment, Gender and Identity, 1
Talking Bodies Vol. II: Bodily Language, Selfhood and Transgression, 1
Talking Bodies III: Transformations, Movements and Expression, x, 1
technological innovation, 2, 98
technology, 200–201
television, 57, 79, 119–121, 137, 218
tomboy, 151–152
Tosh, John, 143, 155–157

Index

tradition, 2, 101, 109, 113, 114, 141–142, 144–146, 148, 151, 153, 155–156, 159–162, 208, 217–218, 226, 239, 245, Chapters 9 and 10
transformations, 67, 201, 232, 237, 239, 243–244
'ugly laws', 37
transgender, 10, 175, 217, 219
    fertility, 10
    pregnancy, 10
    visibility, 10, Chapter 2
transgenerational, Chapter 10
    bond, 189–192, 196, 199, 201
    connection, 189, 204, 209
    conversations, 193
    entanglement, 189
    trauma, 192
travelling, Chapter 9, 244

UN, 33–34, 38, 40, Chapter 3
    Rapporteur, 40, 41
    Convention on Rights of Persons with Disabilities (CRPD), 38, 43
    Refugee Agency, 33–34
    UNHCR, 38
universities, 16, 17, 79, 82, 157–158
University of Chester, 243
Uwajeh, Anita-Joy, 219, 229–232, 239

vagina(s/l), 20, 102–103, 122–125, 128, 130–136
    vaginal woman, 135, 136
Vallone, Lynne, 149, 151, 152
vessel(s), 201, 207–208
vibrator(s), 127–130, 133–134, 136
da Vinci, Leonardo, 199
violence, 35, 52, 53, 56–60, 63, 65, 85, 96, 113, 120, 228, 230, 237
Virgin Mary, the, 198
visibility, 58, 244
voice, 1, 27, 166, 215, 226, 236
vulnerability, 13, 25, 27, 39, 81, 85–87, 89, 181, 189, 193, 208, 209, 237, 239

Walz, Chapter 9
weigh-ins, 78
weight, 85, 87, 108
   emotional, 87
   of experience, 8–9
Western art, 189, 193–194, 201, 209–210
White Supremacy, 51, 54, 61–65, 70, 245
WHO, 34, 37
Winnicott, Donald, 190–191, 193, 195, 201, 202, 205, 209
woman/women
   and identity, 142, 146, 159, 189, 220, Chapters 6, 7, 9, 10
   older, Chapter 7
   violence against, 120
womanhood, 120, 149–150, 153, 157
'Woman Question', 153, 147
Women's Refugee Commission, 33–34, 40

youth, 142, 145–146, 152–153, 162